Gods and the One God

Library of Early Christianity

Wayne A. Meeks, General Editor

Gods and the One God

Robert M. Grant

The Westminster Press
Philadelphia

Book design by Gene Harris

First edition

Published by The Westminster Press®
Philadelphia, Pennsylvania

PRINTED IN THE UNITED STATES OF AMERICA

9   8   7   6   5   4   3

Library of Congress Cataloging in Publication Data

Grant, Robert McQueen, 1917-
  Gods and the one God.

  (Library of early Christianity ; 1)
  Bibliography: p.
  Includes index.
  1. Gods, Greek. God—History of doctrines—Early
church, ca. 30-600. 3. Jesus Christ—History of
doctrines—Early church, ca. 30-600. 4. Trinity—
History of doctrines—Early church, ca. 30-600.
I. Title. II. Series.
BL785.G69 1986   261.2′2   85-11443
ISBN 0-664-21905-5
ISBN 0-664-25011-4 (pbk.)

I dedicate this book to Peggy,
intrepid companion and surveyor
of the Roman world.

We know that "an idol has no real existence" and that "there is no God but one." For although there may be so-called gods in heaven or on earth—as indeed there are many "gods" and many "lords"—yet for us there is one God, the Father, from whom are all things and for whom we exist, and one Lord, Jesus Christ, through whom are all things and through whom we exist.

1 Corinthians 8:4–6 (RSV)

Contents

Foreword

This series of books is an exercise in taking down fences. For many years the study of ancient Christianity, and especially of the New Testament, has suffered from isolation, but happily that situation is changing. For a variety of reasons, we have begun to see a convergence of interests and, in some instances, real collaboration by scholars across several academic boundaries: between Roman historians and historians of Christianity, between New Testament scholars and church historians, between historians of Judaism and of Christianity, between historical and literary scholars.

The Library of Early Christianity harvests the fruit of such collaboration, in several areas in which fresh approaches have changed the prevailing view of what the early Christians were like. Much of what is presented here has not been brought together in this fashion before. In order to make this information as accessible as possible, we have not burdened the books with the sort of argument and documentation that is necessary in scholarly monographs, in which such new work is ordinarily presented. On the other hand, the authors do not condescend to their readers. Students in colleges and seminaries and at more advanced levels will find in these books an opportunity to participate in a conversation at the growing edge of current scholarship.

The common perspective of the series is that of social history. Both words of the phrase are equally important. The objects of study are the living Christian communities of the early centuries in their whole environment: not just their ideas, not only their leaders and heroes. And the aim is to understand those communities as they believed, thought, and acted then and there—not to "explain" them by some supposedly universal laws of social behavior.

The opponents of early Christianity often denounced the new cult as "a superstition" and its members as "atheists." From our per-

spective that seems odd. In what ways did the Christians fail to seem
"religious" to their neighbors? What did ordinary people believe
about the gods? What did they do about it, and what did the gods
do for them? Was the Jewish notion of the One God really so
strange to educated "pagans"? And were the angels and demons in
which many Jews and most Christians believed so different from the
polytheism of the "pagans"? Did the theology of Greco-Roman
paganism as well as of traditional Judaism contribute to the making
of the distinctive Christian doctrines of the Person of Christ and the
Trinity? Robert M. Grant has attacked these questions and others
with rare clarity.

WAYNE A. MEEKS
General Editor

Preface

In this book we start with the early Christian movement, especially as described in Acts, and fill in the story of religious conflict from some of our information about other religions and their theological ideas. Finally we trace the rise of Christian theology and some of its relations to its environment. The upshot is neither institutional history nor doctrinal history but a mixture of both. Members of a class who heard most of the manuscript tended to divide into pagans and Christians, though they might have done so without the readings.

For the New Testament I have used, with or without modification, the Revised Standard Version. The quotations of Plutarch and Lucian are reprinted from the Loeb Classical Library by permission of the Harvard University Press; and all translations, with or without minor revision, of Origen's *Contra Celsum* come from Henry Chadwick's translation, by permission of the Cambridge University Press.

The abbreviated names of periodicals and collections generally follow the example set by the *Oxford Classical Dictionary*.

R. M. G.

PART ONE
Early Christians and Pagan Gods

1
Gods in the Book of Acts

Paul at Athens

If you lived in the Roman empire during the first century of our era or the second, especially perhaps in the eastern half of it, you would probably share the sentiment that Luke ascribes to the apostle Paul when he stood at the foot of the Acropolis in Athens. "Men of Athens, I perceive that in every way you are very religious (*deisidaimones*)" (Acts 17:22). The Greek word is ambiguous, but in a character sketch on *deisidaimonia* the philosopher Theophrastus defines it as "a sort of cowardice with respect to the divine" and describes many practices that he, like us, would classify as superstitious. After him the Roman Stoic Seneca wrote a dialogue, *On Superstition*, of which the Christians Tertullian and Augustine were fond because it was in Latin and went farther in denigrating pagan religion. Plutarch too wrote to show that superstition was worse than atheism.

On the other hand, the word could have a descriptive or even favorable sense, and that is probably how Paul is described as using it. He was trying to win the favor of his audience, not lose it,[1] even though "his spirit was provoked within him as he saw that the city was full of idols" (Acts 17:16). The modern traveler is likely not to be provoked but to share the awe felt by both Greeks and Romans when they saw the magnificent buildings that expressed the religious sentiments of Greeks and foreigners alike. At the top of the Acropolis was the fifth-century B.C. Parthenon with its statue of Pallas Athena by Phidias—now known only from copies or imitations. Below could be noted the huge temple of Zeus Olympios, begun in the sixth century B.C. and still not quite finished. Its 56-foot columns owed something to foreign kings such as the famous Antiochus Epiphanes; even Roman robbery in the last years of the

19

republic had left them largely intact. Throughout the city were countless smaller shrines.

The ambivalence, to rate it no higher, of Paul was like the ambivalence prevalent in Greek society from the sixth century B.C. On the one hand, religious art and architecture reached their peak in the fifth century B.C. The Doric order, especially characteristic of Greek temples, and the Ionic flourished in this century, and toward the end of it Corinthian (for Zeus Olympios) was developed from Ionic. Phidias was especially famous for his statues of the gods. On the other hand there were sophists, philosophers, and politicians who felt free to criticize the cults and their artistic expressions. Heraclitus and Xenophanes attacked anthropomorphic ideas of the gods. Trials were held at Athens for what was in effect "heresy."[2] Anaxagoras and Protagoras were accused of impiety because of their ideas about astronomy. Diagoras was under attack because he was an atheist who revealed part of the Eleusinian mysteries. Socrates was accused of not worshiping the city's gods and of introducing new ones. Within a century, however, civic "heresy" acquired a new shade of meaning. After the death of Alexander the Great, those who had favored deifying him or others were suspect. Demades was fined and Aristotle fled, casting suspicion on his pupil Theophrastus, who was acquitted.

These ambiguities show that the situation was rather more complex than the sermons of Paul against idolatry would suggest. The Stoic Chrysippus thought that anthropomorphic sculpture was childish, while Plutarch criticized superstitious people who had images made and dressed them and worshiped them.[3]

Paul and Paganism Generally

The book of Acts tells of encounters of Paul with both Greek and oriental paganism. First, at Salamis on Cyprus the apostle met a Jewish magician named Bar-Jesus, or Elymas (Eleim), and blinded him, thus producing the conversion of the Roman proconsul (Acts 13:6–12). Even more striking, when Paul cured a cripple at Lystra in Asia Minor, astonished crowds cried out in their native Lycaonian, "The gods have come down to us in the likeness of men!" They identified Barnabas with Zeus (evidently he was tall and stately), "and Paul, because he was the chief speaker, they called Hermes." The priest of the Zeus whose temple was before the city joined the crowds, bringing oxen and garlands to the gates in order to offer sacrifice (Acts 14:8–13). The two missionaries were barely able to prevent the sacrifice, giving instead a brief homily on the providence of the living creator God (Acts 14:15–17; cf. 17:22–31).

In a third case, at Philippi in Macedonia, Paul drove out "a spirit of divination" from a slave girl who formerly had been profitable to her owners. They stirred up a crowd to attack Paul and Silas, who were beaten and imprisoned in spite of their Roman citizenship but then released (Acts 16:16–40). Acts tells that when Paul was at Athens he conversed with Epicurean and Stoic philosophers and preached a sermon based on religiosity but aimed against idolatry. His text came from an altar inscription supposedly reading "To an unknown god," and Paul proceeded to make the unknown known: the god is the Creator who does not live in shrines. He is not "like gold, or silver, or stone, a representation by the art and imagination of man" (Acts 17:22–31).[4]

The most significant encounter took place at Ephesus, where controversy arose because of a silversmith who attacked Paul for winning converts and decreasing the revenues from "silver shrines of Artemis." There was danger, the silversmith said, not only to his fellow craftsmen but also to the prestige of the goddess "whom all Asia and the world worship." The other smiths offered the shout of loyalty "Great is Artemis of the Ephesians!" and a riot led to a mass meeting in the theater. Two of Paul's companions were forced to go there, but the Asiarchs, important local officials, kept Paul from attending. When a Jew, or perhaps a Jewish Christian, tried to defend him, the mob drowned him out by shouting "Great is Artemis of the Ephesians!" for two hours. The town clerk then asked them, "Who does not know that the city of the Ephesians is temple keeper of the great Artemis, and of the sacred stone that fell from the sky?" In his view the prestige of the goddess had not been harmed by the Christians, and they were "neither sacrilegious nor blasphemers of our goddess." Any legal problems that may have existed were related only to the silversmiths' craft (Acts 19:23–41).

Finally we are given a bit of ancient folklore in the story of a Maltese viper that fastened on Paul's hand but did not bite him. The natives imagined that Paul was a murderer punished by Justice for his crime. After Paul shook off the viper "they waited, expecting him to swell up or suddenly fall down dead; but when they had waited a long time and saw no misfortune come to him, they changed their minds and said that he was a god" (Acts 28:3–6).

These six examples provide a wide geographical range throughout the eastern Mediterranean world. They also depict diverse forms of encounter and presumably supply a fairly representative picture of paganism in conflict with Christianity. The motives involved are varied. Cypriot magic is due simply to deceit and villainy.

The Lycaonians respond to Paul's miracle with naive enthusiasm, though perhaps the priest of Zeus was not so naive. The spirit of divination at Philippi is a source of income to slave owners, and they want to keep it. The Athenians supposedly spend their time "in nothing except telling or hearing something new" and inadvertently compare Paul with Socrates (Acts 17:21, 18). The Ephesians defend Artemis for civic and financial reasons. Finally, the pagan analysis of the Maltese viper is simply mistaken. When the Maltese get a better idea of Paul they fall into another error however and, like the Lycaonians, regard Paul as a god.

In these stories told by Luke there is no direct denunciation of paganism, though magic and divination are self-evidently wrong. The Lycaonians wrongly identify apostles with gods, but all that the apostles need to do is insist that they are men "of like nature with you." The encounter at Athens begins negatively, with Paul provoked by the sight of idols, and ends ambiguously, with some Athenians converted and some not. The Ephesian silversmith who defends his trade and the goddess is not criticized as dishonest or particularly greedy. The story simply sets forth plausible motives for opposition to the Christian mission and makes a distinction between the silversmith and the ignorant and excitable crowd.

This is not to say that Luke accepted paganism any more than his heroes did. Paul and Barnabas have clearly stated that they turned to the Gentiles, and Luke notes that "as many as were ordained to eternal life believed" (Acts 13:46–48). A violent attack on pagan religion, however, could not have produced a favorable response. Luke is setting forth an ideal pattern for pagan and Christian relations. He believes it existed in early times, for the Gentile church survived—which is the subject of most of his book.

It is significant that Luke keeps silent about the goddesses Aphrodite and Athena. Aphrodite was born near Old Paphos on Cyprus and worshiped in a great temple there; Luke tells only about Paul's encounter with a magician and with the Roman proconsul of Cyprus at New Paphos. The Parthenon, sacred to Athena, we have seen, stands on the Acropolis above the court of the Areopagus; Luke discusses the Areopagus and an unknown god, not the known goddess. He also quotes a line about Zeus but deletes the god's name.

Paul, Gods, and Goddesses

We now follow the sequence of stories in Acts, beginning with Aphrodite in what was really her context in Paphos (Acts 13) and

Corinth. After that we shall turn to Zeus and Hermes at Lystra (Acts 14), Athena at Athens (Acts 17), and Artemis at Ephesus (Acts 19).

Aphrodite

Magic at Paphos

At the western end of Cyprus lay two cities of Paphos, as we have said: the old and the new. Old Paphos was a Mycenaean city famed for its temple of Aphrodite, whose birthplace was found on the coast to the east where foam still surges among the rocks. Supposedly, veterans homeward bound from Troy had founded the temple. New Paphos, on the other hand, was a harbor town to the north; under the Ptolemies and the Romans it was the administrative and trading center of the island. It was the seat of the proconsul of Cyprus.

It is significant that when Paul went to "Paphos" he obviously went to New Paphos, where he encountered the proconsul. Luke has nothing to say about the shrine of Aphrodite but has much to say about a magician who tried "to turn away the proconsul from the faith" (Acts 13:8). Paul cursed him and he became blind "for a time," while the proconsul "believed, when he saw what had occurred, for he was astonished at the teaching of the Lord." Luke was laying emphasis on the triumph of Christian miracle over pagan magic.

The cult of Aphrodite in Old Paphos was much criticized by the church fathers, for it involved not only what Strabo mentions, the presence of crowds from all over the island, but also phallic mysteries which Herodotus says resulted in the loss of virginity. There were also celebrations for the goddess by hermaphrodites.[5] All in all, it was not what Paul would be likely to visit.[6]

Prostitution at Corinth

When he wrote 1 Corinthians, Paul was well aware of the interest his readers took in the gods of paganism. He reminded them that one might imagine that there were "many gods and many lords" (1 Cor. 8:5), and that they themselves had formerly been led astray in the worship of mute idols (1 Cor. 12:2). But he said nothing explicit about one of the most famous objects of worship at Corinth. This was again the goddess Aphrodite, associated with "sacred prostitution" there.

We do not know that the Corinthian Christians were concerned with the worship of Aphrodite, even though many were ex-pagans. According to 1 Cor. 6:12–20, however, Paul knew converts who believed they could justify dealings with prostitutes on religious and philosophical grounds. They seem to have argued that sexual inter-course was an "indifferent" and natural affair, comparable to eating whatever one chose. This viewpoint had already been expressed by the Cynic sage Diogenes, famous at Corinth.[7]

At least in pre-Christian times the mountain called Acrocorinthus beside the city was the site of a temple of Aphrodite, "so rich that it owned more than a thousand temple-slaves, prostitutes, whom both men and women had dedicated to the goddess." Because of them, Strabo says, the city was crowded and grew rich. A proverb widely circulated held that "not for every man is the voyage to Corinth," but ship captains spent money freely there. One of the slaves, accused of not liking her work, replied that she had "taken down three masts in a short time," or so Strabo says.

It is a question, however, whether the temple and its holdings survived the destruction of Corinth by the Romans in 146 B.C. Strabo says he visited the city and climbed the mountain, where he found ruined walls and only a small temple of Aphrodite, not the famous one.[8] Late in the second century Pausanias mentions a tem-ple of Aphrodite and comments only on its art.[9] It is possible that the sacred trade revived, for in the second century the rhetorician Favorinus speaks of Corinth as a "most Aphroditied city,"[10] and Aelius Aristides alludes to the same features.[11] It is not clear whether those involved were sacred or profane. Paul obviously made no such distinction. A Christian man was united with Christ, not with a courtesan of either sort.

Nothing remains of Aphrodite's temple but some early walls. Later the site was used for a church, two mosques, a Venetian battery, and a house. It is likely that, as in the case of other temples where fourth-century Christians found or suspected sexual immor-ality, the buildings were leveled and their contents smashed.[12]

In any event, sacred prostitution was not a Greek practice. This is why Herodotus and other ethnologists found it so remarkable in the Orient. Athenaeus cites the comic poet Alexis (fourth century B.C.) to show that at Corinth there was a special festival of Aphrodite for prostitutes, who were accustomed to get drunk on it.[13] While this is not sacred prostitution, it is prostitution especially sanctioned by a goddess.[14]

The mixed population of Roman Corinth, especially Latin in ori-gin, also enjoyed gladiatorial combats, not known elsewhere in Greece.[15] Lenschau cites the so-called 35th letter of the emperor

Julian (409A), which criticizes the Corinthians' purchase of bears and panthers for "hunts" in theaters. If this letter really comes from the first century,[16] it is all the more valuable for our point. In any event, such activities are also mentioned as Corinthian by Apuleius and Lucian in the second century.[17] There was a certain non-Greek flavor to life in Corinth. After all, it was a Roman colony.

Paul's first letter to the Corinthians shows that he was well aware of the prevalence of temples and images. He was willing to let the stronger-minded Corinthian Christians eat meat that possibly had been sacrificed to a pagan deity if they did not know that it had been so "consecrated." In that case, they had to abstain. Christians denied the reality and power of these gods, but they presented a threat to the "weaker" members.

Zeus and Hermes at Lystra

Barnabas and Paul came to Lystra in Lycaonia (Galatia) and were hailed as Zeus and Hermes after a miracle of healing. Presumably the natives, though they spoke Lycaonian at times, were acquainted with the Phrygian folk tale describing the coming of Jupiter (Zeus) and Mercury (Hermes) in mortal guise, seeking a place for rest that they found only with the aged Baucis and her husband Philemon. They became the priests of the temple of both gods.[18] Two inscriptions show that these gods were worshiped together in this region. One from the third century of our era, published by W. M. Calder, describes a dedication of a statue of Hermes Megistos and a sundial to Zeus (Helios).[19] Another, found not too far away, just below the top of the acropolis at Isaura, provides a dedication "to Zeus Bronton [the Thunderer, a title of Zeus in Phrygia] and Hermes, [by] the priest Celer, son of Chrysanthus." It also contains a worn depiction of the two gods, Hermes the shorter with his caduceus, Zeus the taller with scepter or bolt of lightning.[20] The common worship suggests that some would be ready to hail a common epiphany.

The temple of Zeus at Lystra is described as "before the city"; that is, outside the gates. The words practically constitute an adjective. Temples of this sort were fairly common in Asia Minor. We can mention Dionysus at Thera, Hecate at Aphrodisias, Artemis the Great at Ephesus, Demeter and Dionysus at Smyrna, Dionysus and Tyrimnus at Thyatira, and Apollo outside the same city.[21] Conceivably the temple was later than the city, hence outside, but this makes little difference. "The priest of Zeus, whose temple was in front of the city, brought oxen and garlands to the gates and wanted to offer sacrifice with the people" (Acts 14:13).

The crowds had shouted ("in Lycaonian," a touch of local color), "The gods have come down to us in the likeness of men," as Ovid (*Metam.* 8.626) had said Zeus and Hermes came *specie mortali*. They thought Barnabas was Zeus, Paul—"because he was the chief speaker" (*hegoumenos tou logou*)—Hermes. The latter indeed was the principal messenger of the gods, and allegorizers, Stoic and other, therefore understood him to be the word (*logos*) of the gods.[22] It is this kind of interpretation that underlies the identification in Acts. With it we may also compare Paul's opponents' comment in 2 Corinthians: His speech (*logos*) is "of no account" (2 Cor. 10:10). If Luke knows this verse, he cannot believe the statement. As for the apostles' rejection of such an ascription of divinity, S. Loesch provided valuable parallel materials, partly from the romance about Alexander the Great. This great king insisted on his own humanity when he was hailed as a god.[23]

Thus we find a genuine encounter between the new Christian mission and the old ideas about the gods and their epiphanies. The mistake of the crowd was easy enough to make. A remarkable healing might well be ascribed to some divine power or other, and they were not well acquainted with the gospel, if at all. We might have expected them to identify Paul or Barnabas with Asclepius or some other god of healing, but they must have had in mind the two gods they worshiped in the region. This exciting beginning drew attention to the new religion. In spite of Jewish pressure on the churches there were conversions to Christianity at Lystra and nearby Derbe (Acts 16:1–5).

Athena and the Unknown God at Athens

As Paul stood before the court of the Areopagus, he could see the Acropolis of Athens, crowned with the world-famous temple of the city's patroness. When he made his defense, apparently against the charge of religious innovation, he said nothing about Athena but preferred to discuss an obscure and ambiguous inscription. Why did he do so? Like Artemis, Athena was essentially a local goddess who, however, had captivated the minds of poets, artists, and travelers and won the attention of philosophers. Her significant role in Homer's *Iliad* meant that schoolboys knew about her and the aid she gave the Hellenes. And according to the *Eumenides* of Aeschylus she established the court of the Areopagus itself. There were thus several reasons why Paul should have refrained from attacking the worship of this goddess of wisdom.

Artemis of Ephesus

The book of Acts describes an early apostolic encounter with Artemis, the great goddess of Ephesus whose temple dominated the city. Her defender in the Acts story was a certain Demetrius, whose occupation Luke gives as "making shrines." This seems to reflect the official temple title "shrine maker," *neōpoios*, held by each of the twelve members of a board of wardens of the temple.[24] It may be equally significant for social history to observe that the Christians were being blamed for financial problems. The prestige of the goddess might suffer and her income decline along with that of the shrine makers. We may compare the report of a Roman governor that after the arrest of Christians the sale of animals for sacrifice picked up.[25]

Several inscriptions from about the year 44, not long before Paul visited Ephesus, deal with the efforts of the Roman proconsul to straighten out the finances of the temple. The situation was bleak, at least from the viewpoint of the temple treasury. "Many divine abodes have been destroyed by fire or through earthquake, and the temple of Artemis herself, the monument of the whole province because of the size of the building and the antiquity of the worship of the goddess and the generous income restored to the goddess by the Augustus [Claudius], is deprived of its own funds, which would suffice for maintenance and the adornment of the offerings. For they are diverted for the unjust desire of those who preside over the common wealth while they plan to make themselves rich. As often as glad tidings come from Rome they misuse [the money] for their own benefit," and so on.[26] A problem about the usual sale of priesthoods has led to a demand for reimbursement. This is the kind of situation in which we should expect the board of shrine makers to be involved.

Thus the shrine makers of Artemis at Ephesus were not moved just by "petty economic jealousy"[27] but by more serious economic problems related to the temple of the goddess. The inscriptions show that precisely during the reign of Claudius, when Paul visited the city, diversion of funds from the temple to private pockets had reached such a high level that the Roman proconsul had to intervene. He was eager to preserve the fame of temple and goddess alike, just as Demetrius was (Acts 19:27). The town clerk in the Acts story urged plaintiffs to go to court or appeal to the proconsul (Acts 19:38), as Ephesians were doing in the case of the missing funds.

A later Ephesian inscription shows continuing difficulties in regard to the worship of the goddess. About the year 160 the Roman proconsul tried to encourage the cult,[28] presumably in decline more because of changes in religious fashion than "the growing power of Christianity" to which Lily Ross Taylor pointed.[29] In any event, enthusiasm for the goddess fluctuated.

Artemis had brought great fame to Ephesus. Her temple was not only the pride of the province of Asia but first among the Seven Wonders of the World. Long ago King Croesus had contributed to its construction and had dedicated the columns of which parts are preserved in the British Museum. That temple burned down in 356 B.C. but was rebuilt with greater magnificence. The Artemis of Ephesus, a unique local goddess unlike the Artemis known elsewhere as the sister of Apollo, was also worshiped in distant ports, such as Massilia (Marseilles), and went thence to Emporion (Ampurias) in Spain as well as to Rome, to the Aventine temple of Diana.[30] The goddess is portrayed in many extant works of art as a deity of vegetation and fertility, wearing a vest with countless large fruits attached to it.[31] A few Christians mistakenly identified these as breasts. Minucius Felix was one; Jerome, who had seen her statue but copied Minucius, was another.[32] Ultimately the great church of St. John took the place, as well as much of the masonry, of the temple at Ephesus. Only in the nineteenth century could parts of it be rediscovered.

2

Mediterranean Religions Westward

Puteoli on the Way to Rome

The book of Acts tells us that the apostle Paul believed he had to visit Rome because of a divine plan (Acts 23:11; 27:24) which confirmed his own judgment (shared with many provincials): "I must see Rome" (Acts 19:21). From Caesarea and Sidon in Palestine he sailed by way of Cyprus to Myra in Lycia, next to Crete and Malta, then to Syracuse in Sicily and Rhegium on the Italian coast, and finally up to Puteoli (Acts 28:13). There he found a welcome from Christian "brothers" already in Puteoli. These events apparently took place around the year 56.

Puteoli, like Corinth in Greece, lay on an important transit route and attracted religions during the late Hellenistic age and under the Roman empire. Some of those who brought them explicitly said they did so by divine command, but all must have shared a similar sense of mission.

The Religious Background in Puteoli

If Paul had preached to Gentiles at Puteoli, he might have found an even better text than the inscription he used at Athens. This one comes from Puteoli: "Sacred to all the immortal gods and goddesses."[1] Paul could easily have described the people of the city as "very religious."

As a port leading to Rome, Puteoli had been an important religious way station for a long time. An inscription from the year 105 B.C. refers to the temple of the Egyptian god Sarapis as a well-known landmark.[2] Sarapis had been in motion for several centuries, as we shall presently see.

Josephus happens to indicate that sixty years before Paul there was at least one Jewish community in Puteoli. A man who pretended to be a son of Herod the Great arrived there on his way to Rome, and the Jews, especially those who had known Herod, welcomed him enthusiastically.[3] Evidently they manned a Jewish trading and shipping center. We do not know whether or not such people were also mission-minded, like the Pharisees of Matthew 23:15, who were said to "cross sea and land to gain one convert."

A later magical tablet from Puteoli which uses Hebrew names tells us nothing about Jews there, for the use of these sacred and potent terms was widespread. The superscription begins with an attempt to write "Sabaoth" three times. Then come the names "Iao El Michael Nephtho," and the wish that an individual may be afflicted by numerous enemies, all of whom are named.[4] The table proves no more than the high regard in which magicians held Hebrew sacred terms.

The Baal of Sarepta to Puteoli

About twenty years after Paul's visit another religion made its way from the eastern shore of the Mediterranean to Puteoli. Only a broken stone now preserved in the Kelsey Museum of the University of Michigan bears witness to this religious transition. "Under the consuls Lucius Caese [nnius and Publius Calvisius] and in the Tyrian year 204, on the 11th of the month Artemision, the holy god of [S]arepta sailed in from Tyre to Puteoli. One of the Eleim brought him at the command of the god."[5] The consul named held office in A.D. 79, equivalent to the 204th year of the Tyrian calendar. This was the time when the god made his journey, and indeed on May 29, only three months before the eruption of Vesuvius that took place across the Bay of Naples on August 24. The circumstances were hardly auspicious, but the god did find a home. A Latin addition attests the loyalty of the cult to a new emperor. It reads thus: "For the security of the emperor Domitian [Augustus], the place permitted by decree. . . ." This implies a date on or after September 14, 81, when Domitian came to the throne.[6]

An undated inscription also from Puteoli refers to the priest Siliginius and to the greatness of the city of Tyre and ends fragmentarily with a dedication to "the holy god C . . . ." The word "holy" occurs in other dedications from Puteoli itself: "To the most holy god of the city" and "To the most holy god the Genius of the colony."[7]

Later Difficulties of the Tyrian Cult

Nearly a century later another inscription (in the Capitoline Museum, Rome) tells us of the Tyrian cult's problems and shows that religious missions were not always private, related to traders and merchants, but were also public, with colonies seeking support from mother cities.[8]

The Tyrian colonists at Puteoli started the correspondence by sending a letter to Tyre. The inscription contains a copy of it, addressed "to the rulers, senate, and people of the Tyrians, of the sacred and inviolate and autonomous metropolis of Phoenicia, ruler of ships and supreme motherland" from "the settlers in Puteoli."

> By the gods and the fortune of our lord emperor [Marcus Aurelius], most of you know that compared with any other station in Puteoli, ours is superior to the others in rank and size. Formerly the Tyrian settlers in Puteoli in charge of it were numerous and rich, but now our number has become small. When we spend money on the sacrifices and worship of our ancestral gods enshrined in temples here, we are not able to provide the rent for the station, annually 250 [,000] denarii, especially since the expenses for the contest of the ox-slaughter at Puteoli have been assigned to us.
>
> We therefore request that you will make provision for the permanent continuation of the station; it will continue if you provide an annual allowance of 250 denarii for the rent. As for the rest of the expenses and what is spent on the holidays of the lord emperor, we reckon them as falling on us, so that we may not burden the city. We remind you that the station here, unlike that in the imperial city of Rome, receives no income from sailors or merchants. We therefore urge and request you to take thought for your own fortune and this matter. Written at Puteoli on 23 July in the consulship of Gallus and Flaccus Cornelianus [174].

Within four months the city fathers in Tyre gave their answer.

> From the acts of the senate, enacted 18 November of the year 300 [= 174], Gaius Valerius Callistrates president pro tem, Pausanias presiding. The letter of the Tyrian settlers was read, submitted by one of them named Laches, in which they asked . . . [here the content of the petition is repeated]. After the reading Philocles son of Diodorus said: "The settlers in Rome have always been accustomed to provide those in Puteoli with 250 denarii out of their income. Now the settlers in Puteoli ask for this sum to be preserved for them, or that if those in Rome are unwilling to provide it for them, they may make the two stations into one." Shouts of: "Philocles said it well. The petition of those in Puteoli is just. It has ever been thus, let it be so now. This helps the city. Keep the old custom." The document submitted by

Laches [son of] Primogeneia and Agathopus, Tyrian settlers of the
Tyrian station in the imperial colony of Puteoli, was read, in which they
explained that our native city has two stations, one in imperial Rome,
the other [in Puteoli . . .].

Tyre is evidently not going to contribute to expenses in Italy.

The settlers' request seems modest enough, and we note that they
intend to keep paying for the sacrifices and worship of the ancestral
gods, no doubt including the Baal of Sarepta.

The alteration of circumstances at Puteoli after nearly a century
is less surprising than the report of Pliny around the year 110 that
persons accused of being Christians (in Bithynia) claimed to have
given the religion up "two or more years previously, some of them
even twenty years ago."[9] Religious allegiance is not always immutable. More important, the Tyrians at Rome seem not to have been
as generous as the Christians there. By 160 the Roman church was
well known for its support of other churches. We know about the
practice from the church of Corinth, to which, as to others, the
Roman church did make grants.[10] Corinth was a colony of Rome
just as the Tyrians in Italy were settlers from Tyre. The Tyrians
expected support that they were not receiving.

Gods from Asia Minor to Rome

Puteoli was not the only port of entry for religions moving west.
Examples from the third and second century B.C. show the Roman
republic importing gods from the east in time of need, during an
epidemic or a potentially disastrous war. The gods came in response
to official action taken by the consuls or the Roman senate. Those
invited were thus officially approved, while other foreign deities
were usually not made welcome.

Asclepius to Rome 293 B.C.

The historian Livy tells us that in a time of pestilence "the [Sibyl-
line] books were consulted to find what end or remedy would be
given from the gods. It was found in the books that Aesculapius had
to be summoned from Epidaurus to Rome, but nothing was done
about it during that year because the consuls were engaged in war,
except that a supplication to Aesculapius was held for one day."[11]
The ancient summary of Livy's lost eleventh book gives a fuller
account. "When the city was burdened with a pestilence envoys sent
to bring the image of Aesculapius to Rome from Epidaurus brought

over a snake which had got into their ship and was regarded as containing the divine being itself. When the snake came out on the Tiburtine island a temple to Aesculapius was erected there."[12]

Such a manifestation was not confined to the remote past. In the second or third century of our era the well- publicized healing of a blind man at Rome brought rejoicing "that living miracles took place under our Augustus Antoninus."[13]

The Great Mother of the Gods, 204 B.C.

Livy also says that the Sibylline books were once more consulted during a critical period in the war with Hannibal of Carthage, when "stones" kept falling from the sky. They were understood to say that "if a foreign enemy should ever invade the land of Italy he could be driven out and defeated if the Idaean Mother were brought from Pessinus [in Asia Minor] to Rome." Roman envoys brought a gift to Delphi and, when they offered sacrifice, reported favorable omens, as well as a voice from the shrine that "a much greater victory was in prospect for the Roman people than the one from whose spoils they were bringing gifts."[14]

A temple to the goddess on the Palatine was not dedicated until 191, but two centuries later Augustus was proud of having restored it.[15] (It now lies in ruins.) The orgiastic cult, however, was forbidden to Roman citizens, primarily because in myth Attis, the youthful consort of the goddess, castrated himself and so in ritual did some of her devotees. Under Claudius the cult of Attis entered the Palatine.[16]

Three centuries after that, the emperor Julian was on his way to Persia when in Pessinus he composed a hymn to the Mother of the Gods. He began with a semihistorical account of how her cult came from Phrygia to Athens and Rome (apologizing for it as perhaps "unworthy of a philosopher or theologian"). He then turned to identify Attis with "the substance of generative and creative Mind which generates everything down to the lowest level of matter," the Mother of the Gods as "the source of the intellectual (*noeroi*) and creative gods, who in turn guide the visible gods." She is "enthroned by the side of King Zeus." He concludes with a prayer to her for human happiness, for the Roman religion and empire, and for his own fortune in politics and war, with a painless and glorious death at the end as he journeys to the gods. The Great Mother has now transcended her primitive origins and entered the world of Greek allegory and mysticism.

Gods of Egypt to Greece and Rome

The gods of Egypt did not come to Rome by official invitation but were imported by traders and merchants who privately found them meaningful and/or advantageous. The Roman government gave no encouragement to these cults.

Isis to Athens

As early as the fourth century B.C., Isis had crossed the Mediterranean to Greece. She reached Athens (Piraeus) before 333, for merchants from Citium, asking permission to found a shrine of Aphrodite, relied on the precedent given by an Egyptian shrine for Isis.[17] An Attic decree of that year ends thus: "It seemed good to the deme [only, not senate and deme]: Lycurgus, Lycophron, Butades said: 'In regard to what the merchants of Citium considered it legitimate to request, asking the deme for the acquisition of an area in which they will build the temple of Aphrodite, just as the Egyptians built the temple of Isis.' "

Isis to Rome

Attempts to bring Isis into Rome during the first century B.C. were not successful. Tertullian mentions that the Egyptian gods Sarapis,[18] Isis, and Harpocrates were prohibited and tells of consuls who overturned altars erected to them and checked the vices characteristic of "disgusting and pointless superstitions." Though by the end of the second century A.D. Sarapis had become a Roman[19] (obviously Isis and Harpocrates had received the citizenship too), there had been a lengthy struggle over admitting such alien gods.

At various times between 59 and 48 B.C. the Roman Senate took action to keep the worship of Isis away from the Capitol,[20] but during the year after the murder of Caesar the triumvirs provided a temple for her,[21] presumably as a sop to the dead leader's popular partisans. Sixty years later a scandal led to the destruction of a temple, perhaps this one, and the crucifixion of Isiac priests with whom a Roman knight had connived in order to seduce a simpleminded Roman matron. He pretended to be the Egyptian god Anubis, who "loved her."[22]

Note that this woman—who, according to Josephus, was of noble ancestry, rich, and beautiful—believed that the god wanted her to share his bed; her husband approved; her friends marveled. Whether or not the Roman knight convinced her of his identity by wearing the jackal mask of Anubis, the affair obviously set the Isiac mission back.

The story was evidently famous. Josephus correlates it with a case of fraud in the Jewish community at Rome, while Tacitus refers very briefly to both cases, speaking of "superstition" and "profane rites."[23] Both religions survived and flourished, however, in spite of remaining prejudices or new ones. The satirist Juvenal, expressing older Roman attitudes, describes women as meeting admirers "near the shrine of the wanton Isis" and tells how the goddess can order her worshipers to make pilgrimages to Egypt, while Anubis stands by to procure pardon from Osiris for sexual sins.[24]

We see the earlier fears of the consuls realized to some extent at Pompeii, where as a group the devotees of Isis took part in town politics and wrote on walls to promote their candidates for office.[25] Like the Christians they were unquestionably loyal to the empire. Apuleius tells how the "scribe" read prayers for the emperor, the senate, the equestrian order, and the whole Roman people, as well as for safe sailing throughout the Roman world.[26]

The Invention of Sarapis

Sarapis is significant because he was a deity invented, or at least discovered and named, during the Hellenistic age. In spite of his artificial character he was immensely successful. His statue was brought to Alexandria by one of the Ptolemies, presumably in an attempt to unite Greeks and Egyptians in a common worship. He became one of the great savior gods but differed from the others in that he really had no divine origin. Historians took pleasure in describing how he came to Egypt, if not into existence.

The only moderately reliable date we have for the beginning of the cult of Sarapis occurs in the *Chronicle* of Eusebius as revised by Jerome.[27] There the arrival of Sarapis at Alexandria is set in the last year of the reign of Ptolemy I Soter (286 B.C.); that is, just before the accession of Ptolemy II Philadelphus.

The Roman historian Tacitus offers many details about the origins of the god, discussing it in relation to cures wrought by the emperor Vespasian at Alexandria on persons whom the god Sarapis had inspired to ask for aid. He relies on medical testimony to show that the cures could have taken place naturally, though he admits that something miraculous happened. Reliable eyewitnesses were still providing testimony in his time (Tacitus, *Histories* 4.81).

He does not explain the role of the Egyptian god in the cures but calls Sarapis the god worshiped by Egypt, "this most superstitious of all nations." Egyptian priests have told him that "a young man from heaven" appeared in a dream to Ptolemy I and told him to send for his statue from Pontus. Thus he would ensure the prosperity of the Ptolemaic kingdom and the city of Alexandria. Egyptian priests at the time could not explain the vision, but fortunately the king had brought an Athenian from Eleusis to be overseer of sacred rites *(antistes caerimoniarum);* this man was able to identify the statue as one of Jupiter Dis, a god of heaven and the underworld worshiped at Sinope with Proserpina. (This explains why Sarapis looks like Zeus.) The king's envoys to Pontus passed through Delphi, where Apollo instructed them to bring Jupiter but leave Proserpina behind.[28] The Pontic ruler, reluctant to part with the statue, finally yielded after he received a terrifying vision accompanied by disasters. The statue then spontaneously went aboard an Egyptian ship and reached Alexandria in two days. There a temple was built in the Rhacotis quarter where "a shrine had been consecrated to Sarapis [presumably Osiris] and Isis from ancient times."

Tacitus calls this "the best known account of the origin and arrival of the god," though he knows other versions in which the statue came from Seleuceia under Ptolemy III Euergetes or from Memphis.[29] Tradition about the origin of Sarapis was obviously not uniform or well controlled by priests.

Plutarch, Tacitus' Greek contemporary, offers an even richer assortment of conflicting materials. First comes a bit of antiquarian lore about the god. "Pluto is none other than Sarapis and Persephone is Isis, as Archemachus of Euboea and Heraclides Ponticus have said."[30] A second account is fairly close to Tacitus. "Ptolemy (I) Soter saw in a dream the colossal statue of Pluto in Sinope . . . and the statue ordered him to bring it with all speed to Alexandria. . . . When it had been brought to Alexandria and exhibited there, Timotheus the exegete and Manetho of Sebennytus [in Egypt] and their associates conjectured that it was the statue of Pluto, basing their conjecture on the Cerberus and the snake with it, and they convinced Ptolemy that it was the statue of no other god but Sarapis."[31]

Third comes an etymological exercise based on names in the myths. This might have reached the true solution had Plutarch been willing to stop looking for etymologies. Unfortunately he goes on into philosophical fantasy. The temple of Sarapis at Memphis, he says, was built over the shrine of the sacred bulls and his name is undoubtedly composed from Osiris and the bull Apis. "Phylarchus writes that Dionysus was the first to bring two bulls from India to Egypt. The name of one was Apis and the other Osiris; but Sarapis is the name of him who sets the universe in order *(onoma tou to pan kosmountos)*, and it is derived from *sairein*, to sweep, which some say means to beautify *(kallunein)* and to put in order *(kosmein)*. . . . More moderate is the statement of those who say that the derivation is from *seuesthai*, to shoot, or *sousthai*, to scoot, in reference to the whole movement of the universe."[32] None of the Greek etymologies make any sense.

The Christian author Clement probably relied on Plutarch at times, but in his description of the origin of the god he supplies four different accounts, none from Plutarch, in order to show how discordant the tradition was.[33] First, some say the god "was sent by the people of Sinope as a thank offering to Ptolemy Philadelphus king of Egypt, who had earned their gratitude by sending them grain from Egypt when they were worn out by hunger; this image was a statue of Pluto. When he received it he set the image on the promontory now called Rhacotis, where the temple of Sarapis is honored; the spot is near the tombs." Second, "others say that Sarapis was an image from Pontus, conveyed to Alexandria with the honor of a solemn festival." Third, "Isidore alone states that the statue was brought from the people of Seleuceia near Antioch when they too had been suffering from lack of grain and had been supported by Ptolemy." Fourth—a bit of art history—"Athenodorus the son of Sandon . . . says that the Egyptian king Sesostris, after subduing most of the nations of Greece, brought back a number of skilled craftsmen to Egypt. He ordered them to make a statue of Osiris his own ancestor. . . . The artist used a mixture of various materials. . . . He stained the mixture dark blue (and therefore the statue is nearly black) and, mingling the whole with the pigment left over from the funeral rites of Osiris and Apis, he molded Sarapis, . . . 'Osirapis' being a compound from 'Osiris' and 'Apis.' " Much of what Clement reports seems to be true, but he was in no position to differentiate one thing from another.

The later Christian theologian Origen rightly concludes:

> Concerning Sarapis the story is lengthy and inconsistent. It was only recently that he appeared through some trickery of Ptolemy, who wanted to show a visible god, as it were, to the Alexandrians. We have read in Numenius the Pythagorean about the construction of [the statue of] Sarapis, where he says that he [the god] partakes of the being of all the animals and plants cared for by nature.[34]

What Numenius said was probably not worth quoting as far as origins were concerned.

In all probability, then, Sarapis was the invention of Greek theologians at the court of Ptolemy I. He flourished in the Hellenistic world, in large measure because of frequent miracles and assiduous propaganda related to them. The orator Aelius Aristides claims that it would take forever to collect all the stories of the works of Sarapis.[35] We shall later discuss some examples.

Sarapis and the Ptolemies 258/7 B.C.

"When I was serving the god Sarapis for your health and success with the king," writes a certain Zoilus of Aspendos, "Sarapis warned me in dreams that I should sail to you and give you this oracle: that a temple of Sarapis and a grove must be erected for him in the Greek quarter by the harbor, and a priest must oversee it and sacrifice for you." To be sure, someone else proposed to build such a temple and even gathered stones for the task. "Later the god told him not to build and he went away." The letter, preserved incompletely on papyrus, is from Zoilus to the finance minister of Ptolemy II. It looks as if the cult was being spread in the same way that it began, though it is not certain where it was going.[36]

Sarapis to the Island of Delos

An inscription from Delos, carved about 200 B.C., allows us to see something of the establishment and growth of the cult of Sarapis on the island. The historical narrative was written by the priest Apollonius "at the god's command."

> Our grandfather Apollonius, an Egyptian of priestly origin, had the god ['s statue] with him as he arrived from Egypt as his servant and continued in ancestral custom; he seems to have lived 97 years. When my father Demetrius succeeded him in line and served the god, he was rewarded by the god for his piety with a bronze image, which was placed in the god's temple. He lived 61 years. When I took over the sacred rites and constantly contemplated the services, the god revealed to me in a dream that his own Sarapeium had to be provided for him and that he would not be in rented quarters as before, and that he himself would find a place where we had to build and would signify the place. This happened. For this place was full of dung and was advertised for sale at the passage through the forum. By the will of the god the purchase was completed and the temple was rapidly constructed in six months' time. But when certain people opposed us and the god, and brought a public suit against the temple and me, claiming punishment or damages, the god announced to

me in a dream that we would win. When the contest was finished and
we won in a manner worthy of the god, we praised the gods by returning proper thanks. Maiistas writes on behalf of the temple on
this subject.

Then there are sixty-five hexameters in praise of the "countless
marvelous deeds" of Sarapis and his temples, not only on Delos but
everywhere else.[37]

The Advent of Dionysus

Dionysus at Alexandria

Dionysus was a god highly favored by the various Ptolemies,
especially at Alexandria. Athenaeus describes a great procession
arranged by Ptolemy II Philadelphus in honor of the god about the
year 270 B.C. His son Ptolemy III Euergetes claimed descent from
Dionysus through a remote ancestor, while *his* son Ptolemy IV
Philopator "was called Dionysus"[38] and had Egyptian Jews branded
with the ivy leaf of the god (3 Macc. 2:28–29). No wonder, then, that
he gave the first rank to the Dionysiac tribe in Alexandria; all the
demes of the tribe bore names connected with the stories about
Dionysus. The biographer Satyrus, who tells us about this, also
traces the king's ancestry back to Dionysus.[39]

The close watch kept over Dionysiacs by the king (presumably
Philopator) is plainly indicated in a decree preserved on papyrus.[40]
"Persons who perform the rites of Dionysus in the interior" are to
be registered at Alexandria and to "declare from whom they derived
the sacred rites for three generations back and to hand in the sacred
book (*hieros logos*) sealed, with each inscribing his own name on it."
This may be some religious book or, as A. D. Nock suggested, an
account book of the cult. In either case, the concern of the Ptolemies
for Dionysiac affairs is evident.

Much later, Mark Antony in the east identified himself with
Dionysus, triumphally entering Ephesus as Dionysus Charidotes
("giver of joy") and Meilichios ("beneficent"). Others had other
names for him. When he came to be associated with Cleopatra, the
New Isis, he was called the New Dionysus.[41] The Roman senator
and historian Dio Cassius notes that this sort of behavior was "alien
to the customs of his country."[42] During the Hellenistic age most
Romans had little use for Dionysus or his cult.

Dionysus in Italy

In Italy the cult was not officially accepted before the end of the Roman republic. Its gradual movement into Roman circles was due to private initiative, not to public approval. It may have arrived when Greek prisoners taken by the Romans at Tarentum in 208 B.C. brought the Greek cult of Dionysus to south Italy in a secret and dangerous form.[43] Within two decades it became clear that the Bacchanalia were not compatible with the Roman character. In 186 B.C. the consuls put down the Dionysiac rites, practiced by slaves and some others, because they were secret and dangerous, not controlled by reason or authorized by the state. It may have been Julius Caesar who first authorized the cult. In the second century it was fully respectable. An inscription from Campania, now in the Metropolitan Museum, names a Roman lady of high rank, Julia Agrippinilla, as the patroness of nearly five hundred Dionysiac initiates, including her slaves and freedmen.[44] The religion was now legitimate because it was under stronger social control and higher social auspices. A generation after Agrippinilla the Latin Christian Tertullian could note that although under the republic the consuls and the senate had driven "Liber pater" with his mysteries not only from the city but from all Italy, in his time offerings were being made to the same god, Bacchus, "now Italian."[45]

The Persian Mithras Westward

According to Plutarch, the Cilician pirates who dominated the Mediterranean in the early first century B.C. had more than a thousand ships and captured four hundred cities. They were hostile to traditional Greek religion, attacking such oracles as those at Claros, Didyma, and Samothrace as well as other temples of Chthonian Earth, Asclepius, Poseidon, Apollo, and Hera. "They offered strange sacrifices on [Mount] Olympus and celebrated certain secret rites. Those of Mithras which they instituted are continued to the present time."[46]

We do not know whether or not Mithras was known at Rome at that time. He is next mentioned by Tiridates, king of Armenia, who paid a state visit to Nero in A.D. 66 and addressed him with the words, "I have come to you, my god, to worship you as I do Mithras."[47] Franz Cumont claimed that Tiridates initiated the emperor into the mysteries of Mithras, but this is mere conjecture. There is no trace of Mithraism at Pompeii and none at Rome before the second century. From that point the evidence is extensive, not least in the Christian apologists. Mithras is mentioned by the Greeks Justin, Tatian, Athenagoras, Theophilus, Clement, and Origen and the Latins Minucius Felix, Tertullian, and Firmicus Maternus. Justin at Rome already knows of bread and a cup of water in his mysteries, of his birth from a rock, and of initiations in caves.[48]

By the early fourth century the emperors were already called *Iovii*, under the auspices of Jupiter, and *Herculii*, under the auspices of Hercules. In a further search for divine aid the embattled tetrarchs restored a Mithraeum at Carnuntum near Vienna and set up an inscription to "the god the unconquered Sun Mithras, defender of their empire, from the *Iovii* (Diocletian, Galerius, Licinius) and the *Herculii* (Maximian, who was not present), the most religious Augusti and Caesars."[49] Neither the *Iovius* Maximin nor the *Herculius* Constantine attended the conference, and nothing came of the inchoate plan, if there was one. In distant London, however, the Mithraists of the Walbrook erected an inscription (now in the London Museum) probably expressing their loyalty and addressed to the four Augusti who held office in 310.[50] Soon afterward, these Mithraists began burying their treasures to preserve them from Christian looting. Initiations continued at Rome during most of the fourth century. The end came with the death of Julian.[51]

Roman Religion and Judaism

Judaism was fairly well known to Hellenistic writers, who usually did not admire it because of its exclusiveness and its lack of linkage with philosophy. By the end of the second century B.C., however, Jews at Alexandria had translated much of their Bible into a rather exotic Greek; some had begun to advocate using allegorical exegesis to remove difficulties; and some apparently began the revision of history in order to contrast ideal Judaism with its current form. Allegorism is advocated by Aristobulus and in the so-called *Letter of Aristeas*. The revision is reported in Strabo's *Geography*. There we learn that the Egyptian priest Moses founded an imageless cult at Jerusalem. Originally it lacked any idiosyncrasies, but Moses' superstitious and tyrannical successors captured Canaan and introduced circumcision for males, excision for females, and dietary laws for all.[52] The theory aroused little interest among Gentiles.

The Roman politician Cicero did not much care for Judaism. In his view what was wrong with it was not just its peculiar rites or its lack of statues but the very fact of being different. He says that "each state has its own *religio;* we have ours."[53] This "chauvinism" pervades Roman religiosity. Seneca, writing "on superstition" (as quoted by Augustine), regrets that the customs of this "highly criminal people" have been received in all parts of the world. "The conquered have given laws to the conquerors." He grudgingly admits that "they know the reasons for their rites" whereas most people do not.[54]

The most peculiar feature of the temple at Jerusalem was that it contained no statues. This lack made possible the inventions of Greco-Roman writers, who variously describe what was "really" inside. Tacitus tells us that they had a statue of the ass which supposedly guided them in the wilderness. He is not even consistent with himself, elsewhere stating that "the Jews conceive of one god and that with the mind alone." He adds that "they set up no statues in their cities, still less in their temples."[55] According to a tale related by Diodorus Siculus, when the Syrian king Antiochus IV "entered the innermost sanctuary of the god's temple" he found "a marble statue of a heavily bearded man seated on an ass, with a book in his hands" and concluded that this was Moses.[56] A little later the anti-Jewish author Apion claimed that the king had found a golden ass's head.[57] A further fiction concerned the king's discovery of a kidnapped Greek who was being fattened in the temple so that the Jews could eat him.[58] As Josephus points out, all this is incredible.

Christianity too would exclude images, and presumably this attitude encouraged the pagan notion that Christians were "godless."

PART TWO
Praise and Denunciation of the Gods

3
Christian Missionaries Against Idolatry

The Christian movement went out into a world that as we saw was "full of idols." Even when modern archaeologists try to restore Greco-Roman cities, they cannot bring back the full glory of the ancient gods. Temples dedicated to gods and goddesses were everywhere, and so were statues of the deities. One might, with the Cynic Oenomaus,[1] guess that there were thirty thousand of them, but Oenomaus is merely paraphrasing Hesiod for the figure.[2] In any event, countless statues were lost or destroyed after the triumph of Christianity, in spite of the efforts of many, pagan and Christian alike, to preserve them. Temples were usually preserved. A decree of the year 408 ordered the removal of statues from the temples while admitting that "this regulation has very often been decreed by repeated sanctions."[3] They were destroyed because of the early Christian denunciation of idolatry.

Idolatry in Conflict and History

The model for the New Testament view of idols was set in the Old Testament, which tells how the Israelites emerged from the desert to attack not only the Canaanites but also their deities. The books generally reflect an ideal determination to remain free from the cult of alien gods. This general Old Testament picture is not confirmed by archaeology or the passages that point toward assimilation. Perhaps the most significant evidence of deviation comes from the Jewish shrine at Elephantine in Egypt, where the god Yahu is accompanied by two consorts, one female. (We shall discuss these deities in more detail; see chapter 8.) Though popular faith, as at Elephantine, did not always maintain a conservative monotheistic or at least monolatrous attitude, the Bible as a whole does stand firm against idolatry.

Bodo von Borries devoted a few pages of his dissertation on idols to the "commonplaces" about idolatry that Jews and Christians shared.[4] Idolatry was treated as fornication, breaking the covenant with God which was like a marriage covenant. Though pagans claimed that the statues were made "in God's honor," anthropomorphic statues have nothing to do with the real god. Their very attractiveness leads men astray—or so said Jewish authors; some Greeks favored such statues. It was a matter of debate whether the statues were or were not thought to be the gods themselves.[5] Jews (notably the Hellenistic author of Wisdom) and Christians attacked the idols as impotent, notably unable to defend themselves from robbers or animals; the satirist Lucian naturally made the same point. Since the idols lack sense perception, they are "dead" and "false." They are made of matter, whether expensive or cheap; they are made by human sculptors and do not deserve worship because of the bad characters of their makers or priests. Demons inspire them and give the illusion that they work miracles.

Such a bill of attainder meant that compromise between defenders and attackers of idols was virtually impossible.

Paul as Opponent of Idolatry

We find idols denounced in the early letter of the apostle Paul to the Thessalonians. He tells them what he thinks has happened to them as converts. Perhaps with some exaggeration he says that all the believers in Macedonia and Achaea report how the Thessalonian Christians "turned to God from idols, to serve a living and real God, and to await his son from the heavens, the one whom he raised from the dead, Jesus who delivers us from the wrath to come" (1 Thess. 1:9–10). Every item in this statement requires amplification and proof, and presumably received it in the apostle's preaching. His Greco-Roman converts cannot have accepted it passively. Why was his God living? Why real? What son? Which heavens, and why there? What resurrection? Who was Jesus? How does he deliver? What wrath? Why due? Every item would raise questions and require the apostle to develop some fairly systematic thought, to move toward consistent theology in combating the worship of idols.

Paul's statement has an implicit logical structure and context, and we attempt to indicate some possibilities before passing on. There is obviously a contrast between the God described first as living, next as real, and the idols who are on the one hand dead (like the gods they represent) and on the other hand "nothing."[6] Conversion has brought the converts from the realm of death and unreality to the realm of the life and reality of God. Presumably the reality of the living God was inferred from his miraculous creation and governance of the existing world as well as by his continuing revelation through his prophets. Above all it was expressed when he raised his son from death and exalted him even to the heavens, where he now is. The story of the resurrection must have been a cornerstone, presumably *the* cornerstone, of Paul's preaching, and so it was, according to 1 Corinthians 15. It showed that God's work had not come to an end but continued into the very recent past. This work would continue further, for God would send his son Jesus again to deliver Christians from the wrath due to sinners for their disobedience. The name "Jesus" (mentioned after a pause as "Jesus Christ" is in Rom. 1:3–4) implies that Paul's converts knew something, perhaps a good deal, about Jesus' life and teaching. From this teaching, as from the prophets, they would learn about God's moral demand and his anger, to be expressed at the final judgment, against those who neglected it.

At the least, then, we find in this brief summary statements about God's reality and power, his revelation through the son whom he raised from the dead, and his continuing moral demand. In all these regards God was different from the gods of contemporary paganism. They were not really powerful, for stories about their immoral behavior and their vulnerability or even death gave the lie to other stories about their creative activities. If they had sons they usually fought them and never protected them. And neither fathers nor mothers, neither sons nor daughters, generally gave divine sanctions to morality.

Elsewhere Paul tells the Corinthians that when they were pagans they were under the control of mute idols, whereas as Christians they are now able to say, by the power of the Holy Spirit, "Jesus is Lord" (1 Cor. 12:2–3). The contrast is obvious between the silence of the idols and the creative speech of the divine Spirit.

Paul also speaks of the invisible attributes of God as visible in the creation (Rom. 1:20) and refers to sinners who "changed the glory of the imperishable God into the likeness of an image of a perishable man [not to mention] birds, quadrupeds, and reptiles" (Rom. 1:23). Once more he has idolatry in mind. He follows Jewish precedents when attacking the human images of the Greeks and Romans as well as the birds, animals, and reptiles conspicuously adored by the Egyptians. He denounces those who "although they knew God did not honor him as God or give thanks to him." They "exchanged the truth of God for a lie and worshiped and served the creature [creation] rather than the Creator." What went wrong? "They became

futile in their thinking and their senseless minds were darkened."
Once more, Paul's ideas are basically Jewish. Philo describes the
same situation in his treatise *On the Creation* (45). Men came to be
"intent on what looked probable and plausible, with much in it that
could be supported by argument, but would not aim at sheer truth."
In consequence "they would trust phenomena more than God." As
is often the case, Paul writes as a Hellenistic Jew. Some have argued
that when he says that God's "invisible attributes" (*ta aorata autou;*
i.e., "his eternal power and deity") have been "clearly perceived
from the creation of the world"(*apo ktiseōs kosmou*), the last expression has to do with the time of creation, not the existence of the
world as such. For us the distinction makes no difference, for in
either case he goes on to say that the attributes were "clearly perceived in [or by] the things that were made." Paul is on the verge
of presenting the cosmological argument, though he gives none of
its details and is concerned with consequences rather than ar-
gumentation. We conclude that some of the basic elements of his
theology emerge from his confrontation with idolatry.

This is notably the case when we find a creedal or semicreedal
utterance arising out of such an encounter. Paul is discussing meat
sacrificed to idols and then sold in the market to all, and he insists
upon his own fundamental theological position as taught to the
Corinthians. "We know that an idol is nothing in the world and that
there is no God but one." He then modifies and expands the statement. "And this is so even if there are so-called gods either in
heaven or on earth—as indeed there are many gods and many
lords—

> but for us there is one God, the Father,
> from whom everything comes, for whom we exist,
> and one Lord, Jesus Christ,
> through whom everything exists, through whom we exist."
>
> (1 Cor. 8:4–6)

It is hard to tell what Paul means when he accepts, even for a
moment, the existence of the "many gods and many lords." Perhaps
he carried over "so-called" in his mind. In similar fashion, however,
the Platonist rhetorician Maximus of Tyre says there is "one God
the king and father of all" and there are "many gods, sons of God,
co-rulers (*synarchontes*) with God."[7] According to Maximus, this is a
doctrine universally accepted, held by both Greeks and barbarians.
Perhaps Paul had something like it in mind when he made his own
affirmation. In his thought we see Christian theology being worked
out in relation to polytheistic idolatry, idolatry which Paul includes

in lists of vices (Gal. 5:20) and the vicious (1 Cor. 5:10). A Christian must avoid idolatry (1 Cor. 10:14) as well as those within the church who may have leanings toward it (1 Cor. 5:11). The temple of God (= the Christian himself) has no "agreement" with idols (2 Cor. 6:16). He has to insist that abhorrence of idols does not justify robbing pagan temples (Rom. 2:22).

We shall later see how important the step taken in 1 Corinthians was for the development of Christian theology (chapter 8).

The Theology of Paul in Acts

The best way to approach some of Paul's sermons in Acts is to consider the rhetorical models they were probably following. In a rhetorical school the pupils would be trained in the exercise entitled "Whether the gods exercise providential care for the cosmos." There is a good outline of this topic in the *Progymnasmata* of the second-century rhetorician Theon.[8] Theon begins thus: You should state how easy it is for the gods to perform the task and how daemons, heroes, and other gods help them. Second, all men whether Greeks or barbarians share this belief, and it is confirmed by the existence of votive altars. You then invoke the authority of "the wise," such as Plato, Aristotle, and Zeno, not to mention the traditional "legislators," none of whom advocated irreligion (*asebeia*). The most famous rulers have also believed in providence. More theological arguments should follow at this point. "Since God is just he would not overlook his worshippers without providential care; moreover, the nature of the universe testifies that everything comes into existence by providence for the sake of what is in the universe." The examples are taken from the changing seasons, with a reference to the much-anthologized *Memorabilia* of Xenophon (4.3.5). Providential care suits the gods, who are not lazy or weak. Indeed, it is necessary for providence to exist. Denying its existence means destroying our idea of the gods and of their very existence. Moreover, the world would not have come to be had there been no providence. The house implies the builder. It would be ridiculous to suppose this most beautiful and most valuable world could have come into existence without some "most beautiful and most divine Demiurge." We compare the governance of the world with the work of a steward or a pilot or a general or a political ruler and conclude that God must govern. Then it can be argued *a fortiori* that since heroes and daemons care for cities, the gods must care for the whole world. Next, without providence there would be no justice or piety or keeping of oaths or courage or temperance or friendship or favor or indeed anything related to virtue. If one goes, many go; and intelligent people do not intend to destroy the virtues.

It is clear that not all the arguments are equally persuasive, but the rhetorician or homilist who used them was aiming at a cumulative effect like the one a Christian missionary would have had in mind when giving addresses at Lystra and Athens or any other Hellenized town in the eastern Mediterranean world.

There is not a great deal of explicit theology in the book of Acts, but in the two keynote addresses against idolatry we find materials that resemble popular rhetorical models like the one in Theon's work, as well as the religious discussions by philosophers such as Epictetus or, for that matter, the basic ideas we have already found in Paul's letters. In these addresses the arguments favoring the gods are used on behalf of the one God.

First we look at what is ascribed to Paul as he denies being the hero or daemon Hermes (Acts 14:15–17). He urges his hearers to "turn from these vain things [i.e., idols] to a living God," described as the Demiurge, the one "who made the heaven and the earth and the sea and all that is in them." Though this God allowed previous generations of pagans to "walk in their own ways" and only now presented his gospel through the mission of the apostles, there were always testimonies to his care for humanity "for he did good and offered you rains and fruitful seasons from heaven, satisfying your hearts with food and gladness." In other words, God's eternal providential care was obvious from the goodness of the creation that he made. The positive notes found in Romans 1:19–20 recur. So do those of Greek rhetoric.

The account in Acts 17 goes farther. First, Luke has created a highly sophisticated setting for his report. In the opening chapters of Acts he had used Pythagorean terms to describe the similar common sharing of property, so now he thinks of the trial of Socrates as he sets Paul before the court of the Areopagus. The key verse is Acts 17:18: "Others said, 'He seems to be a preacher of foreign divinities *(xena daimonia),*' since he was proclaiming Jesus and the resurrection." The charge against Socrates was very close to that. He was accused of proclaiming "new divinities *(kaina daimonia).*"[9] Luke clearly is thinking of popular philosophy—and thinking favorably of its hero.

Paul then launches into a discourse much like that at Lystra but somewhat fuller. He attacks Athenian idolatry by speaking of "the God who made the world and everything in it," the one who "gives to all men life and breath and everything [else]." This God made all human beings "from one" (a tacit reference to Adam) and set them in allotted periods and boundaries (rise and fall of empires? different climates?) and encouraged them to seek after him—and find him. Luke, perhaps after Paul, is perfectly willing to cite the Greek poet Aratus as a witness; it was he who wrote "We are indeed his offspring." Obviously poets making statements like this belong among the "wise" of whom the rhetorician spoke. But this is not to say that Luke, much less Paul, knew Aratus either directly or through the anthology in which the opening lines of his poem are still found. For the point of the Athenian address it is necessary to hold that we are the offspring of God, not (as in Aratus) of Zeus. And just this correction had been made by the Jewish apologist Aristobulus, perhaps a century earlier.[10] As his offspring we know that God is not like the idols but is "a living and real God."

The audience, described as including Epicurean and Stoic philosophers (Acts 17:18), gives a mixed response to Paul's address, though some join him, notably a certain Dionysius, a member of the court (Acts 17:34).

The sermon at Athens ends with God's command to repent and a reference to the last judgment. God "has fixed a day on which he will judge the world in righteousness by a man whom he has appointed, and of this he has given assurance to all men by raising him from the dead." This conclusion leads us back to Thessalonica. Surely the situation of an Athenian convert too would be one of waiting, like the Thessalonians, "for his Son from heaven, whom he raised from the dead, Jesus who delivers us from the wrath to come." The two parts fit together and give us the context not only for the early doctrine about the Father but also, to some extent, for the doctrine about the Son.

Theology in the *Preaching of Peter*

The book of Acts and the apocryphal *Preaching of Peter* are certainly secondary sources for the theology of either of these apostles. Some of Paul's ideas, however, are reflected in the sermons in Acts, and no doubt Peter would not have disagreed entirely with the theological notions ascribed to him in the so-called *Preaching of Peter*. This representation of what Peter could have said when he spoke to Gentiles included his proclamation that "God is one, who made the beginning of everything and has power over the end." Then it went on with typically Middle Platonic statements about God (see chapter 6). "He is the invisible who sees all, the uncontained who contains all, the one without needs whom all need and for whom they exist; incomprehensible, eternal, imperishable, unmade who made all by the word of his power [cf. Heb. 1:3]."[11] "Peter" then proceeded to denounce Greek forms of worship because they involved idolatry. "Influenced by ignorance and not knowing God as we do (in accordance with perfect knowledge), they gave shapes to what he gave them to use, wood and stone, bronze and iron, gold and silver, forgetting the material and its use, they raised up what belonged to them as possessions and worshiped them; as well as what God gave them for food—the birds of the air and the fish of the sea and the reptiles on land, along with four-footed beasts of the field, weasels and mice and dogs and monkeys. They offered their own food as sacrifices to mortals, dead things for dead men as to gods and thus displeased God by denying his existence."[12] An attack on Jewish worship follows. It is wrong because it follows a regular calendar and implies worship of sun and moon. According to Clement, Peter is saying that both Greeks and Jews worship "the one and only God" in their own fashion. This is not what the *Preaching of Peter* really teaches. It says that all should worship him in the Christian way, not that there is anything of value in their indigenous usages.

What is important for our purposes here is the way in which idolatry and theriolatry (i.e., worship of deities in animal form) are contrasted with the true monotheistic theology. The crude materiality of the idols and of the animals sometimes worshiped is an affront to the one creator God. In mission preaching no distinction was made between the twin errors which others ascribed to Greeks and Egyptians.

Theology in the Apocryphal *Acts of Paul*

As an example of "popular" preaching later ascribed to Paul we offer the apocryphal *Acts of Paul* from the latter half of the second century. It gives much the same picture. Paul urges his hearers at Ephesus to "repent and believe that there is only one God and one Christ Jesus, and there is no other. For your gods are of bronze and stone and wood; they cannot take food or see or hear or even stand up. Make a good decision and be saved, so that God may not be angry and burn you up in unquenchable fire."[13] The "popular" faith perhaps expressed in the *Acts of Paul* thus agrees with the more learned assaults of the apologists on idolatry and to their presentation of monotheism.

Pagan and Christian Worship

There was a strong emphasis on worship throughout the ancient world. We have mentioned the impressive ruins of temples all over the Greco-Roman world. Often these shrines manifested religious continuity by being converted to Christian use, as in the cases of the Parthenon and the Pantheon, or by losing their stone columns to newly erected churches. Before Christianization the temples performed different functions. Originally they were built for the delimitation of "sacred space," for the housing of great statues of gods and goddesses, for the offering of sacrifices to the deities, and for the culmination of sacred processions in their honor. Common prayers and initiatory rites were also conducted by priests and priestesses on particular holy days. Certain shrines might also provide the performance of miracles through "incubation," sleeping inside in order to receive divinely inspired dreams or when awake to receive oracles from the gods. In the fourth century the closing of the temples marked the real end of pagan religion.

Among Christians, worship was at first relatively simple, partly because it was conducted by laymen (and women) in houses used by the faithful. The baptismal rite, in which converts were united to Christ and became members of the community, did not take place in the house church but wherever water was available for immersion. At first, baptisms took place in the name of the Lord Jesus, later in the name of Father, Son, and Holy Spirit. Worship led to doctrine and was based on it as well. Persons seeking baptism were asked for affirmations of belief before they were baptized and took part in the eucharist. The eucharist-agape was a common meal—more than a common meal, to be sure, but involving eating and drinking together. These basic rites may have united Christians more fully than any pagan cult united worshipers of the gods.

4

Functions of Gods and Goddesses

Claims for the Gods

Worshipers of the gods naturally rejected the Jewish and Christian claim that they were ineffective. The gods and goddesses who won or retained popular devotion in the Greco-Roman world were those who gave or promised benefits to their devotees. Deities of this kind could cure diseases and other ailments and rescue from any kind of danger. They saved life in the face of threatening circumstances. For kings they kept thrones; for others their property; for all they protected marriages and children. In addition, many gods provided oracles and sent dreams through which the future could be known and right decisions taken. They often encouraged moral behavior and rewarded it with a blessed life for the soul after the death of the body. They could save from fate and, so to speak, short-circuit the stars.[1]

Stories about the deeds of gods and goddesses naturally deal with supernatural and striking events, works in which their extraordinary power is made manifest. If the event were not striking there would be no reason to report it, since it would not prove anything. Similarly, unless the god (or his oracle or prophet) predicted some startling reversal in the future there would be no reason to pay attention. This is why miracle stories and predictions of the future play a prominent part in religious traditions. Miracles and predictions are what the gods provide for humanity.

Epiphanies of the Gods

Appearing and power were closely related. The gods manifested themselves for the benefit of individuals or groups, and their manifestations or epiphanies were recorded on stone and in books.

Thus there were books entitled *Epiphanies of Apollo, On the Epiphanies of Zeus,* and *The Epiphanies of the Virgin Goddess.* [2] An inscription describing epiphanies of Athena at Lindos even includes references to historical authorities for the miracles.[3] The epiphanies themselves involved a magistrate's dream and a rainfall that helped the Lindians against the Persians, the instructions of the goddess about a corpse in the temple, and her order to a magistrate to ask King Ptolemy for help against an invader from Macedonia.

Other inscriptions refer to the epiphanies of such deities as Apollo, Artemis, Asclepius, Athena, and Zeus. A second-century papyrus contains "the praises of Imouthes-Asclepius" and ends with a reference to the god's "wondrous epiphanies, the greatness of his power, and the gifts of his benefits."[4]

The anti-Christian author Celsus devotes more space to oracles than to epiphanies, and indeed the oracles of the Greco-Roman world had a certain reliability about them that appealed to defenders of paganism. Celsus insists that at shrines of heroes "gods are to be seen in human form, not deceitful but plainly evident." They do not merely make "a single appearance in a stealthy and secretive manner like the fellow who deceived the Christians, but are always conversing with those who are willing."[5] A little later he insists on the importance of such revelations.

> Why need I list all the events which on the ground of oracles have been foretold with inspired utterance both by prophets and prophetesses and by other inspired persons, both men and women? or all the wonderful things that have been heard from the shrines themselves? or all the revelations by means of victims and sacrifices? or all those indicated by other miraculous signs? To some persons there have been plainly evident appearances. The whole of life is full of these experiences.

Celsus then proceeds to note the effect of oracles on the history of cities and colonies, on rulers and people, and on the health of individuals.[6] It is an argument from "consensus."[7] Similarly a Stoic speaker in Cicero's *On the Nature of the Gods* began his defense of divination with public examples and went on to those taken from private life.[8]

A less "realistic" view is expressed by a Stoic representative in Cicero's treatise *On Divination.* He cites examples of oracular responses but later adds this significant comment: "Do we expect the immortal gods to converse with us in the forum, on the street, and in our homes? While they do not, of course [*quiden*], present themselves to us in person, they do diffuse their power far and wide, sometimes enclosing it in caverns of the earth and sometimes imparting it to human beings."[9] In this kind of thought there is room for divination but not for real epiphanies.

Praises of the Gods

During the reign of Hadrian, the rhetorician Alexander, son of a certain Numenius, explained how to set forth the praises of the gods.[10] He began his discussion with the supreme or first god, then turned to the "younger gods," who are concerned with the affairs of mortals.

A speaker should praise such a god on the ground that he is worshiped by all nations, or at least the most famous or strongest ones, and he is visible in statues made by famous sculptors. One should praise "the sovereignty of the god and the subjects of his rule in the sky, in the sea, and on earth." What art does he teach? (Athena teaches all the arts, while Zeus and Apollo teach divination.) What relationship does he have to other gods? (Zeus has primacy of power, while Hermes deals with heralding.) "Then how he appeared to men, and his love for them" (no examples are given). Finally one should discuss animals, trees, and special places sacred to him, as well as his association with other deities, as in the case of Apollo and the Muses.

Three points deserve emphasis in Alexander's outline. First, he claims that "some gods are older while some are younger." This statement points to the importance of mythology as a substitute for theology in much Greek thought about the gods. Asclepius was a powerful healer, but his father Apollo also could achieve healings. To call Zeus "father of gods and men" was not an idle statement, for one could trace genealogies not only among heroes and kings but among the gods themselves. To be sure, mythographers sometimes disagreed with one another over these relationships. The general principle that there were relationships remained intact.

Indeed, it had been intact for many centuries, ever since the *Theogony* of Hesiod provided a helpful analysis of the gods' family relationships. It was Hesiod who explained that Athena was the daughter of Zeus and Metis (*Theogony* 886), Apollo and Artemis the children of Zeus and Leto (*Theogony* 918), Hermes the son of Zeus and Maia (*Theogony* 938), Dionysus the son of Zeus and Semele (*Theogony* 940), Heracles the son of Zeus and Alcmene (*Theogony* 950). In the *Eoiae* he probably described Asclepius as son of Apollo and a certain Arsinoe, not the more usual Coronis,[11] but it was his divine father who made the difference. The relationship of aliens like Isis, Sarapis, and Mithras to the Greek gods depended on how they were identified with the Greek deities.

Second, the statues of the gods were important. In the dream visions of Aelius Aristides, the various gods appeared to him as depicted in art. How else would he know who they were? Athena appears "with her aegis and the beauty and size and the whole form of the Athena of Phidias at Athens" (*Orations* 48.41, tr. Behr). Asclepius too sometimes appears "in the posture in which he is represented in statues" (*Orations* 50.50).

Third, it was necessary to speak of the god's "power [*dynamis*], what it is and what works prove it. . . . what things have been rectified through the art which he practises and established . . . whatever works he has done among the gods or for the gods . . . in what way he appeared to men, and his love for mankind." Here there would be discussions of epiphanies made not just for the sake of divine manifestation but for the benefit of gods or human beings. (Under "art," one would naturally mention the medical skill of Asclepius.)

What Did People Generally Think?

It is hard to find out what ordinary people thought the gods did for them. Dio Chrysostom says that "you might reasonably expect (and people report) that founding heroes or gods would often visit the cities they have founded, invisible to others both at sacrifices and at festivals." He refers to Heracles as attracted by a magnificent funerary pyre built in his honor.[12] But the gods would be "invisible to others" (whoever they were), and the statement proves nothing about the more random appearances of the gods to aid even their devotees. Literary figures gain and hold the center of the stage, and only an occasional papyrus letter proves what others had in mind.

Cases from Letters and Inscriptions

Often the letters too are highly stereotyped. In the sampling given by A. S. Hunt and C. C. Edgar, people regularly inform their correspondents that "before all" they are praying for their health either "with all the gods of this place" or "with the Lord Sarapis." They give thanks to Sarapis for rescue from shipwreck or pray to him about health; they pray to "ancestral gods," especially when they are away from home. Does "stereotyped" mean "insincere"? Probably not. When a woman in deep trouble with her husband says, "Every day and evening I make supplication on your behalf before [the hippopotamus goddess] Thoeris who loves you," she must be writing what she believes.[13] Oracles could give personal advice: inscriptions from Dodona show Zeus and his consort Dione being asked about the legitimacy of prospective offspring, about sickness, about real estate, about raising sheep, and about prospective travel.[14]

Some Important Witnesses

Plutarch

Early in the second century the philosopher Plutarch placed the lesser gods between gods and men. Following the Platonic philosopher Xenocrates, he held that between the two groups there were *daimones*, usually beneficent but sometimes harmful. Second-century Christians who discussed such beings invariably had evil *daimones* in view; Plutarch recognized both kinds but laid emphasis on the good. Another Middle Platonist, Albinus, treated them as created by God the Demiurge.[15]

Plutarch thus discusses the meaning of Isis as a good *daimon* before she became a goddess.

> She was not indifferent to the contests and struggles she had endured, nor to her wanderings or her many deeds of wisdom and courage, and she would not accept oblivion and silence for them. With the most holy rites she mingled portrayals and suggestions and imitations of her sufferings at that time, and sanctified them as a lesson in piety and an encouragement for men and women who are overpowered by like disasters.[16]

Oddly enough, as we shall see in chapter 9, Plutarch also called Isis in some sense a cosmic deity.

Artemidorus

To avoid undue concentration on what philosophers said, we turn to the second-century *Dream Book* of Artemidorus, even though it too is a learned treatise, classifying the gods as well as describing them. The advantage his work has for us is that some people must have dreamed the kinds of dreams he interprets. He reveals a thoroughly religious world.

Artemidorus classifies gods in several ways.[17] They can be divided into the many known by the mind (*noetoi*, a term later used by Neoplatonists) and the few known to the senses. They can be treated as Olympian or etherial, heavenly, earthly, sea and river, subterranean, and "outside these categories." Olympians are self-evidently gods like Zeus, Hera, Heavenly Aphrodite, Artemis, Apollo, Etherial Fire, and Athena; heavenly are Sun and Moon, and so forth ("all these are known to the senses"). On earth there are also gods known to the senses, such as Hecate, Pan, Ephialtes ("nightmare"), and Asclepius (he is mentally known too), as well as gods perceived by mind such as the Dioscuri, Heracles, Dionysus, Hermes, Nemesis, Ordinary Aphrodite, and so forth. Among the subterranean deities he names not only the Eleusinian gods Pluto, Persephone, Demeter, Kore, and Iacchus but also (without making any distinction) the Egyptians Sarapis, Isis, Anubis, and Harpokrates. At the end he mentions the primordial gods who go beyond classification: Oceanus, Tethys, Kronos, the Titans, and the Nature of the universe.

The difference between gods perceived by mind and gods perceived by sense is most obscure. The heavenly gods in the sky are obviously perceived by sight. Apart from that, the classifications break down. Artemidorus soon turns to different kinds of distinctions.[18] When the Olympians appear they confer benefits upon the highest class of men and women, while the heavenly gods aid the middle class and the earthly gods help the poor. The subterranean gods are usually good only to farmers and those who are trying to escape detection. Sea and river gods aid sailors and others who work with water. The unclassified gods are harmful to all except philosophers and seers, those who stretch their minds to the limits of the universe.

What kind of help can one expect from the gods according to Artemidorus' book? Just what one would hope for: wealth, health, skill in one's work or profession, happy marriage and safe childbirth, maintenance of family relationships, emancipation from slavery, safe journeys. According to Artemidorus, the Egyptian deities are especially powerful.[19] Dreams about them "and their shrines and mysteries, and everything that has to do with them and those who share temples and altars with them, mean troubles, dangers, threats, and conspiracies—from which they provide security beyond expectation and hopes. For the gods are thought to be saviors of those who have tried every means and have come to the ultimate danger; they are especially the saviors of those who are in such circumstances. Their mysteries are notably predictive of grief; if the physical explanation of their story contains something else, the mythical and the historical interpretations show this."

Thus the gods about whom stories were most often told were not the supreme gods of either Greece or Rome but the deities who in

some sense had lived among humans before and were likely to
appear and give aid now. With the passage of time and the development of theology these lesser gods assumed additional roles that
brought them close to the Olympians or the Twelve Gods of Rome.

Galen

Not everyone was so devoted to the gods. If we look through the
multivolumed works of the physician Galen, we find remarkably
little said about the gods of popular mythology. For Galen only
Asclepius is important, especially because in myth Apollo gave the
gift of healing to him and in turn he revealed it to humanity.[20] He
hardly ever mentions the other gods, though he refers to some of
them as legislators for particular peoples.[21] Though he firmly believes in providential formation and governance by the Demiurge of
Plato's *Timaeus*, whom he calls "Nature," he does not believe in the
wonder stories about divine aid or harm. Those who believe them
rely on "so-called histories" and do not try to understand causes.[22]
He is willing to allegorize Athena's birth from the head of Zeus and
here follows the lead of the Stoic philosopher Chrysippus.[23] The
stories about the birth of Zeus are merely etymological.[24] Aphrodite
was born from foam (*aphros*), but this too is a myth.[25] Ordinarily
Galen discusses aphrodisiacs rather than Aphrodite.

Deified Emperors

Before turning to the beneficent works of the divine sons of gods,
we note that on the borderline between gods and men there also
stood not only *daimones* of varying rank but also great human heroes
or benefactors such as the emperor Augustus. As early as 9 B.C. the
Greek cities of Asia hailed his birthday in religious language: "Since
the providence that has ordained everything in our life . . . the
birthday of the god was the beginning of the good news (*euangelion*)
for the world on his account."[26] A coin issued in Spain to honor his
wife Julia Augusta (Livia) calls her "mother of the world," *genetrix
orbis.*[27] Suetonius tells a tale of his last visit to the Bay of Naples.
When an Alexandrian ship met him, passengers and crew alike put
on white clothing and crowns. They offered incense and shouted
that "through him they lived, through him they sailed, through him
they enjoyed freedom and fortune." He responded with a gift of
gold—not to the Alexandrians but more practically to his companions, whom he asked to spend the money on Alexandrian goods.[28]

The language shows that there was no rigid distinction between gratitude and cosmic affirmation. There was good news for the world at Augustus' birth.[29] His wife could be called the world's mother. The Alexandrians owed their very existence to him. If such was the case with a heroic emperor, the gods could obviously be described in similar terms.[30]

Hellenistic rulers had sometimes been deified, especially in Egypt, but under the Roman empire the senate regularly deified deceased emperors who had cooperated with it. During the first century there was some resistance to the process. Tiberius was not deified. Seneca ridiculed the idea of Claudius as a god. Vespasian on his deathbed exclaimed, "Alas! I think I am turning into a god."[31] By the second century the situation had been regularized and much pomp and circumstance accompanied the ceremonies. Christians, Jews, and others remained skeptical.[32] When they criticized older emperors, however, they confined their attacks to those who had not been deified, Nero and Domitian. (Caligula, generally regarded as crazy, was not worth naming.)[33]

The practice of deification in the Hellenistic age and in the Roman empire led scholarly Greeks and Romans to suppose that all the gods were originally heroes, deified after death because of their aid to humanity. The theory was usually ascribed to an early Hellenistic novelist named Euhemerus, who claimed to have visited an island in the Indian Ocean where he found a golden column with records of the deeds of Uranus, Cronus, and Zeus. These had been kings, deified by grateful subjects like the Hellenistic peoples of Euhemerus' own time. This confirmation of a widespread suspicion about the gods was made popular by the historian Diodorus Siculus, while the Latin poet Ennius relied on Euhemerus for his own prose study, which included the Roman god Jupiter Optimus. Obviously the theory was useful to Christian opponents of paganism. The first Christian apologist to mention Euhemerus was Theophilus of Antioch, who unfortunately confused him with the atheist Diagoras. More fortunately, the later Latin apologist Lactantius used Ennius' version.

5

The Deeds of Individual
Gods and Heroes

Zeus

We begin with Zeus, not Zeus the supreme father in heaven, who did not usually manifest himself to individuals, but Zeus the local deity of Stratoniceia in Caria, Zeus Panamaros. When the city was under attack, probably in 40 B.C., flames from the temple drove the enemy away by night, and fog and rain followed the next day. An inscription ascribes the miracle to the local Zeus.[1] Martin P. Nilsson notes other "political" miracles of the time.[2]

Another event related to Zeus is the "rain miracle" on the Danube under Marcus Aurelius. Various parties claimed credit for it. The column of the emperor in Rome depicts Jupiter Pluvius with wings outspread and rain falling on thirsty Roman soldiers. Dio Cassius refers to "Arnuphis, an Egyptian magician who was with Marcus," who invoked various deities and especially "the aerial Hermes." Contemporary Christians assigned it to God and his response to the prayers of a whole legion of Christian soldiers.[3]

Beyond this there is of course "the epiphany that never was," when Barnabas and Paul were misidentified as Zeus and Hermes (see chapter 1).

Children of Zeus

We now turn to the most important "sons and daughters" of Zeus and some of the other gods, to see how they helped humanity.

Apollo

The god Apollo, son of Zeus, was associated with many of the arts and identified with the sun as early as the fifth century B.C.[4] He was best known, however, as inspirer of oracles, especially the one at Delphi. This was the principal Greek oracle, presided over by a priestess called the Pythia. She sat on a tripod and in a state of ecstasy delivered brief speeches, usually enigmatic, which were put into verse by a "prophet." Before the Hellenistic age many questions came from the rival Greek city-states, though also from individuals and in regard to morality. On the temple walls were inscribed "Know thyself" and "Nothing too much." It may be that in the Hellenistic period the shrine was a center where slaves were fictitiously sold to the god until they had worked off the full price paid their masters,[5] but the arguments of F. Bömer have weakened the case for such a practice.[6]

The oracle at Delphi lost influence and wealth in a period when religious cults were generally growing. Cicero stated that the oracle was in decline, and Strabo noted that "at present the temple at Delphi is very poor."[7] Apparently the oracle had favored the Greek cities and kings in their struggle with Rome, and in consequence the Romans rarely consulted it.[8] Augustus venerated Apollo not at Delphi but at Actium, where he had won the empire. Nero's attitude was ambivalent. On one occasion he "abolished the oracle," filling with corpses the fissure from which the vapor of prophetic inspiration supposedly arose. For a possibly favorable oracle, however, he gave a fairly large sum. His successor Galba was able to recover it for the imperial treasury.[9]

Plutarch discussed the decline of Delphi in two famous dialogues, one on the failure of the oracles, the other on the reason the oracles were not given in verse. Soon afterward the emperor Hadrian, devoted to Greek traditions, tried to revive the oracle. From about the same time, however, come the fragments of the *Refutation of the Charlatans* by the Cynic critic Oenomaus of Gadara. These denunciations of oracles, especially at Delphi, were preserved only by the Christian author Eusebius.[10] Christians like Origen, who vigorously criticized the priestess (see chapter 11), were of course hostile to the oracle, but their attacks suggest that the oracle was still active and highly regarded by many. The pious pagan emperor Julian naturally denounced Oenomaus' work.[11]

Apollo did not give oracles just at Delphi, however. At Miletus and Didyma his shrines flourished throughout the third century.[12] The politically inept oracle at Miletus advised Diocletian to persecute Christians and apparently was forced to recant later.[13]

Apollo was also associated with wisdom, philosophy, and the arts. There were those who even regarded him as the divine father of Plato. According to Origen, the story ran that Plato was the son of

Apollo and a human mother.[14] Jerome went even farther. Not only Plato's nephew and successor Speusippus, he relates, but also the Peripatetic Clearchus and Anaxilides, author of a treatise *On Philosophers,* insisted that Plato's mother was overcome by a vision of Apollo. They thought he would not have been the greatest of philosophers unless born of a virgin mother.[15] Since a closely similar report provided by Diogenes Laërtius (3.2) lacks the reference to a virgin mother, it probably comes from Jerome himself. He has "Christianized" the story.

Christians were not the only ones to collect such information, carefully preserved among Platonists in the second century and later. Plutarch, Apuleius, and Olympiodorus refer to the story, telling how the god as an apparition had intercourse with Plato's mother and then commanded his father not to approach her until the child was born.[16]

Athena

Athena was a daughter of Zeus and Metis, although the god swallowed Metis because he feared her destiny to produce Athena and then a god to rule the gods. In consequence, Athena was born out of the top of his head. The story seems rather confused and presumably combines a swallowing motif with an allegory.[17] Christians took a special interest in the story of her birth, which as we shall see was often treated allegorically by those interested in philosophy and therefore led to a cosmic interpretation.

She was the great patroness of the city of Athens and its art. Many of the gods were concerned with the foundation of Athens, says Aelius Aristides, but Athena above all "granted the city superiority in wisdom."[18] She is the goddess to whom belong both reason (*logos*) and the city itself.[19]

As noted earlier, in Luke's story of Paul at Athens there is no mention of Athena. Perhaps for him the philosophical setting of his story excluded such a local goddess. In any case there was no reason to mention her if no conflict arose. The goddess was present and known as a miracle-worker elsewhere, however—for example at Lindos, where there is a temple chronicle with lists of gifts and another list with three of her epiphanies. Each one (490 B.C., fifth to fourth century B.C., and 305 B.C.) is confirmed by a bibliographical note. The longest now extant states that the events were narrated by no fewer than seven authorities. The listing of these literary references suggests that some may have raised questions about such accounts, but in spite of any doubts the temple adornment was still

paid for because of "the epiphany of the goddess."[20] Another Hellenistic inscription tells of an epiphany of Athena Bringer of Victory.[21]

Dionysus

Ancient authors do not seem to have made anything of the fact
that Zeus's daughter Athena was born out of his head and Dionysus
out of his thigh. Even allegorizers kept silence. The resemblances
were more important: both gods were uniquely close to their father
and both helped humanity. The difference in the kind of help was
more important. Dionysus was conspicuous for his association with
wine, revelry, and ecstasy. In art he was often accompanied by satyrs
and maenads. A Silenus from the London Mithraeum depicts the
Dionysiac circle as giving *vitam hominibus vagantibus*, "life to wander-
ing men," and it is not clear whether they are drunk or seeking for
deeper meanings or both. Similarly, the beautiful frescoes on the
wall of the Villa Item at Pompeii depict the wedding of Dionysus and
Ariadne, thus pointing toward the marital bliss often mentioned by
Roman writers. A veiled phallus and a young woman being beaten
with rods do not necessarily point to a deeper, mystical Dionysiac
cult.

Some of the ancients even supposed that the god's name was
derived from *oinou dosis*, "gift of wine." At festivals his gift was
repeated. Priests at Teos, north of Ephesus, claimed that he was
born there, for at fixed times, as late as the first century B.C., a
fountain of wine gushed forth spontaneously from the ground.
Competitors on the island of Andros, north of Delos, claimed that
the water from a spring in the temple of Dionysus always tasted like
wine on January 5, the day they called *Theodosia*, "gift of the god."
For Elis near Olympia, Pausanias gives more details. He did not visit
Elis in time for the festival, but "the most respected citizens of Elis"
and others as well swore to the truth of a miracle. Dionysus himself
attended the festival, at which the priests put three empty pots in
the temple and sealed the doors. The next day they broke the seals
and went in to find the pots full of wine.[22]

Hermes

In the *Cratylus* (407E), Plato explains that the name Hermes is
derived from *hermeneus*, "interpreter"; he was also "a messenger,
wily and deceptive in speech, and rhetorical." Hermes presided
over thieves and businessmen and gave aid to both. He was a fast
talker whom the Romans honored as Mercury. Stoics used the alle-

gorical method to identify him as the *logos* or speech of Zeus, whose messenger he was. In the first century Cornutus called him "the Logos, which the gods sent to us from heaven," though he was not considered an agent in creation, as far as we know, before the fourth century.[23] Justin Martyr had heard of him as "the interpretive Logos and teacher of all."[24] We have seen in chapter 1 that in Lycaonia villagers could suppose that he had come down to them from heaven.

Heroes

Asclepius

Asclepius was a son of Apollo and the nymph Coronis, according to myths, and was noted for the cures he performed. He was originally a man, however, as Homer makes plain. Zeus later killed him with his thunderbolt because he raised a mortal from the dead and might have done so for all humanity. The account does not seem highly consistent, and the Skeptic Sextus Empiricus takes pleasure in listing the contradictory and "false" explanations given by various poets and historians.[25] The Christians had no difficulty in following up this line of attack, but in spite of criticisms Asclepius was widely venerated well into the fourth century.

The public setting of Asclepian religion was extremely important. Without the propagandistic records of healings at Asclepius' shrine at Epidaurus, the history of Hellenistic religion would be much poorer. The inscriptions (about 300 B.C.) record healings performed by the god for pilgrims who slept in the shrine. The god could perform healings elsewhere, as we learn from the orations of Aelius Aristides. When one asks what the gods were supposed to be doing for humanity, these inscriptions provide the kind of definite answer often lacking elsewhere.

Strabo, writing in the Augustan age, says that at Epidaurus "Asclepius, who is believed to cure diseases of every kind, always has his temple full of the sick and of the votive tablets on which the treatments are recorded." Nearly two centuries later, Pausanias tells us that old votive tablets still stood within the enclosure at Epidaurus. "In my time six remained, but earlier there were more. On them were inscribed the names of the men and women healed by Asclepius, the disease from which each one suffered, and the mode of the cure; they were written in Doric."[26] At the end of the nineteenth century two of the six were found complete, part of a third, and a piece of a fourth.[27]

The title given the narratives is *Healings of Apollo and Asclepius*, even though Apollo is not mentioned in what we have. O. Weinreich suggests that "epiphanies" would be a more correct title, but emphasis is being laid on the results of the epiphanies. The cures always took place, though the sleeping suppliant did not always have to dream, nor did the god always have to appear. More often than not, however, the sleeper "saw a vision" *(opsis)* or the equivalent "dream" *(enypnion)*. Often "it seemed to him" or "her" that the god was present. More tangibly, the god could extract the head of a spear or an arrow and put it into the hands of the patient. Some of the stories clearly suggest that when asleep the patients underwent surgery performed by the priests. However the cures were effected, all could agree upon the power of Asclepius to perform them. The priests insisted on advertising the power of the god.

Such healings continued at Epidaurus and elsewhere (notably at Pergamum and at Aegae in Cilicia) for more than six hundred years. In his *Life of Constantine*, Eusebius says of Aegae that "thousands were excited over [Asclepius] as over a savior and physician who sometimes was manifest to sleepers and sometimes healed the diseases of those who were sick." The god led their souls astray, however, and therefore Constantine ordered the temple destroyed. "Not a trace of the former madness remained there."[28] As late as 355 a "hierophant and priest of the Savior, instructed by a dream," still could dedicate an altar at Epidaurus to the Asclepius of Aegae.[29]

Seven years after that, Julian mentioned Asclepius at Aegae in his treatise *Against the Galileans* (200B), and a priest of the god from that shrine asked him to have the pillars of the temple given back by the Christian church there. One column was brought as far as the doorway of the church by the time the emperor died. The Christian bishop then moved it back into the church.[30]

The practice of "incubation" was not confined to the temples we have mentioned. Many other shrines of Asclepius could provide dreams and cures, while other gods and goddesses had similar powers. For the western provinces we mention only the shrine of Nodens (Mars) in Gloucestershire and that of the goddess Sequana near Dijon.[31]

There were also relations of a more private and personal sort between Asclepius and some of his worshipers. Fortunately we possess the six "sacred orations" produced by the hypochondriac Aelius Aristides in the latter half of the second century. These provide an invaluable picture of a personal attitude toward the god

and his powers[32] as well as materials for a medical and psychopatho-
logical analysis.[33]

Heracles

The hero Heracles was regarded as a son of Zeus and a human
mother, Alcmene. Zeus's jealous wife Hera persecuted Heracles
throughout his life, beginning by sending two serpents to kill him
as an infant; he escaped by strangling them. Later he was forced to
serve Eurystheus and at his command achieved the famous Labors,
twelve in number. After many further adventures, his wife Deianeira
got him to wear a garment poisoned with the blood of a centaur.
This caused him frightful pain and he had himself brought to the
top of Mount Deta and burned on a pyre. His divine part ascended
to heaven, where he was reconciled with Hera and married her
daughter Hebe.[34]

The Christian apologist Justin supplies a clear and brief summary
of Heracles' career. "They say that Heracles was strong and wan-
dered over the whole earth; he was born to Zeus by Alcmene, and
when he died he ascended to heaven."[35] In the *Apology* he had said
that "to escape from pain he delivered himself to fire."[36] Justin
simply reports the myth and seems to know nothing of any allegorical interpretation.

About the time of Justin, however, Stoics were treating Heracles
as a great example of moral struggle. Dio Chrysostom idealized his
labors, which he supposedly undertook "for virtue's sake," and said
that he was considered son of Zeus "because of his virtue." Alexander the Great was thought to be descended from him.[37] Epictetus
used him as a model of effort. "What would Heracles have
amounted to without his labors? They revealed him and trained
him." The effort led to deification. "With him he had no dearer
friend than God. This is why he was believed to be, and was, son
of Zeus. In obedience to him he went about eradicating injustice and
lawlessness."[38]

Another example: "Heracles was ruler and leader of the whole
land and sea, purging them of injustice and lawlessness and introducing justice and righteousness; and he did these things naked and
alone."[39]

Epictetus not only provides the moral meaning of the story of
Heracles but also explains away difficult episodes. He explains Heracles' wanderings thus: "It was the lot of Heracles to traverse the
entire world, 'seeing the wanton behavior of men and the lawful'
(*Od.* 17.487), casting out and purging the one and introducing the

other for it." Then he turns to the difficult problem of Heracles' incessant promiscuity. "He was in the habit of marrying [!] on occasion and begetting children and deserting them, not groaning or yearning for them or leaving them as orphans. For he knew that no human being is an orphan but for all always and constantly there is the Father who cares for them." Now, past the difficulty raised by mythology, Epictetus is ready to turn to the relation of Heracles to the Father Zeus. He concludes triumphantly that "to him it was no mere story that Zeus is father of men, for he always thought of him as his own father and called him so and looked to him in all he did. Therefore he had the power to live happily in every place."[40]

Oriental Gods

Isis

The worship of Isis (and Osiris) originated in Egypt and in both art and ritual preserved an Egyptian atmosphere. Isis was not worshiped for the sake of local color, however. She performed many functions for her devotees and these are listed notably in the so-called *Praises of Isis* found in the Greek islands and elsewhere. The version in some manuscripts of Diodorus Siculus[41] suggests that the *Praises* were sent out from Memphis, but this may be part of the fictitious framework for the work, which indicates that they were found on hieroglyphs at Nysa in Arabia.[42]

> I am Isis, the queen of every land, and whatever laws I ordained no one can dissolve. I am the eldest daughter of the youngest god Cronus. I am wife and sister of King Osiris. I am the first inventor of crops for mankind. I am the mother of King Horus. I am she who rises in the star in the constellation Sirius. For me the city of Bubastis was built. Rejoice, rejoice, Egypt that nursed me.

The fullest version of the Isis aretalogy, from Cyme, lists no fewer than fifty-three virtues, powers, or achievements of the goddess and recalls the "praises of Yahweh" to be found in the Old Testament.[43] If we analyze these materials, we find that almost all are basically religious rather than related to philosophical theology. They deal with the myth about the goddess and her achievements for humanity, especially for the women who may have been her principal devotees.

Isis is the supreme Queen goddess, eldest daughter of Cronus and sister of Osiris, brought up in Egypt and given instruction by the wise god Hermes. She differentiated the hieratic language from demotic and also became the wife of King Osiris and mother of

Horus. She founded the city of Bubastis (and is therefore superior to the lioness goddess of that name). She is no merely Egyptian deity, however, for she has complete control over world events and indeed over fate.

A brief cosmological section found in these Greek versions but not well attested in Egyptian sources (lines 10–12) identifies Isis as the divider of earth from heaven and the guide to the stars, sun, and moon on their courses. (We shall discuss these lines in chapter 9 when we come to the cosmic meaning of Isis.) Elsewhere in the *Praises* she appears in the rays of the sun and accompanies it on its course, while in Diodorus and on Cyme she rises as a star in the constellation Sirius.[44] In other words, in the *Praises,* apart from lines 10 to 12, she is not a true creator, though she does rule over rivers, winds, rains, and storms as well as the sea and the islands in it. As a sea goddess she is also concerned with navigation and seamanship.

She cares for the lesser gods and established their initiations, shrines, and sacred groves as well as her own. More to the point, she is concerned with human beings. She gave them agriculture and trade by sea; she founded cities, hence civilization; and she liberates prisoners. She brings down tyrants and rules over war. Her legislation determines the basic principles of morality, and she strengthens what is right.

Most important in regard to the women who worshiped her (she is called God by women), she created their sexual attractiveness, instituted marriage contracts to protect them, designed the nature of pregnancy and birth, and established binding ties between children and parents.

Items repeatedly mentioned must point to essential claims of the Isiac religion. There are repeated references or allusions to Isis' strengthening of what is right, her encouragement of sexual attraction, and her concern for navigation. These must have been key elements in the appeal of the goddess to men, to women, and to humanity generally. Hers was a universal message, based on an Egyptian foundation but pointing toward the whole Mediterranean world. As we have indicated, in the *Praises* there is little philosophical theology or none. For fully cosmic interpretations we must wait for philosophers like Plutarch and rhetoricians like Apuleius.

Sarapis

We have already discussed the origin of Sarapis (chapter 2). In all probability, Greek theologians at the court of Ptolemy I gave shape to the cult of Sarapis. He lacked the allure of antiquity, but he was a famous wonder-worker and benefactor of humanity. He saved people from illness and shipwreck and was known as a friend of sailors. This is shown in *Oxyrhynchus Papyrus* XI 1382, where a pilot recounts a miracle—unfortunately now lost—which is so spectacular that it is to be " recorded in the library of Mercury." Those who hear about it will cry out "There is one Zeus Sarapis." The little account has a title: "Miracle of Zeus Helios the great Sarapis in regard to the pilot Syrion."

Weinreich argued that since the god had "neither myth nor genealogy . . . miracle stories took the place of mythology."[45] Aelius Aristides would probably have agreed. He said in one speech that the genealogy of Asclepius is irrelevant when compared with his miracles of healing and in another pointed out that it would take forever to collect all the stories of the works of Sarapis.[46] The latter sentiment obviously resembles John 21:25, on the deeds of Jesus: "If they were recorded one by one, I think the world itself could not hold the books that could be written."

Some worshipers of Sarapis may have been especially devout. There were men who lived at the principal shrines in Egypt and were called *katochoi*. They "seem to have considered themselves bound to the temple precincts until the god should set them free."[47] Evidence for their existence comes from the papyri.[48] These persons were probably men "possessed" by the god.[49] In the third century of our era there were *katochoi* of Uranian Zeus near Apamaea. At first, Dittenberger thought they simply owned property in the village, but later he changed his mind.[50]

Of course one could add discussions of many other gods and many other forms of myth and ritual. These will suffice, however, to give a picture of the background current in New Testament times and immediately afterward. Now we turn to the theological considerations present among pagans and Christians alike.

PART THREE
Basic Doctrines

6

The Philosophical Doctrine of God

We have discussed the forms of religion that had to do with local or personal relationships between gods and human beings, whether in epiphanies or oracles or divination or cult. In the following chapters we turn to universalizing statements about the gods and their complete power and providence; that is, statements of a theological nature.

A papyrus containing popular "sayings of Sansnos" begins with the counsel to "revere the divine" and to "sacrifice to all the gods."[1] This advice made good sense in a world full of religions. The multiplicity of gods in Greco-Roman paganism is nowhere more evident than in the lists of names that scholarly ancient authors provided.[2] These lists attract attention especially when used by Christians against the gods. Theophilus, for example, inquires "how many kinds of Zeus there are," and relies on a semi-alphabetical list for the names Olympios, Latiaris, Kassios, Keraunios, Propator, Pannychios, Poliouchos, and Kapitolinus, as well as the son of Kronos, buried on Krete (Theophilus, *To Autolycus* 1.10). Clement mentions three Zeuses, five Athenas, and six Apollos (Clement, *Exhortation to the Greeks* 28.1–3).

Philosphers and rhetoricians, on the other hand, gave lists that emphasized the beneficent activities of particular gods under various aspects. Examples for Zeus occur in *On the Universe* ascribed to Aristotle (401A) and in two orations by Dio Chrysostom (1.39–41); 12.75–76). The content of such lists was similar to theologians' list of the names and attributes of God.[3]

Against polytheism stood those who, usually following philosophers, developed ideas about the unity of God or, as it is sometimes called, the divine monarchy. This idea was supported more often not by rejecting other gods in favor of one but by insisting upon the virtual identity of one god with others. There might be one god or goddess, but he or she transcended all the names that could be applied to his or her local manifestations. Isis, for example, was called "myriad named" because of the number of such equations.[4] Apuleius tells that in various places she is known as Mother of the Gods, Minerva, Venus, Diana, and so on.[5] We now turn to the doctrines by which philosophers justified such syntheses.

Anticipations Among the Pre-Socratics

There were anticipations of philosophical theology in the first attempts to coordinate and systematize Greek mythology, not to mention the earlier essays of Orientals in regard to their own myths. Later Greeks often thought that Homer and Hesiod were responsible for such systematization and that they had made it popular by expressing it in poetic form. Later philosophers preserved the memory of the pioneers, notably Xenophanes, who was to be highly regarded by Christians.[6]

Xenophanes the Critical Theologian

Xenophanes described Homer as the poet "from whom all men have learned since the beginning," but he did not agree with what Homer taught about the gods. Instead, "One god is the greatest among gods and men; in neither form nor thought is he like mortals." Indeed, he "ever abides in the selfsame place without moving; nor is it fitting for him to move hither and thither, changing his place." His creative and formative activity is mental, not physical: "But effortlessly he sets all things astir By the power of his mind alone."[7] Werner Jaeger compares a similar idea in Aeschylus about the way the gods work: "Gods act without effort: high from their hallowed seats they somehow make their own thinking come all at once to pass."[8]

Against this background we can readily see why Xenophanes was so hostile toward the old poets, who were providing textbooks for Greece. The problem is first of all moral. "Homer and Hesiod say that the gods perform countless most disgraceful actions: adultery, stealing, deceiving one another." In addition, "mortals suppose that the gods undergo generation; they dress them with clothing like their own, as well as voice and form." Xenophanes therefore denounced anthropomorphic depictions of the gods. "If cattle [and horses] and lions had hands, or could paint with their hands and fashion such pictures as men do, then horses would pattern the forms of the gods after horses, and cattle after cattle, giving them just such bodies as the shapes which they find in themselves." Thus, he says, [the gods of] the Ethiopians are black with snub noses, while [those of] Thracians are blond, with blue eyes and red hair."[9]

This whole attitude passed into later Greek criticism of the traditional gods and was eagerly appropriated by Christian authors. We have just referred to several fragments of Xenophanes. Indeed, Fragment 23 about the one God comes from Clement of Alexandria, who immediately proceeds to quote Fragments 14 and 15 and elsewhere cites Fragment 16, all directed against anthropomorphism.[10] We may add that even if Clement was using anthologies, the fact (if it is a fact) makes no difference in the theological impact. The negative side of Xenophanes' thought was immensely popular among later philosophers and notably with Plato, who rejected poetry from his ideal Republic simply because it was harmful to true theology. We shall later see how influential Xenophanes' positive doctrine of God was with some early Christians.

Zeus as King of Gods and Men

A. B. Cook has traced the history of Zeus from "god of the bright blue sky" through his control over various weather phenomena, as a god of the earth, then the strongest, most powerful, and wisest of the gods.[11] In Homer and later there was a tendency to exalt him, in spite of the many myths about him that are "early and grotesque."[12] Myths and cults can be contrasted with what Zeus meant to "poets and thinkers."[13] A movement toward monotheism is evident even in Homer, who calls Zeus "father of gods and men."[14] Hesiod too reveres him, and the works of both poets continued to influence schoolboys throughout antiquity. Some of the great tragic poets encouraged thought about Zeus and his mysterious workings in human life. A fragment of Aeschylus preserved by Clement of Alexandria says that "Zeus is ether, Zeus is earth, Zeus is heaven; and Zeus is everything beyond these."[15]

Christians, however, could also cite a line of Euripides from *Melanippe the Wise*.[16] In it Euripides referred to "Zeus, whoever he is, for I know him only by report [*plen logoi*]." The word *logos* permitted different kinds of exegesis. The more pious Stoics took *logos* to mean "reason"; one knew God only by this means.[17] Epicureans, on the other hand, took the word as "report" or "hearsay" and viewed Euripides as their own forerunner.[18] Plutarch tells a story (from the prologue to the play) about how the poet changed his mind and later substituted the line "Zeus, as he is called by the voice of truth."[19] In any event, Zeus was a cosmic power for Euripides, not a god active in human affairs.

Hellenistic philosophers often gave praise to Zeus. The devout Stoic Cleanthes invoked Zeus in two hymns, one quoted in an anthology, the other by later Stoics such as Seneca and Epictetus.[20] The poem of Aratus on weather prediction begins with the praise of Zeus. Cornutus, theorist of allegory in Roman times, devoted much space to Zeus, his names and his deeds. He explains that Homer calls Zeus "father of gods and men" because the nature of the world was the cause of the existence of these beings, "just as fathers generate children."[21] Plutarch is more precise, noting that they were not made through semen. The language is analogical; "God begot in matter the principle of generation."[22]

The praise of Zeus continues in the rhetorician Aelius Aristides, who has a hymn explicitly directed to him.[23] We shall return to Aristides later in this chapter.

Cosmic Theology in the Treatise *On the Universe*

A treatise from the early years of the Christian era, wrongly handed down among Aristotle's works, is entitled *De Mundo*, or *On the Universe*. Its philosophical origins are not readily identifiable, and it thus reflects the interrelationships of the schools in Roman times. It also shows how one could move from "God" to "Zeus" or the reverse.

The basic theological doctrine is set forth in chapter 6 *On the Universe*.[24] "All things are from God and were constitued for us by God." Indeed, "God is the preserver *soter* of all things and the creator *genetor* of everything in this universe, however it is brought to completion." He is Supreme, because Homer says he dwells "on the highest peak" of the whole heaven. The primary purpose of Pseudo-Aristotle is thus to lay emphasis on God's transcendence.

On the Universe ends with a brief but climactic statement about God and his names and functions.[25] "God being one yet has many names, being called after all the various conditions which he himself inaugurates. We call him Zen [here understood as derived from the verb "to live"] and Zeus, using the two names in the same sense, as though we should say 'him because of whom we live.' " He is the god known in mythology and from natural phenomena and his participation in human affairs. After a list of examples we see that he "derives his names from all natural phenomena and good fortune, since as he is the cause *(aitios)* of all things." A quotation from "the Orphic Hymns"[26] confirms the point, and the author goes on to simplify the theological tradition by identifying God with Necessity, Fate, Destiny, Lot, Nemesis, Adrasteia, and Dispensation and explaining that the names of the three Fates refer to God's actions in past, future, and present. Quotations from Plato round out the account. "God, as the old story has it, holding the beginning and the end and the middle of all things that exist . . . brings them all to accomplishment; and with him ever follows Justice."[27] This picture of Zeus as the "cause" of all obviously carries his transcendence beyond the simple assertions of supremacy and power to be found in mythology. The Orphic hymn makes it especially clear that he is above all else.

Plutarch's Doctrine of God

Plutarch's Platonic doctrine of God is set forth in the treatise *On the E at Delphi.*[28] We quote only the beginning, though all of the work is relevant.

> God exists, if one needs to say so, and he exists for no fixed time but for the everlasting ages which are immovable, timeless, and undeviating, in which there is no earlier or later, no future or past, no older or younger. He being one has completely filled "forever" with one "now"; and being is really being only when it is after his pattern, without having been or about to be, without a beginning and not coming to an end. Therefore in our worship we ought to hail him and address him with the words "Thou art," or even, by Zeus, as some of the ancients did, "Thou art one."

Plutarch goes on to explain that the name of Apollo, the god of Delphi, denies multiplicity. There is really one god, the god of Platonic theology.

Later Middle Platonists

By the middle of the second century, Middle Platonic doctrine about the supreme transcendent God was being expressed by a number of teachers, among whom we may mention Albinus, Apuleius, and Atticus.

Albinus, who taught Platonism toward the middle of the second century, has left an introductory manual in which the gods are discussed (ch. 8), in a section "on first principles *(archai)* and the theological theorems," specifically in relation to what Albinus calls "the third principle" (ch. 10). The gods have nothing to do with the world of sense perception, and since Mind is even better than Soul, the transcendent cause of Mind is the First God, who works un-moved (the Aristotelian principle). He always knows himself and his own thoughts, and this activity is called Form.[29]

> The First God is eternal, ineffable, self-sufficient—that is, without needs, ever-sufficient—that is, always perfect, all-sufficient—that is, completely perfect; Deity, Substantiality, Truth, Symmetry, Good. I mention these aspects not as providing definitions but as naming aspects in every respect characteristic of the one under consideration. And he is Good because he benefits all things as he is able, being the cause of every good thing; beautiful, because his form is by nature perfect and symmetrical; Truth, because he is the source of all truth as the sun is of all light; he is Father because he is the cause of all and sets in order the heavenly Mind and the soul of the universe toward himself and toward his own thoughts.
>
> For in accordance with his will he filled everything with himself, raising up the soul of the universe and turning it toward himself as being the cause of its Mind. The Mind, arranged by the Father, in turn arranges the whole of nature in this world. It is ineffable and appre-hensible only by Mind, as was said, since it has neither genus nor form nor distinction; nothing has happened to it, nor any evil, for it would not be right to say this; nor any good for this will involve participation in something, notably good.

Albinus goes on to offer further exercises in negative theology. Obviously they were popular in the philosophical or theosophical circles where religious thinkers sought philosophical support. For instance, the rare word *ousiotes* appears not only here but also in the contemporary *Corpus Hermeticum* (12.1), where we read that "the Nous is not cut off from the substantiality of God but is deployed, so to speak, from this source like light from the sun." Here we also find ourselves in the imagery used by the Christian apologists in speaking of the generation of the Son from the Father or the Logos from God. From a Hermetic fragment we learn that " the soul is an incorporeal substance which when in a body does not depart from its own substantiality."[30] Again, this was a doctrine which Christians and others found attractive.

In chapter 15,[31] Albinus speaks of God as maker of the whole universe, including gods and daemons. He sustains the whole by his will. The beings called his sons do what they do by his command and in imitation of him; they are responsible for divination. They also took part with him in the making of man.[32]

Apuleius[33] says that in Plato's doctrine, God is "incorporeal, one, immeasurable, begetter of everything, . . . blessed and beneficent, the best, in lack of nothing, himself bearing all things, celestial, ineffable, unnameable, and as he himself says, 'invisible, unconquerable'—'whose nature is difficult to find and if found cannot be expressed among the many' (*Tim.* 28E)."

Similar teaching is expressed by Atticus, head of the school at Athens around 176.[34] "Plato connects everything to God and from God. For he says he 'holds the beginning and middle and end of everything that exists and completes his circuit in a straight course' (*Leg.* 715E). And again he says he is good, but for the good there is no grudging about anything."

Such a monotheistic emphasis did not keep Platonists after Plutarch from differentiating the supreme God from the Demiurge or Creator. Albinus treats "the God in the heavens" as different from "the God above the heavens," who like Philo's Demiurge does not possess virtue but is above it.[35] Numenius (wrongly) claims that Plato made such a distinction. "As Plato knew that among men only the Demiurge is known, while the first Mind, called Being in itself, is entirely unknown among them, for this reason he spoke like one who might say this: 'O men, he whom you conjecture as Mind is not the First; another, older and more divine Mind is before him.' " It was not Plato who said this but Numenius himself.[36]

For authors like these there were thus at least two gods, not just one. Numenius, for example, writes that "if it is not necessary for the First to create, one must consider the First God as the Father of the one who creates." He then works out the implications of this thought.[37]

Rhetoricians and Satirists

Similar doctrines appear in the writings of rhetoricians such as Aelius Aristides and Maximus of Tyre, as well as those of the satirist Lucian and of Celsus, the critic of Christianity. We look at Aristides first.

There is a close connection between Aristides' prose hymn to Zeus (*Or.* 43) and the theories of the fourth-century rhetorician Menander. Aristides produces praise of Zeus; Menander tells us how it should be done.[38] The points to be treated are essentially the same. After briefly discussing the divisions of rhetoric, Menander turns to "hymns to the gods." Some are invocations, some the reverse; there are hymns "natural" or physical, or mythical, or genealogical, or fictitious. Finally, some hymns are petitions for favor, some the reverse. Menander provides examples by naming poets who favored one form or another. Thus among the "natural" or physical hymns are poems by Parmenides, Empedocles, Orpheus, Plato, and the Pythagoreans. They deal with the nature (*physis*) of Apollo or Zeus. Fictitious hymns, on the other hand, associate personified abstractions with the gods (Flight the friend of Fear, Sleep the brother of Death; Reason the brother of Zeus). The analyses are rather mechanical and do not reflect lively concern for the gods.

At the end of the second century, Maximus of Tyre deals with theological topics in several of his essays. The titles themselves show what he has in mind. The best examples are *Oration* 2: whether shrines should be built for the gods; *Oration* 4: poets and philosophers on the gods; *Oration* 5: whether to pray; *Orations* 8–9: the *daimonion* of Socrates; *Oration* 11: God according to Plato; *Oration* 17: should Plato have expelled Homer from the Republic; and finally *Oration* 41: since God does good things, whence come evils? The subjects and the manner of treatment are completely traditional.[39]

Oration 2 ends with the statement that "God, the Father and Demiurge of what exists, older than the sun, older than the heaven, superior to time and the age and every transient nature, is anonymous for any legislator and ineffable to voice and invisible to the eyes. We have no means of ascertaining his nature." For this reason "we use words and names and animals and products of gold and ivory and silver and plants and rivers." The same doctrine recurs in *Oration* 11.

Finally, the Cynic philosopher Menippus, a figure in the *Icaromenippus* (ch. 9) of the satirist Lucian, discusses divergent views about the gods just as if he were a Christian apologist. He relies on the lists of theories to be found in the doxographical literature (lists of opinions) used in schools.

> To some [Pythagoreans] a number was god, while others [Socrates] took oaths by geese and dogs and plane-trees. And some banished all other gods and assigned the rule of the world to one only [Jews? Christians?], so that it made me a little disgusted to hear that gods were so scarce. Others [Numenius] again lavishly declared them to be many and drew a distinction between them, calling one a first god and ascribing to others second and third rank in deity. Some thought the divine was without form and substance, while others defined it as a body.
>
> They did not all think that the gods exercise providence in our affairs; there were some who relieved them of all responsibility as we are accustomed to relieve old men of public duties. . . . A few went

beyond all this and did not even believe that there were any gods at all, but left the world to run on unruled and ungoverned.

Lucian's contemporary the Christian bishop and apologist Theophilus provided a similar list of opinions in his treatise *To Autolycus*. From doxographical sources he listed the inconsistent and pointless opinions of various philosophers on God (*To Autolycus* 2.4) and providence (3.7). He also ridiculed Socrates' oath "by dog and goose and plane-tree" (3.2). In such similar settings we expect to find similar theological ideas.

7

Christian Doctrines of God

The Creator God of Judaism

We expect Jewish authors to play an important part in the discussion of God as creator. Emphasis on the universal rule of God was expressed among Jews, who reverentially read Adonai (Lord) for the more sacred name Yahweh or in the Greek translation rendered Adonai as *kyrios*. Above all, the whole structure and content of the Old Testament revolves about the power and goodness of the God of Israel, who was also the Creator. The Bible begins with his act of creation.

By the early first century A.D., even Greek authors recognized that Moses painted a sublime picture of divine creativity at the beginning of Genesis. The rhetorical treatise *On the Sublime* discusses the point (9.9). "The lawgiver of the Jews, no ordinary man, since he had formed a proper conception of divine power, expressed it at the outset of his laws where he says, 'God said'—what? 'Let there be light, and there was light. Let there be earth, and there was earth.' " The author regards the picture as sublime, of course, because it agrees with his own viewpoint. He is a typical first-century rhetorician influenced by increasing emphasis on absolute divine power. Similarly, Jews like Josephus insisted on the solitary oneness of the God who "created . . . not with assistants of whom he had no need."[1]

The Cosmic Yahweh and Philosophy

Such Jewish philosophers were eager to explain Old Testament ideas in relation to the highest levels of Greek theology, notably in Middle Platonism. Thus Philo's treatise *On the Creation of the World* tells us that according to Moses "the active cause is the perfectly pure and unsullied Mind of the universe, transcending virtue, transcending knowledge, transcending the good itself and the beautiful itself" (*On the Creation* 8). This is God, the Father and Maker, who first made "an incorporeal heaven and an invisible earth and the essential forms ('ideas') of air and void" (*On the Creation* 29). Philo concludes that Moses teaches the eternity of God, his unity, the created nature of the world, its unity, and God's exercise of providential care (*On the Creation* 170–72). In this work, however, he refers to mediators as implied by Genesis 1:26: "Let *us* make . . . ," and elsewhere he lays emphasis on the work of such subordinates as Logos and Sophia.

Did Philo's Basic Doctrine Come from Philosophy?

Philo was thus a Jewish philosopher who taught about the creative activity of the supreme God. He should have done so, for the Old Testament insists that God is the sole creator. John Dillon and others, however, have supposed that Philo was relying on Eudorus, a Pythagorizing Platonist of the first century B.C.[2] The Neoplatonist Simplicius ascribed to Eudorus the doctrine that the One was "the causal principle of matter," and Dillon finds such a doctrine reflected in Philo. It is by no means certain, however, that Philo had ever read Eudorus, whom he never mentions, any more than other philosophers just before his time.

Admittedly some Middle Platonist did come to lay emphasis on the creative power of God. In the *Timaeus* (28C), Plato had already called "the supreme god" the "father and maker of all things." In the second century of our era Plutarch explained that this god is not only father of engendered gods and men, as in Homer, "but maker of irrational beings and of inanimate things." Whose exegesis of Plato is this? According to Cherniss, the statement formulated Plutarch's "own theology and theodicy."[3] Plutarch proceeded to criticize "most students of Plato," those who try to conceal his true doctrine about "the generation and composition of the universe and its soul, which have not been compounded from everlasting or in their present state for infinite time." People who speak of an eternal world or soul "confuse or rather utterly ruin the reasoning of Plato's case for the gods." Plutarch's own doctrine is that "the universe was brought into being by God, whereas the substance and matter out of which it came into being did not come to be but was always available to the artificer . . . , for the source of generation is not what is non-existent (*ek tou me ontos*) but . . . what is not in good and sufficient condition."[4] Plutarch was defending his own view, not Plato's, against what he thought was majority opinion.

We know that this was his own special view, because later Neo-platonists who discussed the origin of the world named not Eudorus but Plutarch himself and a few later second-century Platonists as holding this doctrine.[5] Cherniss notes that "the 'creation' in the *Timaeus* had already been taken literally by Aristotle and a few others but so far as is known not by anyone regarded as a Platonist." Plutarch himself—and his contemporaries?—thus significantly heightened emphasis on divine power.

Early Gnostic Theology

The first Christian theologians after Philo to echo and use Middle Platonic theology (after Philo) were the Gnostic teachers who, like the major Middle Platonists, flourished in and after the reign of Hadrian.[6]

The theology of the earliest teachers such as Simon and Menander did not amount to much, but in the advanced doctrine of Basilides and the *Apocryphon of John* we encounter full statements about God's transcendence. Basilides goes so far along the *via negativa* as to speak, at least according to Hippolytus, of the nonexistent god making the nonexistent universe out of nothing.[7] From the *Apocryphon* we learn that God is the Monad, more than a god, completely perfect, illimitable, unsearchable, immeasurable, invisible, eternal, ineffable, unnameable. He has no definable attributes.[8]

There are clear reflections of Platonic theology in Gnostic doctors such as these, and notably in the theologian and biblical critic Marcion, who was in Rome in 137 and was expelled in 144. Marcion differentiated the just *(dikaios)* Demiurge of the Old Testament from the truly Good *(agathos)* who was the Father proclaimed by Jesus. Tertullian commented that Marcion's God was "the better for his tranquillity."[9] A distinction not unlike Marcion's had already been drawn by Philo in order to explain the major divine names in the Old Testament. In Philo's view, "God" *(theos)* referred especially to God's goodness, whereas "Lord" *(kyrios)* usually involved his justice.[10] He was certainly wrong, but he supposed that *theos* came from *tithemi* ("to place" or "to put") and therefore associated the name with the creation. Marcion as an opponent of Judaism maintained the distinction but increased the confusion by transposing Philo's terms (with the rabbis!) and making a philosophical or Gnostic distinction between the Highest God and the inferior creator. The distinction is not based on the Old Testament but is essentially Middle Platonic, as we have seen.

The Valentinian teacher Ptolemaeus, introducing a certain "Flora" (whether a Christian woman or the church at Rome) to his doctrine, also differentiates "God the Father" or "the perfect God" from the Adversary, the devil, ascribing the basic moral law to an intermediary, "the Demiurge and Maker of this universe." The perfect God is the Father of All; that is, of the Gnostic aeons. He is "good" and "unbegotten," and his essence is "imperishability and light-in-itself, simple, uniform."[11]

These examples suffice to show how Gnostic teachers appropriated the basic Middle Platonic doctrine in the second century. As we have already suggested, the most important difference between their teachings and those of the Christian apologists lies in the Gnostic refusal to accept the simple and obvious teaching of the Bible. In spite of their inadequate semiphilosophical theology, the apologists did maintain much of the biblical teaching.

The Christian Apologists from Justin to Theophilus

The first significant Christian apologist was Justin Martyr, who wrote at Rome around the year 150. Alongside his biblical doctrine he set forth a high view of divine transcendence evidently related to Middle Platonism. L. W. Barnard has listed the basic points. God is "the eternal, immovable, unchanging Cause and Ruler of the Universe, nameless and unutterable, unbegotten, residing far above the heavens, and is incapable of coming into immediate contact with any of his creatures, yet is observant of them although removed from them and unapproachable by them."[12] In addition, as in Gnostic and philosophical thought, Justin says that the titles God bears, such as Father, God, Creator, Lord, and Master, refer to his activities, not to his essence.[13]

Both Tatian and Athenagoras express similar ideas about the nature of God, although Tatian's doctrine seems strangely expressed when we find him using the term "the perfect God" and speaking of the Logos as "the God who suffered." As we have seen, the Gnostic Ptolemaeus used the former term; he also spoke of Sophia as "the Aeon who suffered."[14] Athenagoras conveniently and conventionally summarizes: God is "uncreated, eternal, invisible, impassible, incomprehensible, and infinite." He "can be apprehended by mind and reason alone." He is "encompassed by light, beauty, spirit, and indescribable power." He created and adorned the universe and now rules it.[15]

Other orthodox authors made use of categories both Platonic and

Stoic. Theophilus, bishop of Antioch, illustrates such a combination. He lists "negative attributes" of God in Platonic fashion while he treats the Logos, or Son of God, in a Stoic manner, differentiating the *logos endiathetos* within God from the *logos prophorikos* expressed by him. His Logos doctrine will be discussed in chapter 10, on Antiochene Christology.

Here we note that in *To Autolycus* 1.3, Theophilus insists on the transcendence of God and points out that all of God's "appellations" refer to his characteristics, attributes, or activities, not to his nature in itself.

> If I call him (God) Light, I speak of his creature;
> if I call him Logos, I speak of his beginning [or first principle];
> if I call him Mind, I speak of his intelligence;
> if I call him Spirit, I speak of his breath;
> if I call him Sophia, I speak of his offspring;
> if I call him Strength, I speak of his might;
> if I call him Power, I speak of his energy;
> if I call him Providence, I speak of his goodness,
> if I call him Kingdom, I speak of his glory;
> if I call him Lord, I speak of him as judge;
> if I call him Judge, I speak of him as just;
> if I call him Father, I speak of him as all things;
> if I call him Fire, I speak of his wrath.
>
> (*To Autolycus* 1.3)

All these terms are symbolic because they refer to the ineffable transcendent God—who, unlike Marcion's God, is just as well as good.

Similar teaching is to be found in Albinus and the *Corpus Hermeticum* (2.14). But like Justin, Theophilus is not an orthodox Platonist philosopher. His list of names and attributes ends on a biblical note. "If I call him 'fire' I speak of his wrath." The interlocutor asks, "Will you tell me that God is angry?" Against the overwhelming majority of philosophers, not to mention the Marcionites,[16] Theophilus replies, "Certainly: he is angry with those who commit evil deeds but good and merciful toward those who love and fear him.[17] For he is the instructor of the pious and father of the just, but judge and punisher of the impious." Here he is on firm Stoic ground, at least: Plutarch notes that in the Stoic view "God punishes evil and does much to punish wicked men."[18]

Theophilus then returns to philosophy and continues with school definitions and etymologies (*To Autolycus* 1.4). "God has no beginning because he did not come into existence; he is immutable because he is immortal. He is called 'God' (*theos*) because he has set (*tetheikenai*) everything on his own stability (Ps. 103:5), and because of *theein*, which means to run, to move, to energize, to nourish, to exercise forethought, to govern, and to give life to everything. He is Lord because he lords over everything, Father because he is before everything, Demiurge and Maker because he is the founder and maker of everything, Most High because he is above everything, All-controlling because he controls and surrounds everything." The section ends with a string of Old Testament passages illustrating God's creative power. "Most High" and "All-controlling" probably reflect Theophilus' close relationship to Hellenistic Jewish thought, but the rest of the discussion contains nothing specifically Jewish. The derivation of *theos* from *tithemi*, though found in Philo, is as old as Herodotus (2.52), while that from *theein* comes from the *Cratylus* (397D) of Plato, where it refers to star gods. It hardly fits a Jewish or Christian context, but Theophilus' additional verbs change the meaning entirely. In any case, given such insistence on divine transcendence, the Christian apologist could then denounce the stories about the all too human gods as found in mythology—and so he does (*To Autolycus* 1.9–10; 2.3; etc.).[19]

Irenaeus and the Influence of Xenophanes

One fragment of Xenophanes (B24) was especially popular in the Greco-Roman period. God "sees as a whole, understands as a whole, and hears as a whole." In other words, as Christians were to take the doctrine, his functions cannot be divided and there is no place for any Gnostic divisions in the Godhead. Irenaeus of Lyons found this language so attractive that he referred to it no fewer than four times, ascribing it to the scriptures and to "religious men" as well. Irenaeus is not concerned with pagan idolatry as much as with Gnostic idolatry, but the arguments are somewhat similar and the appeal to philosophy by a Christian theologian is the same.

In the first example, Irenaeus describes the Gnostic emanations —from Bythos (Depth) to Ennoia (Thought) and Thelesis (Will), then to Monogenes (Only Generated) and Aletheia (Truth)—and rejects such a way of speaking about God; for God perfects what he wills as he thinks. Everything is simultaneous. For "He is all Thought, all Will, all Intellect, all Eye, all Hearing, all Source of all good things."[20] In the second example he contrasts divine and human psychology and criticizes the Gnostics for confusing the two. "If they had known the scriptures and if they had been taught by the

truth, they would know that God is not like men and that the
thoughts of God are not like human thoughts." The first allusion is
to Numbers 23:19 and is employed by Philo (*On Immutability* 53); the
second has no parallel in Philo but comes from Isaiah 55:8–9. Irenaeus goes on to say that God is "simple, not complex, without
diversity of members [1 Cor. 12?], completely like and equal to
himself, for he is all Mind, all Spirit, all Intellection, all Thought, all
Logos, all Hearing, all Eye, all Light, and all Source of all good
things, as it is right for religious and pious men to say of God."[21]
"Religious" is Irenaeus' term for those who, though not always
Christians, share Christian attitudes or doctrines; Plato was one of
them.[22] In the third example Irenaeus claims that the Gnostics are
simply using human psychology for their pictures of the spiritual
world. In the case of human beings it is quite legitimate to differentiate faculties. "But since God is all Mind, all Logos, all active Spirit,
all Light, always identical with and similar to himself—as it is right
for us to think of him, and as we learn from the scriptures—pro-
cesses and distinctions of this kind could not exist in him."[23] Irenaeus' mention of the scriptures is striking. Perhaps what he means is
that the terms "Logos" and "Spirit," which he has just brought into
the formula, come from scripture. Surely he does not imagine that
any definition like this occurs there. It may also be the case that he
has in mind Paul's remarks about human beings and the body of
Christ in 1 Cor. 12:17: "If the whole body were an eye, where would
be the hearing? If the whole body were an ear, where would be the
sense of smell?" So it is with man, not with God.[24]

Much later in his work, and quite unexpectedly, Irenaeus brings
in the definition again. He is speaking of the law, which offered
human beings the opportunity to grow in maturity, and he turns
aside to contrast humanity with God. God creates, man is created.
God gives benefits, man receives them. God is perfect in every
respect, equal and similar to himself, "all Light, all Mind, all Substance and Source of all good things," while man "receives progress
and growth toward God."[25] In these passages, then, we see a pagan
theological formula being baptized into Christian service.

Clement of Alexandria

Clement of Alexandria has an even higher doctrine of the transcendence and ineffability of God.[26] For him, God is incorporeal,
formless, and possesses no attribute. He transcends the world of
sense perception and is above space and time. As One, he is even

above the monad. He is also above virtue; that is, beyond goodness. He cannot be comprehended by the human mind and thus he is "unknown" and he is ineffable. The best way the human mind has to approach him is the negative process *kat' aphairesin.*

All these points are closely paralleled in Philo, whose works Clement knew and copied. They are also present in Middle Platonism and often in Gnostic thought.

S. R. C. Lilla notes that "Clement's God recalls, under many aspects, the 'one' of Plotinus." There are two differences, however, between the two ideas of God. Clement identifies the supreme God as a Mind, the locus of Ideas,[27] but Plotinus sets the One above Mind as its source. The Mind God of Clement thinks the Ideas, whereas for Plotinus the One has no noetical activity.[28] Lilla traces Clement's doctrine to that of Ammonius Saccas, better known as a teacher of Plotinus and two Origens, one the Christian theologian. We thus see that at every turn Christian Alexandria was closely related to currents in pagan thought.

Lilla also points to the deep influence of Gnostic ideas on Clement, an influence later overcome by Origen because of his emphasis on scripture and church teaching and firmer grasp on philosophy.

Origen on God

Origen himself is probably our best witness to early Christian theology because of the relatively systematic nature of his treatise *On First Principles.* He begins precisely with scriptural problems, criticizing those who suppose that God is a body because "our God is a consuming fire" (Deut. 4:24) and "God is spirit" (John 4:24). Origen explains that "light" is spiritual and so, therefore, are "fire" and "spirit." There is nothing corporeal about God. Indeed, "God is incomprehensible and it is impossible to think of him." As H. Crouzel points out after Jean Daniélou, this is "a commonplace of Judaism and Christianity as of Gnosticism and Middle Platonism." We are in an area, and a time, in which "the religious" share common ideas.

God transcends all his works, for he is "a simple intellectual nature without any admixture." He is "entirely a monad or, I might say, a henad, a Mind and a Source from which proceeds the beginning of the whole intellectual nature or mind." (This reiterates the doctrine of Clement.) God needs no place, just as our intelligence needs no place. As Intelligence, God is invisible. Someone may object that "Blessed are the pure in heart, for they shall see God"

(Matt. 5:8). But what is seeing with the heart if not understanding with the intelligence? "Frequently the names of organs of sense are referred to the soul."

In Book II of *On First Principles*, Origen explicitly states that heretics read the Old Testament and criticize its pictures of God as angry or repenting or experiencing some other human passion. They think they are attacking the orthodox, since all share the belief that God is "absolutely impassible and free of all feelings of this sort." We know, however, that the anger of God in either Testament must not be taken literally. This is not to say that the passages referring to it should be deleted, but there must be an interpretation worthy of God (*On First Principles* 2.4.4). He has allegorization in mind.

In Book IV, where Origen deals with scriptural exegesis as such, he explains that "the Word of God intentionally inserted in the law and the history something like stumbling blocks and passages shocking and impossible, to keep us from being drawn away by the style with its faultless charm." (This is what philosophers said poets added to truth.) In that case "we might learn nothing worthy of God and would therefore abandon the doctrines; or else we might not be moved by the literal meaning and would learn nothing more divine." We must "look for a meaning worthy of God in the scriptures inspired by him" (*On First Principles* 4.2.9).

About twenty-five years later, in the treatise *Against Celsus*, Origen referred to "the doctrine of Jews and Christians which preserves the unchangeable and unalterable nature of God" (*Against Celsus* 1.21) —as based on "Thou art the same" (Ps. 102:27) and "I change not" (Mal. 3:6). This is Philonic; we have already referred to Philo's treatise on immutability. In the Jewish-Christian tradition, Origen also upheld the doctrine of the Creator and vigorously attacked idolatry (*Against Celsus* 3.40), though he was not far from his opponent at either point.

A Change in Origen's Position?

At the same time, Origen seems to have been reconsidering his basic position. In the late *Commentary on the Gospel of Matthew* he wrote of the divine Logos that "as loving mankind the impassible one suffered with compassion."[29] More than that, in his *Homilies on Ezekiel* (6.6) he came to ascribe emotions to God the Father himself because of the sufferings of the Son. This marks a striking change. The material cause of it, so to speak, must be sought in Origen's discovery of the letters of Ignatius. In his earlier writings he mentions neither them nor their author, but later he explicitly approves what he calls the letters of the martyr Ignatius and indeed defends Ignatius' statement that "My *Eros* has been crucified"—a statement he understands as referring to Christ.[30] This is from Ignatius' letter to the Romans, where there is a reference to "the passion of my God" which Origen would not have liked when younger, though now he apparently accepted it.

Origen is proving the passibility of God and he begins with a human example. If one makes a petition to a human being, the recipient, if not a merciful person, is unsympathetic *(nihil patitur)*. The Savior, however, "came down to earth, taking pity on the human race, and experienced our passions before he suffered the cross and condescended to assume our flesh. For if he had not suffered he would not have entered into human life." The point is quite clear: the Savior experienced suffering in his divine, preincarnate state, not just during his earthly life. Origen carefully adds, "First he suffered, then he came down and was seen." The idea may be verbally based on Ignatius (*Epistle to the Ephesians* 7.2), who says that Jesus Christ our Lord was "first passible and then impassible," with reference to the incarnate Lord and the risen Lord (cf. 1 Cor. 15:42–44). Origen prefers to speak of the time before the incarnation. Conceivably he has in mind Galatians 2:20: He "loved me and gave himself for me."

"What is that passion which he experienced for us?" Origen asks. It is the passion of love *(caritas)*, for which he cites Psalm 103:8, a reference to God's mercy and love (Ex. 34:6–7 would have done as well). As for God's experiencing *caritas* as a *passio*, this may be related to his notion that Eros in Ignatius (*Epistle to the Romans* 7.2) means Christ. "Or don't you know that when God deals with human affairs he experiences human passion?" This is proved by Deuteronomy 1:31: "The Lord your God put up with you, as a man puts up with his son." Philo allegorized this analogy,[31] but Origen now prefers to take it literally. Therefore, he concludes, God puts up with our ways just as the Son of God puts up with our passions. "The Father himself is not impassible.[32] If he is asked, he takes pity and commiserates, he suffers something of love and enters into circumstances in which by the greatness of his nature he cannot enter, and for us human beings endures passions."[33]

Apparently the threat of Patripassianism (see chapter 8) did not bother Origen, at least at this point. We have already seen that in his work *On First Principles* he did not hold a rigid doctrine of divine impassibility. Since Origen advised the exegete to look for a spiritual understanding of passages ascribing emotions to God "in order to think worthily of God," he must have believed that there are realities in God corresponding to these emotions.[34]

Our point in discussing this evident change is to show that even in the third century Christian doctrine was still fluid and able to admit contradiction on the part of theologians. We usually think of struggles between orthodox and heretics, or vice versa. Here is something of a struggle between Origen and Origen, and over a crucial problem.

8

Christ: Deeds and Names

Miracles

Jesus was well known in his lifetime as a healer and a wonder-worker who said that the God he worshiped, and whose Son some claimed he was, was at work through him. "If I by the finger of God cast out demons, then the reign of God has come upon you" (Luke 11:20). He set forth his teaching about the reign of God in enigmatic parables, but his adherents were strongly impressed by the miracles and kept repeating stories about them.[1]

Jesus' career as a prophetic and charismatic figure ended in Jerusalem, where the Temple authorities cooperated with the Roman governor to have him put to death. His followers held that he then rose from the dead and appeared to many of them.

It is sometimes claimed that there is an authentic proclamation of Jesus without the superfluous miracles and that the apostle Paul speaks of this when he describes the Jews as demanding signs and the Greeks seeking wisdom—"but we preach Christ crucified" (1 Cor. 1:22–23). This is unlikely exegesis, since in the next verse Paul speaks of Christ as both the power and the wisdom of God. Even the signs of a true apostle involved "signs and wonders and mighty works" (2 Cor. 12:12). Miracle was an essential aspect of the gospel.

Miracles in the Gospels

All four of the Gospels written about Jesus and generally accepted by his followers include narratives about his resurrection and all contain other miracles. (The so-called *Gospel of Thomas* contains nothing but sayings and dialogues and is not really a "Gospel.") The three Synoptic Gospels, ascribed to Mark, Matthew, and Luke, contain many accounts of the exorcism of demons (apparently popular in Palestine); healings, including the raisings of dead persons; and stories about the multiplication of bread and fish and walking on the Lake of Tiberias.[2] Rudolf Bultmann assigns twenty synoptic stories to this group. Thirteen of them are miracles of healing. Out of these, four are exorcisms, eight are healings, and one is the raising of a dead man (Luke 7:11–17). The other seven are "nature miracles," with the stilling of a storm, the walking on the water, two feedings (five thousand and four thousand), a miraculous catch of fish, finding a coin in the mouth of a fish, and the cursing of a fig tree for not giving miraculous fruit. Few of these stories find exact counterparts among stories told of the Greek and Roman gods or even heroes. None is necessarily based on a pagan original. The similarities, as Bultmann points out, indicate the "atmosphere" in which such stories were told.[3]

It must be confessed that we cannot trace such stories to alien areas whether Jewish or Christian, and we must assume that those who told them were convinced that the miracles took place. On the other hand, the freedom with which later evangelists retell earlier stories shows that their idea of reliable narrative did not involve vouching for every detail.

Miracles in the Gospel of John

Unlike the Synoptics, the Gospel ascribed to John contains no exorcisms. Instead, the author uses seven startling wonders, called "signs," as key points in Jesus' career. "The first of his signs" took place at Cana in Galilee, where "he manifested his glory." This was the transformation of water into wine at a wedding. The story occurs only in John (2:1–11).[4] It is the only account of Jesus' miracles in John, or indeed in any of the Gospels,[5] for which a fairly striking pagan parallel has been found. The exception is thus all the more important, for once more it points toward environments through which such stories might pass, no matter how they may have originated. The second sign in John was the cure (at a distance) of an official's son (John 4:53), the third a healing of a man paralyzed for thirty-eight years (John 5:5).

The fourth sign was Jesus' multiplication of bread and fish to feed five thousand people (John 6:10) and the fifth was his walking on the surface of the sea to meet the disciples who were in a boat (John 6:19). Versions of these two miracles are also to be found in the Synoptic Gospels, and they are perfectly attuned to the circumstances of Mediterranean life. "Mediterranean man," writes Fernand Braudel, "gains his daily bread by painful effort." The same social historian notes the dangers of travel by sea during the winter, and during other seasons as well.[6] The miracle of the loaves and fishes also corresponds to the realistic petition of the Lord's Prayer, "Give us this day our daily bread." Only in a mistakenly futurist context, as in the apocryphal *Gospel of the Hebrews,* could the petition be changed to ask for "the bread of tomorrow."

The sixth sign was the healing of a man born blind (John 9:1–17), and the seventh, climactic, sign was the raising of Lazarus, who had been dead for four days (John 11:39). The evangelist tells all the stories in an allusive, mysterious manner in order to indicate that they point beyond themselves; they are not "mere" miracle stories but lead to belief in Jesus. "Jesus did many other signs in the presence of the disciples, which are not written in this book; but these are written that you may believe . . ." (John 20:30–31).

Various Approaches to Miracles

The other evangelists do not make the point so definitely. Mark, as Martin Dibelius said, is "a book of secret epiphanies."[7] "Who is this that wind and waves obey him?" (Mark 4:41). The point that all are making is much the same. They tell the stories in order to lead hearers to faith. A century later the apologist Justin was aware how closely some of these stories resembled stories about the gods. He notes that Jesus' crucifixion is like the disasters that overwhelmed several sons of Zeus, while his birth from a virgin is like the birth of Perseus. His healings of people who were lame and paralyzed or blind from birth, or even already dead, are like what Asclepius was said to have done.[8] Still later, Tertullian says that some people supposed Jesus was a magician because of his power: he drove out demons, healed the blind, lepers, and paralytics, raised the dead, and controlled the elements—showing himself to be the Son and Logos of God.[9] Around the year 248, Origen argues that these stories are not fictitious, because if they were there would have been more of them.[10] These three analyses reflect the controversies that the miracle stories naturally aroused. Some critics could see nothing new beyond pagan parallels. They might think of magic or imaginative storytelling.

The basic point of telling miracle stories is given in the words of John which we have already quoted. Significantly enough, they seem to be the "signs" for which, according to Paul, Jews were seeking. Their presence in this Gospel at least reflects a variety in Christian approaches to the mission. John ends his statement about "signs" with the words "That you may believe that Jesus is the Christ, the Son of God."

Who was Jesus? Which titles among those given him, such as Messiah or Christ, were best suited to the story and the continuing experiences? How could they be coordinated in relation to an increasingly logical theology?

Beginnings of Christology

The Earlier Names Given Jesus

The word "Christology" indicates our starting point, for it is based on *Christos,* the Greek and Christian translation of the Hebrew term *meshiach,* meaning someone "anointed"; that is, with oil. There were various meanings of unction in biblical antiquity, but essentially an anointed one was an agent of God for rule or message or both. As G. F. Moore long ago noted,

> "Messiah" is essentially an adjective meaning consecrated or appointed by God, and was not the prerogative title of any single person until later than the time of Christ. It was applied in various forms of literature to expected scion of the house of David, to the supernatural Son of Man, and to the High Priest; but its use does not show that these figures were habitually identified with each other in Jewish thought.[11]

While "Christ" became a second name for Jesus of Nazareth, the one whom early Christians considered to be God's agent in the world, the revealer of God's will to them, it was not a term used by the earliest disciples. Indeed, an early sermon in Acts suggests that it was first employed after the resurrection of Jesus. The reference is to the way "God has made him both Lord and Christ, this Jesus whom you [the house of Israel] crucified" (Acts 2:36). To put it rather crudely, as later Adoptionists did put it, Jesus finally became Christ. In the earliest Gospel, Jesus is called Messiah (Christ), but the messiahship is treated as a secret (cf. Mark 8:29–30). This kind of Christology will recur at Antioch (see chapter 10).

Another term sometimes employed, though not by Paul, is "Son of Man." Essentially the term means nothing but "man," or "human being." It occurs in Daniel 7:13, where a dream shows Daniel "one like a son of man" who is presented before God and given everlasting world power. The human figure, Israel, is contrasted with the beastlike nature of other nations. The meaning of the term is clear from two addresses to the prophet himself in Daniel 8:16–17. First he is called "man," then "son of man."[12] More specifically, those who receive world power are "the people of the saints of the Most High" (Dan. 7:27). The idea that there was a particular Son of Man is based partly on Gospel expressions, partly on the parables of Enoch, chs. 37–71 of the apocalypse called 1 Enoch. As a whole this work may come from the first century B.C., but in spite of the discovery of several imperfect copies at Qumran (evidence for the first century A.D.), no pieces of chapters 37–71 have turned up. Their absence supports the thesis that this section is later. We are probably dealing with a Christian interpolation, based on the Gospels, not prior to them. In another apocalypse, 2 Esdras (4 Ezra), we also find "as it were the likeness of a man" (2 Esdras 13:3), but this is no individual Son of Man figure.

Sometimes another title later used of Jesus was employed "corporately." This was "Son of God." In Exodus 4:22, the Hebrew people collectively are called the Son of God. The king too could be called God's son (Ps. 2:7–8), for he not only had a unique status in relation to God but also represented the people as a whole. Later, the wise man as well could be called son of God, as is the case in Wisdom of Solomon 2:18. And angels are called sons of God in the Old Testament—for example, in Job 38:7 ("when the morning stars sang together, and all the sons of God shouted for joy"). The term seems not to have been used of Jesus during his ministry. Paul tells us, perhaps expressing doctrine he knew the Romans would find acceptable, that Jesus was "designated Son of God in power according to the Spirit of holiness by his resurrection from the dead" (Rom. 1:4). That is to say that he became (or was recognized as) the unique Son of God only after his death. The passage reminds us of the statement in Acts 2:36 that Jesus became Christ. "Son of God" sometimes points toward Christ's special relationship with the Father; he is God's "own" son (Rom. 8:3, 32; Gal. 4:4; 2 Cor. 1:19) or "the son of his love" (Col. 1:13).

The most likely sequence of the Gospels shows us a Sonship gradually pushed back in time.[13] Mark 1:11 tells of a divine voice at the time of Jesus' baptism: "Thou art my beloved Son; with thee I am well pleased," while Luke 3:22 has a variant reading: "This day have I begotten thee."[14] (This is the royal language of Ps. 2:7.) The temptation stories in Matthew and Luke represent the devil as somehow trying to identify Jesus as Son of God in relation to startling works of power. Jesus refuses to supply such proofs and cites scripture against his adversary. Both of these evangelists trace his Sonship not to his baptism but to his conception and birth. It goes back before the creation of the world in the Gospel of John. This is not surprising in the light of Paul's language about himself in

Galatians 1:15 ("He who had set me apart from my mother's womb")[15] and about Christ in 1 Corinthians 8:6. But there is a tendency to meditate upon the cosmic meaning of what was later called "the incarnation."

The evangelists disagreed when they tried to explain the purpose of Jesus' mission, especially his death. Mark says that "the Son of man came not to be served but to serve, and to give his life as a ransom for many" (Mark 10:45). Luke paraphrases and has Jesus say, "I am among you as one who serves" (Luke 22:27). There is thus no more fixity about a doctrine of atonement in the Gospels than in the rest of the New Testament.

Indeed, there was nothing fixed about Christology, presumably because Jesus proclaimed not himself but the coming of God's reign. All three Synoptic Gospels lay emphasis on his gospel of the kingdom. John does not do so; instead, he concentrates upon the doctrine of Jesus as Logos and Son of God. This difference arose because John may have been later but, in any event, grew out of a different and less historical kind of tradition.

Jesus did not clearly identify himself. Early Christians wanted to assign titles to him and they therefore called him Messiah (Christos), Son of Man, Son of God, and so on. Other speculations about a "man from heaven" or a "second Adam" proved to be less important. For the future, the term to which we now turn, "Wisdom," proved especially meaningful.

Wisdom Christology

Wisdom in Proverbs and Later Writings

The title given Christ in 1 Corinthians 1:24 and 30 is Wisdom (*sophia*). This title goes back to the figure of Sophia as God's personified Wisdom in Proverbs 8:22–31, a passage that was to prove remarkably fruitful for early Jewish and Christian Christological speculation. It begins thus:

> The Lord created me at the beginning of his work, the first of his acts of old. Ages ago I was set up, at the first, before the beginning of the earth. When there were no depths I was brought forth. . . . When he established the heavens, I was there. . . . I was beside him, like a master workman; and I was daily his delight, rejoicing before him always.

This is the basic Old Testament locus for the personified figure of divine Wisdom, God's aide in the work of creation. Such a picture of the cosmic Christ explains how Paul could write to the Corinthians (1 Cor. 8:6) that "for us there is one God, the Father, from whom everything comes, for whom we exist, and one Lord, Jesus Christ, through whom everything exists, through whom we exist." He is speaking of the Lord Jesus Christ as the preexistent Wisdom of God, the agent of creation. This personified Wisdom recurs in the Christology of Colossians 1:15–18, where Christ, the Son of God's love, is described as "the image of the invisible God, the first-born of all creation."

The influence of the "praises of Wisdom" was very strong later, especially on newer wisdom literature, on Philo, and on early Christians.[16] In the second century B.C., Sirach too has Wisdom describe her origins. She says, "I came forth from the mouth of the Most High, and covered the earth like a mist. I dwelt in high places, and my throne was in a pillar of cloud. . . . In every people and nation I have gotten a possession. Among all these I sought a resting place; I sought in whose territory I might lodge. . . . From eternity, in the beginning, he created me, and for eternity I shall not cease to exist."[17]

In the mid-second century B.C., the Hellenistic Jew Aristobulus gave Greek exegesis of Genesis and pointed out that God made the universe. He opened the way for the use of a mediator by the supreme god, however, when he said that what was said about light (first God said, Let there be light) might be transferred to Wisdom, "For all light is from her." Some Peripatetic philosophers, he claims, hold that wisdom has "the rank of illuminator." His main point is that according to Solomon (Prov. 8:22) she existed before heaven and earth. Aristobulus thus speaks of the one creator God and refers to his use of Wisdom as an instrument. For him, the creative word of God was to be understood as Wisdom, not the kind of word that a human being might utter.

Around the beginning of the Christian era the Wisdom of Solomon moves toward philosophical language in describing the divine Wisdom. First the author describes the "spirit" in Wisdom in terms like those used by the Stoic Cleanthes concerning "the good." Then he tells of Wisdom herself, with emphasis on light, as in Aristobulus.

> She is a breath of the power of God, and a pure emanation of the glory of the Almighty; therefore nothing defiled gains entrance into her. For she is a reflection of eternal light, a spotless mirror of the working of God, and an image of his goodness. (Wisd. of Sol. 7:25–26)

In addition, "she glorifies her noble birth by living with God, and the Lord of all loves her."[18]

In Proverbs, Wisdom is created by God and helps in the work of creation. In Sirach, and perhaps in Wisdom too, she comes forth from his mouth—like words or, more specifically, the words, "Let there be light." "God made all things by his word and by his wisdom formed man."[19] When Philo dealt with these matters, the passage in Proverbs led him to think of a female agent in creation, although his ideas were not well worked out. He called Wisdom the daughter of God "because both in Greek and in Hebrew the word for wisdom is of feminine gender."[20] Her mythic function in creation must have been more important than the grammatical point, but the passage cited by H. A. Wolfson shows Philo meditating on her gender as feminine and trying to differentiate it from the masculine.

For Philo, Wisdom as God's daughter is "the first-born mother of all things" or "the mother of all in the world," who nourishes them with her breasts. In *On Flight and Finding* he says that God is the father, Sophia "the mother through whom all things came into being." In *On Drunkenness* he uses the term *episteme* ("understanding," "knowledge"), not Sophia, when he speaks of the female principle with whom God ("not like a man") had intercourse so that she brought forth "the only and beloved perceptible son," this cosmos. A quotation of Proverbs 8:22–23 makes it clear, however, that he has Wisdom in mind. And he goes on to refer to her as the mysterious "nurse" and "mother" of Plato's *Timaeus*. [21]

We should note after John Dillon, though citing different texts, that Wisdom is clearly analogous to the creative Athena of Greek rhetoric and philosophy. Philo calls her "motherless" and "virgin," both epithets of the goddess.[22] Dillon says that "we can see Sophia coming very close to Plutarch's concept of Isis."[23] This is more especially true in regard to Athena. (See chapter 9.)

Was Wisdom Based on the Goddess Isis?

What was the context of this kind of speculation? Did it lie in philosophy, as Aristobulus tries to suggest, or in ancient religion? Before we look at philosophy we should discuss an attempt to relate Wisdom to oriental religion, specifically to ideas about the Hellenized Egyptian goddess Isis. According to the hypothesis of W. L. Knox, a cosmic presentation of Isis served as a model for the goddesslike figure of Wisdom in Proverbs and related books.[24] On this view, the creation of the world was ascribed first to Isis, then to Wisdom. Knox's theory is hard to prove, however, for cosmic theologizing about Isis comes almost entirely from the Greek world. The personal opinions of Plutarch and the religious experiences of Apuleius were not set forth until the second century of our era, when the dossier of Greek texts provided by Werner Peek also arose,[25] as did the cultic equivalences noted in *Oxyrhynchus Papyrus* XI 1380. All these are much later than the Proverbs passage and reflect Greek philosophical meditation rather than "oriental" musing.

Jan Bergman has tried to connect the aretalogies with older "Memphitic" theology, propagated by native Egyptian priests,[26] but the studies of D. Müller do not confirm his conclusions.[27]

We do not question the reality of Isis as a cosmic goddess in Greek circles. In the longest inscription containing her praises, the one from Cyme on the island of Euboia, she describes herself as "the eldest daughter of Kronos," the one who "separated earth from heaven, showed the stars [their] courses, ordained the path of sun and moon." At Cyrene she declared that she was "sole ruler of eternity" and that "all call me the highest goddess, greatest of all the gods in heaven." "Nothing happens apart from me." The goddess is also addressed in a hymn to Anubis from Bithynia and is called "blessed goddess, mother, many-named, whom Uranus son of Night bore on the marbled waves of the sea but Erebus brought up as a light to all mortals; eldest of the blessed ones in Olympus, bearing the sceptre," and so on. The time sequence seems confusing.

These examples suffice to show that in *Greek* circles Isis could be regarded as daughter of either Kronos or Uranus, as the supreme goddess, as one who had taken a leading part in the creation of the universe and now ruled over heaven and earth and whatever happened in either. The last passage cited shows that she was sometimes identified with Aphrodite, and such equivalences become fully clear in the Oxyrhynchus papyrus already mentioned. There, after 119 lines (only a part of the original) of identifications, the author supplies nearly two hundred more on the powers and functions of the goddess. She is "ruler of the world, . . . greatest of the gods, the first name . . . ruler of heavenly things and the immeasurable." The author says that "you bring the sun from east to west, and all the gods rejoice" and that "you made the power of women equal that of men."[28] "You are the ruler of all forever . . . you have power over winds and thunders and lightnings and snows . . . you made the great Osiris immortal."

One should not suppose, however, that such descriptions were universal. Worshipers did not have to refer to cosmic activities every time they praised the goddess. The aretalogy from Maroneia tells us that "human life knows only you [Isis and Sarapis] as gods,"[29] but speaks of neither one as a demiurge. In addition, individuals could provide their own philosophical interpretations. When Plutarch tells us that "Isis generates Horus as the image of the intelligible world" his language shows that he is expressing his own Platonic view, not reporting any early Egyptian tradition. Isis as Nature brings about the creation of the world in the manner described in the *Timaeus* of Plato.[30]

A hymn from the wall of the birth house at Philae in Egypt does refer to Isis as "the one who originated at the beginning and fills heaven and earth with their beautiful powers of life." She is "leader of the gods of the earth, falcon goddess of the gods of the underworld."[31] This birth house is Ptolemaic and Roman, however, not early Egyptian. Bergman's section on "Isis—die Aktive"[32] does not demonstrate that she was viewed as a creator. Indeed, ordinarily people thought she had been created. Isis therefore cannot be seen as a model for the Old Testament Wisdom.

A better model may perhaps be found in Jewish circles, heterodox to be sure, at a military colony in Elephantine, Egypt, where there was a temple of "Yahu" (Yahweh) in the fifth century B.C. Financial accounts for this temple reveal that with Yahu two other deities were worshiped, one named Eshem-beth-el, the other Anath-beth-el (in another document called Anath-yahu). The names beginning with "Anath" obviously refer to the war goddess worshiped at Ugarit (Ras Shamra), while "Eshem" is probably "Shemesh," the sun. Both deities are thus subordinate to Yahweh, the supreme creator god, though we do not know just what their roles were in the sacred cult or history. Since the sun ruled over the day, and perhaps the universe, on Yahweh's behalf, Anath-beth-el may have performed a similar function. Conceivably a goddess like this, at Carthage and elsewhere called Tanit, was the prototype of Wisdom, but this is mere guesswork. All it shows is that some Jews sometimes thought in pluralistic terms.

Other Christological Language

The language of the wisdom literature also leads directly to the prologue to the Gospel of John, except for the fact that John, correlating this divine principle with the obviously masculine Jesus, feels he should change the gender of the divine principle. We have already seen Philo treating Wisdom as God's daughter and Logos as God's Son. John, making use of a Son of God doctrine in his Gospel as a whole, inevitably uses Logos for his prologue. If he considered the difference between creation and emanation he must have rejected emanation, which would have implied saying that the Logos was in God. Instead, he says that the Logos was *with* God.

A more psychological or mythological doctrine appears in Philippians 2:5–11. Christ Jesus,

> though in the form of God, did not consider equality with God something to be grasped, but emptied (*ekenosen*) himself, assuming the form of a slave, coming to be in the likeness of men; and found in appearance (*schema*) like a man, he humbled himself, becoming obedient even to death, and that a death on a cross. Therefore God highly exalted him and gave him the name above every name, so that at the name of Jesus every knee should bow, of beings celestial and terrestrial and subterranean, and every tongue acknowledge that JESUS CHRIST IS LORD, to the glory of God the Father.

Various expressions from this passage, perhaps a hymn, occur among later theologians, but as a whole it did not win special favor before the rise of the kenotic theologies of the late nineteenth century. There may be echoes in Gnostic myths, always concerned with the preexistent Christ. In any event, the passage makes it plain that before Christ Jesus emptied himself he was not human but divine.

There is a striking parallel (in reverse) to this passage in the impiety of the hero Salmoneus as set forth by the mythographer Apollodorus (1.9.7). He "was arrogant and wanted to make himself equal to Zeus, and because of his impiety he was punished; for he said that he was Zeus." Jesus was obedient, certainly did not want to make himself equal to God, and was exalted.

Christology in the Second and Third Centuries

Ignatius of Antioch

The most "advanced" Christology of the early second century was advocated by Ignatius, bishop of Antioch around the year 110. What he did was to take some of the ideas of Paul and the Paulinist author or authors of Colossians and Ephesians and combine them with some of the language of the Fourth Gospel. We have already seen Paul identifying Jesus with the preexistent Wisdom of God, the agent of creation as well as of redemption, and in Philippians using a remarkable myth of preexistence and condescension. Colossians and Ephesians go even farther in this direction. John, writing a Gospel, paints a portrait of the divine Son in his human existence but begins with a prologue in heaven. "In the beginning was the Logos." He links the two by means of the paradox, "And the Logos became flesh."

A similar Christology of exaltation appears in the letters of Ignatius. While Paul had been reluctant to call Christ God,[33] there is no such reluctance in John, who could write that "the Logos was God" (John 1:1), "I and the Father are one" (John 10:30), and "my Lord and my God" (John 20:28). Ignatius too felt free to speak repeatedly of "Jesus Christ my God." Though he was aware of some of the theological difficulties, as we shall see, his determined devotion combined with a love of rhetorical paradox was able to overcome them. Writing to the Magnesians, Ignatius speaks twice of the preexistent life of the divine Son Jesus Christ. "Before the ages he was with (*para*) the Father and was manifested at the end." He "proceeded from (*apo*) the one Father and is with (*eis*, as in John 1:18) him and departed to the one."[34]

Ignatius was not much concerned with the Johannine theology of the Logos or Word. Once he did speak of "the one God, who manifested himself through Jesus Christ his Son, who is his Word proceeding from silence," but ordinarily he preferred the terms "Father" and "Son" with their reference to personal relations.

Ignatius' Christology was so high that he used traditional God language in regard to the Son. He thus believed that the Son, as divine, was "above seasons, timeless, invisible, intangible, passionless." But he also knew a good deal about the human life of the Son, "truly born, . . . baptized by John, . . . truly nailed in the flesh." Obviously there was something paradoxical about the incarnation, and Ignatius spoke of Jesus as "flesh and spirit, born and not born, God in flesh, real life in death," and so on.[35] In writing to Polycarp he pointed to the foundation of the paradox in the experience of redemption. "Who *for us* became visible . . . who *for us* accepted suffering." The language anticipates that of the "Nicene" Creed: "Who for us men and for our salvation came down from heaven." Ignatius' own precedent is presumably Pauline. In 2 Corinthians 8:9, Paul speaks of "our Lord Jesus Christ, how *for you* though rich he became poor." The thought, but not the language, has parallels elsewhere in Paul. Ignatius' language owes much to the kind of florid rhetoric common in the second century, but rhetoric has never been a stranger to theology.

Gnostic Christology in Ignatian Antioch

There are areas of Christological speculation into which Ignatius does not enter, such as the role of the Son or Word in creation. After the first few verses of John's Gospel, the evangelist does not discuss the subject either. Perhaps Ignatius thinks of such speculations as related to "angelic locations and archontic conjunctions," which he knows about but prefers not to discuss,[36] probably because they come from Gnosticism.

If Ignatius knew the system of the Gnostic Saturninus, taught at Antioch in his time, he doubtless found too much talk about angelic and archontic activities in it.[37] This notorious heretic taught that evil or incompetent angels produced the world and humanity, bungling their copy of a heavenly image. Much later the Savior, somehow related to the image, came to destroy the bad and help the good, those who have the spark of life from above. He was "unbegotten, incorporeal, and shapeless." Obviously Saturninus' Christology was extremely "high," so high that the humanity of Jesus evaporated.

Saturninus' thought obviously owes something to Jewish ideas. His picture of the angels and their work of creation does not come from mainline Judaism, to be sure, but it is probably related to the thought of ex-Jews who were still concerned with Genesis. His picture of Satan as the enemy of the "god of the Jews" comes from the same source. But Saturninus put all such separate points into a system of his own, in an anti-Jewish context. "Christ came to destroy the god of the Jews," he said, identifying himself as an adherent of an extreme version of Gentile Christianity.

This was not Ignatius' doctrine, and we shall not discuss it further. It may have made the memory of his own doctrine suspect, however; simple believers could find it hard to differentiate one high Christology from another. Presumably the incorporeal Savior of Saturninus was essentially the Christ of the Docetists later known to Serapion of Antioch—or to Axionicus the Valentinian, still at Antioch in Tertullian's time.[38]

At least one later Gnostic stood closer to Ignatius, perhaps because he read the letters. Ptolemaeus says that when the Savior came to save the psychic man, he put on a psychic body which became "visible and tangible and passible."[39] This looks like an echo of what Ignatius said in his letter to Polycarp (3.2): "visible, passible, enduring." Of course Ptolemaeus has a Gnostic explanation for what Ignatius was willing to let stand as a paradox.

Ignatius and the Patripassianists

Especially important in Ignatius' doctrine was his insistence that Jesus Christ was God, a view emphasized in his letters to the Christians of Rome, Ephesus, and Smyrna. It may be significant that at the end of the second century these churches were produced or tolerated theologians called Patripassianists, those who held that the Father suffered or even died. One of them, named Noetus, came to Rome from either Smyrna or Ephesus and claimed that his teaching simply glorified Christ.[40] A later critic says he asked, "What harm have I done in glorifying the one God? I acknowledge one God, who was begotten, suffered, and died."[41] He insisted that the Bible, especially the Old Testament, spoke of only one God, and he interpreted Romans 9:5 in this light.

Hippolytus summarizes the doctrine thus: "There is one Father and God of all, who made everything. He was invisible to what was made when he wished [to be so], and then appeared when he wished [to do so]. He is invisible when not seen, visible when seen; unbegotten when not begotten, begotten when born of a virgin; impassible and immortal when he does not suffer or die, but when he encounters passion, he suffers and dies."[42] This language, with its emphasis on divine options, recalls that of Ignatius.[43] The difference is that Ignatius never held that the Father suffered, nor did he confuse the Son with the Father.

No "orthodox" theologian of the second century referred to this kind of theology, and Irenaeus, who cites Ignatius—but only on martyrdom[44]—does not give his name. Opponents of "high" Christology insisted that "the truth of the preaching" about Christ was maintained until Zephyrinus became bishop of Rome and was then falsified. This picture of tradition, given by Eusebius,[45] is partly confirmed by what Hippolytus says about Zephyrinus.

When Noetus' doctrine reached Rome, it was more than tolerated by Zephyrinus and his aide Callistus. According to Hippolytus, Callistus persuaded the ignorant, illiterate, and avaricious bishop to declare, "I know one God Christ Jesus, and apart from him no other, created and passible." At other times he would contradict himself by saying, "It was not the Father who died, but the Son."[46] Similar views were advocated by a certain Praxeas, who according to Tertullian taught that the Father was crucified. What the followers of Praxeas really said, however, was that "the one who died was of human substance, not divine. . . . The **Son** suffers, the Father feels compassion."[47]

The Apologists and the Logos Doctrine: Christ as God

Quite a different emphasis appears in some of the writings of the major apologists, who developed the Logos doctrine and found an ecclesiastical continuator in Irenaeus of Lyons. They are often treated as a monolithic and monotonous group, but their teachings were divergent. Theophilus espouses a "low" Christology (see chapter 10), while Melito of Sardis offers many Christological references but hardly any to the Logos. The Logos doctrine does not necessarily exhaust the theological ideas of any of the apologists. As a group, they wrote in order to make Christian doctrine respectable, not to tell everything they believed. In other words, the nonapologetic works of all must have been rather different from the apologies.

An anonymous author of the late second century discusses some of the apologists among those who held doctrines like his. Since he himself refers to "our compassionate God and Lord, Jesus Christ" as well as to "the compassionate Church of the merciful Christ," he obviously represents a "high" Christology. He claims that Justin, Miltiades, Tatian, and Clement spoke of Christ as God, while Irenaeus and Melito called him God and man.[48] He says nothing about the Logos doctrines of these authors but notes their teaching about Christ's divine nature.

In Philo a Logos doctrine had bridged the gap between his transcendent, abstract God and the world. It also explained how theophanies could be included in the Old Testament revelation. The point was picked up in John 1:18: "No one has ever seen God; the Only-begotten God at the Father's bosom has interpreted [or revealed] him." Among the apologists too the Logos is the one who appears in the theophanies. But Justin describes this Logos as a second God, one who proceeded from the Father before creation in the manner of word or fire or spring water. "The Father of the Universe has a Son, who also, being the first-born Logos of God, is God." Tatian too has a Logos doctrine but speaks of Christ as "the God who suffered." Similarly, Clement refers to Christ as God.[49]

In spite of these points, the Christology of the apologies, like that of the New Testament, is essentially subordinationist. The Son is always subordinate to the Father, who is the one God of the Old Testament. This is related to the fact that in the apologists there is generally no clear distinction between Logos and Sophia or between either of them and Spirit.

Christ in Irenaeus and Clement of Alexandria

A significant passage in Irenaeus' *Against Heresies* sets forth his doctrine of the incarnate Logos.

> God's only begotten Logos, who is always present with the human race, was united and mixed with his creation by the will of the Father,

and became flesh: he is Jesus Christ our Lord, who suffered for us and
rose for us, and will come again in the glory of the Father to raise up
all flesh and to show forth [our] salvation. . . . He recapitulated man
in himself, the invisible made visible, the incomprehensible made com-
prehensible, the impassible passible, and the Logos made man.
(*Against Heresies* 3.17.6)

The phrases near the end seem to reflect ideas expressed by Ignatius, but without Ignatius' doctrine of Christ as God.[50]

In Clement of Alexandria we sometimes find traces of earlier
Docetic ideas—that Christ merely seemed to be human and suffer
—ideas we know were popular also at Antioch in his time. Thus he
provides a quotation from a letter of the Gnostic Valentinus about
Jesus' absolute self-control which meant that he did not evacuate
any of his food, since it did not decay inside him.[51] Clement cites
this, without comment, in support of his contention that continence
involves more than avoidance of sex. Again, in his *Outlines* he related
a "tradition" about the beloved disciple and his discovery that
though the body of Jesus seemed solid it turned out not to be so.[52]
Such notions are hardly orthodox or even intelligent. In addition
there were the interesting notions denounced by Photius, such as
the idea of the Son as a created being and the picture of two *logoi*
of the Father; only the inferior one of these two appeared to men.
Photius attacks a quotation that could be explained differently.
"The Son is called Logos, with the same name as the paternal
Logos, but he is not the one who became flesh. It was not the
paternal Logos but a certain power of God, like an emanation of his
Logos, which became Mind and permeated the hearts of men."[53]
This may not be accurately quoted, but even if it is, the power
emanation could be Sophia-Wisdom as discussed by second-century
apologists and Irenaeus. Apart from these exotic notes, we agree
with Kelly that Clement's Christology is not especially interesting.[54]
He did speak of Christ as God, as we have said, though not often.

Origen and Christology

Origen's doctrine tries to solve more problems. To be sure, it
contains a few Gnostic elements; that is to say, Origen adapts iso-
lated ideas from the Gnostic sphere for use in his own scheme. Like
Clement he begins with Sophia, at least in his *On First Principles*, but
we find some of his most important ideas in the *Dialogue with Heraclides*, where he discusses the Father and the Son without much
philosophical baggage.

According to this conference report he agreed with the bishop

Heraclides that "there is one God, omnipotent, uncreated, over all and maker of all." Problems arose in regard to the preexistence of Christ Jesus. When he existed "in the form of God" (Phil. 2:6), before the incarnation, was he God or not? If so, he was distinct from the God in whose form he was, and as Son distinct from Father. Therefore in one sense one must affirm the existence of two gods, in another only one. Origen insists on the importance of holding that there are two, and he compares the unity with that in marriage. "We must not fall into the opinion of those who have separated from the Church for the fantasy of 'monarchy,' withdrawing the Son [as a distinct person] from the Father and thus practically suppressing the Father, nor, on the other side, fall into another impious doctrine, that which denies the deity of Christ." He goes on to the relationship of the doctrine to the eucharist and states that "the eucharistic offering is always to be made to God almighty through Jesus Christ," because "the offering is made to God through God."[55]

Even though for Origen the Son is God, there is more than a trace of subordinationism in his doctrine. He insists that the Father alone is truly "the God" (*ho theos*) while the Son-Logos is *theos*, as in Philo and Clement.[56] He uses terms with the prefix *auto*, "in himself," of the Father, not of the Son, thus following the precedent of Numenius.[57]

While at Antioch theologians generally insisted on maintaining monotheism even at the expense of the divinity of the Son and the Spirit, and at Alexandria theologians were often willing to speak of two (or three) gods with Origen, the difference must not be exaggerated. All alike were trying to maintain a delicate balance between monotheism and polytheism or at least tritheism. In the second and third centuries, all ran the risk of dynamistic or modalistic Monarchianism. Instead of interurban rivalry, we seem to find intra-urban rivalry, at least in the period we are considering. Unfortunately we do not know just how Origen's Christology differed from that of his bishop Demetrius. This is why we shall presently turn to Antioch for more evidence on Christological debates (chapter 10).

9

The Cosmic Christ

Christ in Paul's Creed

Several decades before the Christian Gospels were written, the apostle Paul, who knew Jesus as one who though crucified had revealed himself to him, made an astounding confession about the cosmic Jesus Christ in a "creedal" passage in 1 Corinthians 8:6. Though pagans might accept "many gods" or "many lords," Christians believed in one supreme God, the Father, and one Lord, Jesus Christ, through whom everything, including us, has come into being. The universe was thus created through the crucified and exalted Messiah whom Paul proclaimed in his preaching. The supreme Father resembles the supreme Zeus, while the work of the Lord Christ is like that of the various demiurgic gods to whom cosmic functions were assigned. Later passages, such as Colossians 1:15–20 or even John 1:1–14, make no higher claims for Christ, though John 17:5 does speak more explicitly about his preexistent life. Jesus possessed glory with the Father before the world was made.

Within about two decades after the crucifixion, then, Paul was teaching his converts that Jesus had been God's agent in creation and, in effect, that he was the divine Wisdom of the book of Proverbs —or the second god of Middle Platonism. The claim might be less surprising if made in regard to Asclepius or some other demiurgic demigod. When made for a man whose crucifixion was "a stumbling-block to Jews and foolishness to gentiles," it is paradoxical, as Paul was well aware. Jewish hearers would ask for attestation by miracles, while Gentiles would ask for some kind of philosophical insight. Paul insisted that "to those who are called, both Jews and Greeks, Christ [is] the power of God and the wisdom of God" (1 Cor. 1:22–24).

Converts to Christianity could recognize that Jesus, the Son of God, did what the cosmic gods did. But since Christians denied the reality of these gods, he was the only Demiurge there was. Similarly, as Christians continued to meditate on the person of Wisdom, God's helper in the book of Proverbs, they became aware that Christ was not one intermediary among many (not one lord among many lords) but the only mediator. Much of later Christology and, ultimately, trinitarian theology was developed because of Christian insistence that both the Father and the Son were active in creation.

The traditional prayer in the fourth-century *Apostolic Constitutions* illustrates their belief. The prayer addresses the God who "brought everything to existence from the non-existent" through the only-begotten Son, who was begotten before all ages and is God the Logos. Both powers were involved in creation.[1] So too the so-called "Nicene" Creed says of Christ, "*Through* whom all things were made," not "*by* whom." The incorrect English translation assigns the work of the Father to the Son.

Middle Platonism, Gnosticism, and Christianity

We have already seen in chapters 6 and 7 that the formulations of second-century Christians stood close to Middle Platonism. So did the ideas of some Gnostic teachers. The oldest account of the Simonians describes their view of Simon's consort Helen as the first Thought that came from him—evidently his first Thought or pattern for the creation. Justin, as we shall presently see, uses the same language in speaking of the relationship between Zeus and Athena. We are therefore not surprised to find that the Simonians had statues of Zeus and Athena, evidently identifying them with their own hero and heroine. Again, Marcion regarded the good "unknown Father" as superior to the just Demiurge. And the Gnostic Ptolemaeus sharply differentiated "the perfect God" from "the Demiurge and Maker of this world."[2]

More orthodox Christians such as Justin, who spoke of the "second God," were also acquainted with this kind of philosophy. Relying on scripture, however, they insisted that "there is no other God above the Maker of all," and they usually referred to the Father as the Demiurge. Very occasionally they would use the term in regard to aspects of the Son's work. Normally, then, Gnostics agreed with Platonists that the perfect god was above the Demiurge, while Christians treated the Demiurge as supreme and his helper or helpers as subordinate to him.

Cosmic Interpretation of Pagan Gods

The doctrine of the cosmic Christ was proclaimed in a setting where the "many lords" were not so much related to one another as to the supreme god Zeus. These lesser gods could be expected to intervene in human affairs for the benefit of humanity and individuals. This is what epiphany and miracle mean. Beyond such interventions we find the supreme example of beneficience, as Plato had already intimated, in the creation of the world. (For the highest god, Zeus, see chapters 5 and 6.) At least some among the lesser gods came to be viewed as cosmic in nature.

In general the ideas were developed and expressed by religious-minded rhetoricians, trying to say as much as they could in praise of various gods. We should not suppose that they were creating a kind of pagan orthodox theology. Erwin Goodenough used to argue that the Jewish Platonist Philo derived some ideas from the Egyptian mysteries, because his ideas resembled those of Plutarch on the same mysteries. A. D. Nock wrote, however, that "the similarities to Plutarch are striking. But there is no reason to believe that initiates were taught anything like what Plutarch says." And he quotes Plutarch himself to the effect that "the true Isiac is he who, when he has duly received the things shown and done in reference to these deities, searches them by reason and philosophizes on the truth contained in them."[3] Nock adds emphatically, "The mysteries, like Judaism and Christianity, were in themselves nonphilosophical and, if they were to be intellectually acceptable at the time, had a like need of the application of philosophical terms and concepts." There was originally neither heresy nor orthodoxy in paganism, Christianity, or Judaism.

Greek Gods: Sons and Daughters of Zeus

As theology, both pagan and Christian, developed in the second century, the functions of Zeus as creator were being shared with his children, and during the next few centuries they came to be even more widely distributed. We now examine the cosmic functions ascribed to some of the gods subordinate to him. We expect to find not the source of Christian theological statements but environments in which Christian statements might be acceptable because not unfamiliar.

Cosmic Apollo

There is a cosmic Apollo in the speech that Plutarch attributes to his teacher Ammonius in the dialogue *On the E at Delphi*. After a thoroughly Platonic discussion of deity as eternal and one, he identifies Apollo as A-pollon—supposedly meaning "not many"—"denying the many and rejecting multiplicity." Those who identify him with the sun rightly recognize "the creative power associated with it" but fail to see that acts and experiences having to do with change "are related to some other god or rather to a daemon set over dissolution and generation." Apollo is above change and is "existent through all eternity."[4] But he is not really a creator.

A third-century manual of rhetoric ascribed to Menander of Laodicea devotes a special chapter to the praises of Apollo and gives him some creative powers. It ends with the numerous alternative names of the god and notes that "Persians call thee Mithras, Egyptians Horus, Thebans Dionysus."[5] Apollo can even be called Sun or Mind or Demiurge of all, for he abolished chaos and brought about order. The contemporary powers of the god seem less impressive: his skills in archery, prediction, medicine, and music. The author does retain the theological notion that the universe moves in tune with Apollo's music.[6]

The cosmic role of Apollo is often expressed in what is said of the sun. In Tractate 16 of the *Corpus Hermeticum* the Sun is described as the Demiurge, subordinate to the supreme God (ch. 18), even though the name Apollo does not occur. The emperor Julian devoted a prose hymn to "King Helios" and identified Apollo with Helios, even though he referred to Apollo by name only as "the leader of the Muses" and said that the god looks up from below to the triad in heaven and offers this acclamation: "One Zeus, one Hades, one Helios is Serapis."[7]

Apollo thus maintained his role among the gods who helped humanity, and retained cosmic functions in spite of the decay of his oracle at Delphi. Sometimes we hear of them among scholars like Macrobius. Better evidence occurs in an oracle of Clarian Apollo from the third century: "Born from himself, innately wise, without mother, unshakeable, enduring no name but many-named, living in fire, that is god. But we are particles of god, his messengers. Whatever persons ask god what he is, he answers, 'Looking upon him, the Aether, the All-seeing god, pray facing east in the morning.' "[8] Apollo is obviously the sun—and more.

Cosmic Athena

Apollo's sister was Athena, and we expect to find her equally creative. In Plato's *Cratylus* (407B) she is already identified as the mind *(nous)* of God *(theos)*, though we never know how seriously Plato wanted his etymologies taken. It is the Stoic Chrysippus who gives us an allegorical explanation of the birth of Athena from the head of Zeus. He took Athena to be Zeus's thought *(phronesis)*, coming out of his head. Chrysippus' pupil Diogenes of Babylon wrote "On Athena" and set forth the same doctrine. He was criticized for it after Cicero by the Christian apologist Minucius Felix.[9]

In slightly different terms the apologist Justin mentions pagans who hold that Athena, the daughter of Zeus, was not generated from sexual intercourse. When Zeus considered *(ennoethesis)* making the world through his reason *(logos)*, his first thought *(ennoia)* was Athena. Justin comments rather feebly that "we consider it ridiculous that the image of a thought should be female in form." So too another Christian knows that "they say Athena is thought pervading all things."[10]

The orations *To Zeus* and *To Athena* by the late second-century rhetorician Aelius Aristides provide excellent parallels to Christian theology and at least indicate the environment in which the latter was acceptable and meaningful. The rhetor states:

> Zeus made everything and all things are works of Zeus; rivers and earth and sea and heaven and whatever is within these and whatever is beyond them, gods and men and whatever has life and whatever appears to sight and whatever one can think of. First he made himself, not the Cretan [Zeus] brought up in sweet-smelling caverns, nor did Kronos plan to consume him or consume a stone in his stead, nor was Zeus ever in danger or ever will be; there is nothing older than Zeus, for sons are not older than fathers nor things produced than those who make them, but he is first and oldest and chief of all, himself produced from himself. One cannot say when he came to be, but he was from the beginning and will be forever, father of himself and greater than one coming to be from another. And as Athena derived her nature from his head and he needed no partner to produce her, thus even earlier he made himself from himself and needed no other for coming to be; on the contrary, everything began its existence from him.[11]

The relation of Zeus to Athena is described more fully in the other oration.[12]

> He had nothing of the same rank from which to make her, but himself withdrawing into himself generated the goddess from himself and bore her, so that she alone is securely the genuine offspring of the

Father, coming to be from a race equal to him and acknowledged. What is yet greater than this is that from the most excellent part of himself, that is, from his head, he produced her . . . therefore it is not right for her ever to abandon the Father, but she is always present with him and lives with him as being of the same origin; she breathes toward him and is present alone with him alone, mindful of her genesis and returning a suitable repayment for the birth pangs.

There are striking Christian parallels to this interpretation, and we shall find the setting of Theophilus' doctrine of Logos and Sophia, notably in his *To Autolycus* 2.10 and 22, in what Aristides says about Athena. In other words, the Sophia of Theophilus is not only the Sophia of Proverbs but also the Athena of Aristides.[13] F. W. Lenz claimed that the Athena of Aristides had the Christian *homoousia* as its model, but since the doctrine of *homoousia* did not as yet exist, this cannot be right. It is as wrong to treat Aristides as an imitator of Christian theology[14] as it would be to suggest that Christians relied on Aristides. The two interpretations reflect similar meditations on similar bases.

Cosmic Dionysus?

At Delphi, according to Plutarch, "the theologians" spoke of Dionysus in verse and prose, defining the god as "by nature imperishable and eternal" but fated to undergo transformations—above all into fire, but also in his form, emotions, and powers. "As to his turning into winds and water, earth and stars, and into the generations of plants and animals, and his adoption of such guises, they speak in a deceptive way of what he undergoes in his transformation as a tearing apart, as it were, and a dismemberment."[15] Plutarch is interpreting the Dionysiac myth in a cosmic manner.

A hymn by Aelius Aristides treats Dionysus as both male and female and asks if he is the same as Zeus. In the way of cosmic interpretation, however, all Aristides says is that "he watches over the limits of night and day, becoming the initiator and leader of sight. . . . Ever in motion and movement he passes through the age. He is the oldest and youngest of the gods, friend of the ever present hour and lot."[16] This is not fully cosmic language.

Sometimes scholars seek to find fixed theological interpretations of the reliefs on Dionysiac and other sarcophagi, but an attack on this kind of overexegesis has been mounted by Hugo Brandenburg[17] and Angelika Geyer.[18] Nock too resisted the temptation to find more in the art than could be proved.[19]

In the fourth century, however, the emperor Julian was able to allegorize the story of Dionysus' birth, which in his view depicts all too human events and is nonsensical as a story of the gods. What counts is the cosmic meaning. Julian argues that "those who sought to discover what kind of god Dionysus is, worked into a myth the truth . . . and expressed in an allegory both the essential nature (*ousia*) of the god and his conception among the 'intelligible gods' in his father Zeus, and further his ungenerated birth in the world."[20] But what he does is not clear.

Cosmic Hermes

By the fourth century of our era there was some speculation about Hermes not only as revealer but also as creator. According to *Kore Kosmou,* a fragment of the Hermetic literature, Hermes in heaven assured the supreme God that he would create "the nature of men" and set Wisdom and Temperance and Persuasion and Truth in them. He was the intermediary through whom and with whom "the Father and Demiurge," the "Monarch," would work.[21]

A contemporary papyrus provides a rather similar picture, though Hermes, not Zeus, is here the Demiurge. The father Zeus created Hermes out of himself and "to him he gave many commands, to make a most beautiful cosmos." While Zeus "rejoiced to behold the works of his illustrious son," Hermes went forth and ordered the elements to separate and live in peace. Then "the son of the all-creator" provided orderly arrangement for the universe. Hermes went through the skies, "but not alone, for with him went Logos, his noble son." Instead of treating Hermes himself as Logos, the author creates a genealogy from Zeus to Logos; the latter is now called "the swift herald (*angelos*) of the father's pure intention (*noema*)."[22]

We thus see that as a god subordinate to the supreme Father, Hermes could act as his assistant in the creation of the universe.

Cosmic Deeds of the Hero Gods

Cosmic interpretation of the two hero gods Asclepius and Heracles was made difficult by the fact that stories about them depicted both of them as mortals. Asclepius, in fact, was killed by Zeus, jealous of his reputation as a healer. Philosophers spoke of Heracles as a man divinized by virtue, one who finally set fire to himself to escape the burden of the flesh. It was hard for most to see how such semihuman beings could have been active in the creation, though there were those who thought they were.

Asclepius

Asclepius was a son of Apollo, and like his father he was sometimes considered a cosmic god. The author of a second-century papyrus text (P. Oxy. XI 1381) deals with the praises of Asclepius (identified with the Egyptian god Imouthes) and is concerned primarily with recording the healings for which the god was famous. There is, however, a "physical treatise" in another book of his. It contains "the convincing account of the creation of the world" and thus extends "the fame of your [Asclepius'] inventiveness." He urges readers to come together if by serving the god they have been cured of diseases or propose to follow virtue zealously or have been blessed by benefits or saved from the dangers of the sea. "For every place has been penetrated by the saving power (*dynamis soterios*) of the god." He therefore intends to proclaim his "manifestations, the greatness of his power, and his benefactions and gifts."[23] Praises for his healings are most important, but they can be supplemented by comments on his cosmic functions.

The rhetorician Aelius Aristides says exactly what we should expect from a devotee healed by the god.[24] "Asclepius has great and many powers, or rather he has every power, not just that which concerns human life. And it is not by chance that the people here [at Pergamum] have built a temple of Zeus Asclepius." On this basis Aristides can proceed to speak of Asclepius as if he were Zeus. "He is the one who guides and rules the universe, the savior of the whole and the guardian of the immortals, or if you wish to put it in the words of the tragic poet, 'the steerer of government,' he who preserves both what always exists and what comes into existence." In a dream Aristides was shown a spot in the sky which was identified as "the soul of the universe" (*Tim.* 34B); when he looked at it he saw "Asclepius of Pergamum enthroned in the sky."[25] This means that Asclepius is still subordinate to Zeus, though possessing powers virtually identical with his.[26]

Heracles

In his discussion of the myth of Heracles, the first-century allegorizer Cornutus treats him as "the Logos in all things, in accordance with which Nature is strong and powerful, since it is immovable and endlessly generative." He mentions the early Stoic teacher Cleanthes, who ascribed the twelve labors not to the life of the hero but to the work of the god. Evidently he identified him as the sun in its heavenly journey.[27] The Neoplatonist Porphyry also identified him with the sun as defender against evils and treated the twelve labors as his passage through the signs of the zodiac.[28] But he was not a cosmic creator.

One wonders how much the emperor Julian owes to his Christian upbringing (as well as to Neoplatonic allegorization) when he writes that all the elements obeyed the "divine and most pure body" of Heracles because they "served the creative and perfecting force of his stainless and pure intelligence." (The example he uses is Heracles' supposed ability to "walk on the sea as if it were dry land.") "Great Zeus, through his Forethought Athena whom he appointed as his guardian, her whom he had brought forth whole from the whole of himself, generated him to be savior for the world."[29] In this picture Athena is more clearly cosmic than Heracles, essentially the grandson of Zeus, not his son.

Heracles becomes truly cosmic only when identified with some other god or principle. Thus the Christian apologist Athenagoras, at this point close to the late Neoplatonist Damascius, refers to the Orphic doctrine that everything came first from water, thence from slime. From both there emerged "a serpent with the head of a lion attached, and between them the face of a god." Its name, they said, was Heracles and Chronos (Time), and it "generated a huge egg which, when filled by the power of him who generated it, broke into two through friction" and became heaven and earth.[30] Though an Orphic hymn applies many "cosmic" epithets to Heracles,[31] he is rarely named in the Orphic fragments.

Heracles, then, was not a significant cosmic creator, even though like other minor gods he was occasionally addressed as such. Late Orphism provided a special environment in which rhetorical praise in hymns was lavishly applied to many deities.

To sum up, we note that the gods and goddesses most often credited with cosmic creativity are children of Zeus who assist their Father. He remains above as the ultimate Demiurge; they do his work. We shall expect the situation of oriental deities not to be very different, since in Greco-Roman times they were ordinarily identified with the Greek gods.

Oriental Cosmic Deities

Cosmic Isis

We have discussed the earlier status of Isis. In Greco-Roman times she acquired cosmic functions. Thus the rhetorician Apuleius speaks of the providential care she bestows on humanity and then explains that she does so by unweaving the web of fate and keeping back the harmful course of the stars. "The gods above worship you; the gods below reverence you; you turn the earth and give light to the sun, you rule the world, you tread upon Tartarus. The stars respond to you, the seasons return, the gods rejoice, the elements give service. By your will the winds blow, the clouds give nourishment, seeds sprout, fruits grow. . . . My voice lacks the strength to express what I think of your majesty, nor would a thousand mouths or tongues continuing to speak forever."[32] No praise can be too high for the god or goddess.

The Christian apologist Athenagoras is acquainted with this kind of interpretation. He knows the "physical explanations" that interpret Isis as "the origin of eternity, from whom all originate and through whom all exist."[33] If all comes from her, she is evidently the supreme cause, not just a mediator.

The explanation Plutarch gives of the work of Isis, however, makes clear that for him she is a secondary creative principle. In his treatise *On Isis and Osiris* he sets forth some of the basic principles he uses for criticizing the old Egyptian myths. The stories about the cutting up of Horus and the beheading of Isis are incompatible with "the nature of the blessed and imperishable, in accordance with which the divine is really known." They are not poetic imaginings, however, but because they "contain narratives of puzzling events and experiences,"[34] they have allegorical meanings which the exegete can set forth. In Plutarch's own doctrine about Isis, she is essentially equivalent to Matter, hence not really a creator deity. He says she is

> the female principle of nature, and is receptive of every form of generation, and therefore is called by Plato "gentle nurse" and "all-receptive" and by most people has been called "of countless names."[35] Because of the force of Reason, she turns to receive all shapes and forms. She has an innate love for the First and most dominant of all, identical with the Good, and she yearns for this and pursues it. She tries to avoid and reject what comes from evil. Though she provides place and material for both good and evil, she always inclines toward the better and offers it opportunity to create from her and sow effluxes and likenesses in her. She rejoices in these and is glad to be pregnant and teeming with the things generated. For genesis is the material image of reality, and what is generated is an imitation of the Existent.[36]

Cosmic Mother of the Gods and Attis

One might speak of the Mother of the Gods from Asia Minor as truly the mother of Zeus or "the great parent of all nature,"[37] but her identification with the rather shadowy Rhea, the consort of Kronos, did not contribute to her popularity, and only late visionaries like Julian and his friends tried to develop her into a cosmic figure. Sallustius called her "the life-giving goddess" and treated her son Attis as the Demiurge of things coming to be and passing away. His self-castration symbolized either "the revolution of the sun between the tropics" or "the separation of the soul from vice and error."[38]

Cosmic Mithras?

Mithras seems cosmic in nature, but the myth about him is a story about nowhere and never. According to Plutarch, Zoroaster taught that Oromazes (Ahura Mazda) was like light, Areimanius (Ahriman) like darkness. Mithras is between the two, and the Persians therefore call him Mediator.[39]

He was only occasionally treated as a demiurge. A writer on Mithraism cited by Porphyry called him "maker and father of the world . . . which he created."[40] If, as J. Bidez and Franz Cumont suggest, the notice comes from Numenius, the idea that he was the Demiurge (or rather, a representative Demiurge) could be Numenius' own, not a testimony to Mithraic thought.[41]

In any case, making the world was not Mithras' basic work. He was born from a rock already in existence. As a young man he struggled with the cosmic bull depicted on many beliefs. It is not quite clear what this means, though Porphyry tells us that "Mithras rides the bull of Aphrodite, since the bull is creator (*demiourgos*) and Mithras is the master of creation."[42] At the bull's death a hostile dog and scorpion try to get vital fluids from it, but Mithras contends with them and then defends humanity when it comes into existence. Finally he joins the Sun in eating the bull's flesh, and the two ascend into the heavens.

The importance of Mithraism should not be exaggerated. Even toward the end of paganism, Mithras was not the chief of the gods, and whatever fame he had was due to his assimilation to the sun-god.[43]

No Cosmic Sarapis

Though Aelius Aristides tells us that "whatever directs and preserves human life is the work of Sarapis," that "from the beginning he led us to light and providentially provided his own beginning," and (as usual) that "being one he is all things,"[44] there seems to be no cosmic myth and Sarapis cannot be considered a creator.

We thus see that the developments of cosmic theology in the background of early Christian thought were not universal and were related not to oriental deities but primarily to the Greek gods who stood on a level just below Zeus. The creative powers of Zeus were extended to them (though not to others) and the work of philosophical theology could begin. This kind of religious thought apparently did not directly influence Christian theology, but the congenial environment permitted theology both Christian and pagan to develop.

10

Divergent Christologies at Antioch

Struggle among various parties, all maintaining what they considered the true Christian tradition, brought about development in the doctrine of Christ at Antioch. We have already looked at the "high" Christology of Ignatius of Antioch, whose roots may lie in apocryphal traditions about the risen Lord as well as in New Testament notions. The defenders of "low" Christology could appeal to equally venerable and authentic traditions, handed down from apostles like Peter and maintained by several later bishops of Antioch.

From early times there were at least these two emphases in Christology at Antioch. The older was expressed in sermons of Peter as set forth by Luke as well as in apocrypha ascribed to Peter himself. Later it was expressed in doctrine developed by two apologists and continued into the third and fourth centuries by Paul of Samosata and Marcellus of Ancyra. The doctrine that is probably newer relies more on Paul and John and states what came to be regarded as the basic emphasis of catholic Christianity on the deity of Christ. Its chief proponent was Ignatius of Antioch. In relation to broader "tendencies" in early Christianity, the first was close to Hellenistic Jewish thought while the second stood nearer to theology as developed among, or at least for, Gentiles.[1] Both doctrines, however, contain Jewish and Gentile elements.

Traces of Early "Low" Christology at Antioch

The first emphasis should be traced back to the apostolic church at Antioch not just because Eusebius says Luke came from there (*Ecclesiastical History* 3.4.6) but because the apostle Paul tells us that Peter was somehow associated with the Jewish or Judaizing Christians of the city (Gal. 2:11–13). Traditions about Peter were impor-

tant at Antioch, where he was later viewed as the first bishop. Antio-
chenes were devoted to his memory. Bishop Serapion, as we shall
see, proves this point.

The speeches ascribed to Peter in Acts set forth a "low" Christology, presented to Jewish Christians or prospective converts. It
appears in Acts 2:22: "Jesus the Nazarene, a man attested from
God," in Acts 2:36: "God made him Lord and Christ, this Jesus
whom you crucified," and in Acts 10:38: "How God anointed Jesus
from Nazareth with Holy Spirit and power, and he went about doing
good and healing. . . . God was with him." Modern critics insist that
Luke did not think of Jesus as "mere man," but he certainly accepted a view of Jesus as essentially human and said nothing about
his preexistence.[2]

Similarly, in the apologetic *Preaching of Peter*, perhaps first used at
Antioch, the basic Christian doctrine is that there is one God, who
was made known through the Lord and his apostles. It is not clear
whether it was "Peter" or Clement of Alexandria who identified the
"first-born Son" with the "Beginning" of the first verse of Genesis
or called the Lord "Law and Logos."[3] In any event, our fragments
provide no developed Logos doctrine.

The author of the *Preaching of Peter* presents a straightforward
Middle Platonic doctrine of God, unhampered by Jewish or indeed
Christian complexities until the end of his affirmation. "There is
one God . . . the invisible who sees all, the uncontained who contains
all, without needs whom all need, for whose sake they exist, incomprehensible, everlasting, imperishable, unmade, who made all by
the Word of his power."[4] "The Word of his power" reminded von
Dobschütz of Hebrews 1:3, but there the term refers to the Son's
word, not the Father's. The expression as found in these two Christian books shows that it need not be taken personally. We therefore
refrain from taking either Law or Logos as an adequate portrayal of
the Son. Probably they are references to the content of his message.
This kind of language will recur in Theophilus of Antioch.

"Low" Christologies Attacked by Ignatius

We have seen in chapter 8 something of the "high" Christology
proclaimed at Antioch by Ignatius. We do not know how much
support he received at Antioch, since no letters of his to or from the
church there have survived, if indeed they ever existed. We do find
hints of the "Jewish" Christologies which probably existed at Mag-
nesia and Philadelphia in Asia Minor. Ignatius denounces his Christian opponents there so vigorously that it is hard to tell exactly

what they thought. Perhaps they were Adoptionists, perhaps not.

It is significant, however, that some of Ignatius' most important statements about the preexistent Son appear in his letter to the Magnesians. Evidently he thought they needed this kind of teaching. He speaks twice about the life of the preexistent divine Son Jesus Christ. "Before the ages he was with the Father and was manifested at the end." He "proceeded from the one Father and is with him and departed to the one."[5]

It is also important to observe that neither to the Magnesians nor to the Philadelphians does Ignatius speak of Christ as God. Since he does so in his other letters, even the one to the Romans whom he does not know, presumably he is affected by the monotheistic views of his readers.

Between Ignatius and Theophilus: Tatian

Only toward the end of the second century do we find more information about Christology at Antioch or even about the church there. Our lack of information does not prove anything about the theological situation. It could be due just to Eusebius' lack of materials from Antioch when he was writing his influential *Ecclesiastical History*. But the situation in his time was not a new one. The extant Christian literature of the late second century and the early third suggests that the church of Antioch between Ignatius (about 110) and Theophilus (about 180) made no favorable impression, or indeed no impression at all, on Christian writers elsewhere.

To fill the gap we venture to make use of Tatian's *Oration to the Greeks*, whether it is orthodox or heretical or in between. The justification for doing so is not so much Epiphanius' remark that Tatian's doctrine was spread from Antioch as the fact that his Christology seems to harmonize with the situation we can imagine at Antioch before Theophilus. Tatian writes that he came from "the land of the Assyrians," and this term was sometimes used of Syria as well.[6] Herodotus says that Greeks used the word "Syrians" for people whom barbarians called "Assyrians."[7] We recall that Tatian insisted that he was a barbarian. He studied with Justin at Rome before 165, said good-by to Rome and Athens, and probably went back to Syria after Justin's death.

Tatian claims to have been converted to Christianity by reading the old and divinely inspired "barbarian writings" of the Old Testament, in which he found stylistic simplicity, an intelligible account of creation, the predictions of the prophets, "the remarkable quality of the precepts," and the Monarchican (monotheistic) doctrine.[8] In other words, he combined the Jewish scripture (in Greek) with a philosophical analysis of it.

Tatian's teacher Justin had developed a semiphilosophical doctrine of God and his Logos but always gave it content by using biblical passages, especially from the Old Testament, and speaking of the life of Jesus. Tatian, on the other hand, did away with much of the biblical content, certainly when addressing strangers as in the *Oration to the Greeks.* What he retained seems close to what was being presented, or was about to be presented, as Christian apologetic theology at Antioch. If Tatian left the Roman Christian community in 172 (so Eusebius-Jerome), Theophilus was probably bishop of Antioch and thus would have taken notice of Tatian's work, whether favorably or not.

Tatian's doctrine of God is straightforwardly Middle Platonic, related to the New Testament only by rather forced exegesis. "God has no constitution in time but is alone without beginning; he is the beginning of everything." Thus philosophy explains the terms of John 4:24, "God is spirit." In addition, God is invisible and intangible. "We know him through his creation and we recognize his invisible power in his works"—an echo of Romans 1:20.

God exercised his creative power through his Logos. He was originally alone, but the whole power or potentiality of things visible and invisible was with him through his logical power. (Conceivably these expressions are built on Hebrews 1:3.) In response to God's pure will, the Logos "leapt forth" (an echo of Justin) as his "first-born work" (cf. Col. 1:15). It originated by division, not abscission. In other words, it remained essentially united with its source. To explain this notion, Tatian relies on two analogies. First, many fires come from one torch; he takes this image from Justin and indirectly from Philo. Second, a speaker is not "empty" of thought when he expresses what is in his mind. This picture comes from what we may call linguistic psychology.

Tatian specifically notes that the Logos, "becoming Spirit from Spirit and Logos from logical power" or, in other words, becoming actuality from potentiality, then made angels and, in imitation of the Father, man. The firstborn of the angels rebelled against God, and by following him man became mortal. By the aid of the divine Spirit, however, the human soul can ascend and live.

The Logos is obviously derived from God, but this fact may not have any direct bearing on Christology. Three passages tell us something about the Christological doctrine. First, Tatian calls the Spirit "the minister of the God who suffered" (*Oration to the Greeks* 13). Similarly, the Gnostic Basilidians called the Spirit "minister," though they did not say whose he was.[9] The idea of the suffering God clearly recalls the devotional language of Ignatius. Second, Tatian says, "If a man is like a temple, God wills to dwell in him through the emissary Spirit" (*Oration* 15). This is clearly based on Pauline thought and language: "You are the temple of God and the Spirit of God dwells in you" (1 Cor. 3:16). Paul is speaking of Christians in general but obviously includes particular individuals in his outlook. Third, Tatian refers to the Christian message about "God in the form of a man" (*Oration* 21), presumably in allusion to Philippians 2:6–7, where Paul describes Christ Jesus as "in the form of God" and "in the likeness of men."[10]

The upshot is that we have a theology of creation with God as Spirit and creative Logos as Spirit, and a theology of redemption with God as Spirit but nothing said about the Logos. In fact, Tatian rewrote John 1:3, "Everything was made through the Logos," to read "Everything was made by God." There is no contradiction, but there is a different emphasis. He referred John 1:5, "The darkness did not comprehend the light," to the human situation generally by changing the verb to the present tense. And he took Psalm 8:5, "for a little, lower than the angels," as referring to humanity, not the Son.[11] In other words, in passages where other early Christians found the incarnate Logos or the Son, Tatian found a God-man or God in man, or simply mankind.

In Tatian's *Oration* there is no trace of Peter or Luke-Acts or a relatively "low" Christology. He naturally used the Gospel of Luke in the *Diatessaron* but treated it as less reliable than the apostolic Matthew and John.

We conclude that Tatian may give us a Christological doctrine as taught at Antioch around 175. Certainly it was not the only one. Saturninus may well have had successors. There were also the forebears of the Docetists whom Serapion would later encounter. And the bishop Theophilus must have been developing his thoughts on these matters. A simple list of Antiochene teachers cannot do justice, however, to the diversity present in the churches. Theophilus certainly knew most of the books in the Greek Bible. He knew and used Hermas, probably the *Preaching of Peter*, possibly Ignatius. Hermas, at any rate, will have broadened his theological horizons.

Theophilus and the "Low" Christology

The curtain of silence over Antiochene Christianity lifts in the three books *To Autolycus* by Bishop Theophilus. They are important because, though Theophilus used Pauline epistles and the Gospel of John, he reverted to the "low" Christology expressed by Peter in Acts and also used Luke's picture of Jesus in setting forth his own doctrine. He thus anticipated much of what scholars have treated as Antiochene in the fragments of Paul of Samosata and Marcellus of Ancyra.

We begin with God. Theophilus resembles Philo when he sets forth a doctrine essentially Jewish in nature even though expressed in the language of Middle Platonism. He says that "we acknowledge (1) a God, (2) but only one, (3) the Founder and Maker and Demiurge (4) of this whole cosmos, (5) and we know that everything is governed by providence, by him alone" (*To Autolycus* 3.9). These five points are exactly the same as those listed by Philo in a "creed" toward the end of the treatise *On the Creation of the World;* in his introduction, Erwin Goodenough pointed to Philo but not to Theophilus.[12] Theophilus is an heir of Hellenistic Judaism and presumably reflects some of its major developments in the second century. His doctrine of God uses biblical texts most of the time for philosophical conclusions. After the *Preaching of Peter* he makes use of the traditional "negative attributes." Indeed, he insists that one can speak only of functions or aspects of God, never of God in himself. For example, one cannot say that God is Logos or Mind or Spirit or Wisdom. These terms express modes of God's working, not God. Justin had already presented this idea in abbreviated form.[13] Because of Theophilus' concern for scripture one might hope for a more detailed picture of how God works, but he does not provide one. Instead, he treats God's Logos as equivalent to his Mind, Spirit, Wisdom, and Forethought.[14] Like Irenaeus, he refuses to differentiate mental activities within God because the Gnostics could then offer their theories about sequential emanations. On the other hand, he is unfortunately ready to analyze God's internal and external Logos, as we shall see.

Theophilus' language is rather loose. Sometimes he treats Logos as different from Wisdom; sometimes he identifies them. Quite in the manner of Philo, he calls Logos and Sophia God's hands but is willing to speak of God's one hand even when discussing the creation.[15]

He strives to be precise when he describes the Logos, and insists that originally the Logos was *in* God. On this point he agrees with Valentinian Gnostics, Tatian, Irenaeus, Clement of Alexandria, and sometimes even Tertullian and Origen. Indeed, Theophilus holds with Irenaeus and Clement that this is exactly what the evangelist

John meant when he said that "the Logos was *pros ton theon*"—which must mean "with God."[16] Tertullian finally denounced the idea, but followers of Paul of Samosata, as well as Marcellus of Ancyra, picked it up.[17] Presumably it won favor for a time because of the Johannine emphasis on the coinherence of the Father with the Son.[18] Later theologians saw that the notion implied that the Son was once not distinct from the Father.

Theophilus goes into more detail than most when he describes the generation of the Logos from God. He says that the Logos was contained in God's "inside parts" or "heart" and that before creation God "disgorged him," a notion supposedly justified by exegesis of Psalm 45:2, "My heart overflows with a good matter."[19] This inelegant metaphor did not appeal to Irenaeus, who denied that anybody knew the mode of the Son's begetting, or to Origen, who denied the relevance of Psalm 45:2 to the Son.[20] Unfortunately Tertullian liked it, probably because of Theophilus' influence on him.[21] The Greek word for "disgorge" is sometimes used of giving birth and for the "inside parts" of the womb. Conceivably Theophilus could have used this kind of language by analogy with the human birth of the incarnate Logos, but we do not know that he did so.

A different way of describing the generation could use language borrowed from rhetoricians and Stoic philosophers and already applied by Philo to human thought (the *Logos endiathetos*) as expressed in human speech (the *Logos prophorikos*).[22] Theophilus goes beyond Philo by applying the analogy to the divine Logos. We note that both Irenaeus and Origen followed Philo by accepting the distinction but reserving it for human psychology.[23]

After creation the Logos appeared in Eden, just as Philo and Justin said he did, for according to Adam he heard the voice of God, who was walking in paradise (Gen. 3:10). God cannot be present in a particular place. It must have been his creative Logos, called Voice and identified as his power and wisdom (cf. 1 Cor. 1:24). The Logos was "assuming the role" (*analambanon to prosopon*) of God. Has Theophilus really thought about the Christological implications? More probably, he is simply playing exegetical tricks. He read in Gen. 3:8 that Adam and Eve hid from the *prosopon*, or "face," of God.

To be sure, Theophilus probably knows that Justin referred to the prophets, inspired by the divine Logos, as speaking "as in the role of God the Father and Master of all" or in the role of Christ or of "the people replying to him or to his Father."[24] Justin's prophet is much like Theophilus' Christ, an emissary of the Father, as we shall see.

What might have been a more suitable interpretation can be found in Clement's *Exhortation to the Greeks:*

> The divine Logos, the most manifest real God [cf. John 17:3], the one made equal [Phil. 2:6] to the Master of all—for he was his Son and "the Logos was in God" [John 1:2]—. . . assuming the role of a man and fashioned in flesh, played the saving drama of humanity. (*Exhortation to the Greeks* 110.1–2)

For Theophilus as for his predecessors, the Logos (or Sophia, or Spirit) inspired the prophets. God sent prophets "from among their brothers" (Deut. 18:15) to "teach and remind" the people of the content of the Mosaic law (*To Autolycus* 3.11). According to John 14:26, the Paraclete, the Holy Spirit, will "teach and remind" of everything Jesus said to his disciples. If we can rely on these allusions, Jesus must have reiterated the law of Moses. This is what we should expect to hear from a reader of the *Preaching of Peter.* [25] With the *Preaching,* Theophilus lays emphasis on the Old Testament law and its complete agreement with the prophets and the Gospels (*To Autolycus* 3.9–14). The *Preaching* says that the Jews do not understand God or keep Sabbath correctly.[26] This would help explain why Theophilus' decalogue does not include the commandments about the name of God and Sabbath observance (*To Autolycus* 3.9).

We now turn directly to the doctrine about Christ. There is some ambiguity about the incarnation of the Word of God. Theophilus avoided Ignatian paradox in his quest for a theology based on philosophy and exegesis. The term "exegesis" reminds us that he was not relying upon tradition as such but upon a Gospel collection which he used against Marcion. This means that he must have accepted both Luke and Acts and defended the opening chapters of Luke, regarded by Marcion as interpolations. Thus he referred to the Lucan "Power of the Most High" as one of the names of the Logos (*To Autolycus* 2.10; Luke 1:35). Justin had already taken the angel's words to Mary to mean that the Spirit and the Power from God were his Logos. They came upon Mary and "overshadowed" her and she became pregnant.[27] Is this what Theophilus thought? It is hard to say, but it seems likely.

Did the Logos really become incarnate however? In Theophilus' view, there was no need for such an action. He could write that "whenever the Father of the universe wills to do so, he sends the Logos into some place where he is present and is heard and seen, being sent by God and [unlike the Father] being present in a place." The phrasing reminds us of the Johannine insistence upon Jesus as the "one sent" by the Father. In the same chapter, when Theophilus denies the existence of "sons of gods born of sexual union" he speaks of the Logos as "always innate (*endiathetos*) in the heart of God" (*To Autolycus* 2.22). Does that mean that the Logos was not born? We have already compared the generation before the creation with the incarnation, but that is a tenuous comparison indeed. Whether Jesus was born of a virgin or not, Theophilus had no reason to suggest that the Logos was born. Even John 1:14, "The Logos became flesh," may not have convinced him.

What did Theophilus think about the life and work of Christ? He says nothing directly, but in his account of Adam there seem to be echoes of the early chapters of Luke, notably the passages on Jesus' growth, progress, and obedience to parents. God gave Adam an "opportunity for progress" (*To Autolycus* 2.24; Luke 2:52). Had he taken it, he could have ascended into heaven and become God.[28] It is a holy duty not only "before God but also before men" (Luke 2:52 again) to obey one's parents (cf. Luke 2:43). If children must obey their parents, how much more the God and Father of all (cf. Luke 2:49)? As one grows in age in orderly fashion, so also one grows in thinking.[29]

Theophilus has applied to Adam, generic man, what Luke said about Jesus' infancy—and for Theophilus, Adam in Eden was an infant. So also in *To Autolycus*, Theophilus takes the apostle's comparison of Adam with Christ (Rom. 5:15–21) and rewrites it to compare man then with man now.

> What man acquired for himself through his neglect and disobedience God now freely [for]gives him through love and mercy. For as by disobedience man gained death for himself, so by obedience to the will of God whoever will can obtain eternal life for himself. For God gave us a law and holy commandments; everyone who does them can be saved and attaining to the resurrection can inherit imperishability. (*To Autolycus* 2.27)

Thus Christ is significant primarily as an exemplary second Adam. The unique role of Christ virtually vanishes.[30] For Theophilus, the essence of religion must be revelation in law, not redemption. This is why he is eager to call Adam, Moses, and Solomon prophets.[31] Like Theophilus, Marcellus of Ancyra called them prophets, and Eusebius ridiculed him for doing so.[32]

To sum up: for Theophilus, God possesses various faculties through which he acts and reveals himself. He thereby shows man what is good and expects him to do it. If Jesus differed from others it was in the obedience for which God finally rewarded him. There is a sharp break between the incarnational Christology of Ignatius and the reticent monotheism of Theophilus. Who could say whether one of them was orthodox, the other not? These problems, beginning in very early times, were to plague the church at Antioch for centuries.

Christians outside Antioch may have been aware of some of these difficulties. Irenaeus, who certainly knew and used the work of Theophilus (but did not mention his name) as well as the writings of Clement, Polycarp, and Hermas, quoted part of one sentence from Ignatius and simply called him "one of our people."[33] Clement of Alexandria used Clement, Hermas, and Barnabas but not Ignatius. Origen seems to have encountered the Ignatian letters only in his last years at Caesarea (see chapter 7). On the other hand, Theophilus' work won some favor among Latin theologians, but little among the Greeks.

Serapion and the Memory of Peter

After Theophilus, Serapion of Antioch expressed reverence for Peter and the other apostles. At Antioch, doctrine handed down from Peter was obviously authoritative. Serapion also knew Docetists, obviously not orthodox, who were willing to help him understand their *Gospel of Peter*. We cannot tell what Serapion thought about "the true teaching of the Savior," to which he appeals. Presumably it was found in writings rightly ascribed to the apostles.[34] To judge from contemporary authors, these would include the sermons of Peter in Acts and also the *Preaching of Peter*. We therefore suppose that Serapion stood in the line of Theophilus.

Paul of Samosata as Traditionalist

Half a century later, former pupils of Origen met at Antioch to depose the bishop there, Paul of Samosata, a successor of Theophilus and Serapion not only in office but also in doctrine. We need not go into details after the work of G. Bardy, F. Loofs, H. de Riedmatten, and T. E. Pollard,[35] not to mention an excellent dissertation by R. L. Sample.[36]

It remains hard to tell which fragments may be authentic, but Fragment 36 Bardy[37] is very close to Theophilus.

> Our Savior has become holy and righteous, having conquered the sin of our first fathers by struggle and toil. Having thus set up virtue again, he has been united to God, having one and the same will and energy as God, for the progress of man in goodness. In order to preserve it

> inseparable, he has obtained the name above every name [Phil. 2:9] which is given him as a reward of love.

Or this (five citations in de Riedmatten):

> The Logos was not a man; he dwelt in a man, in Abraham, in Moses, in David, in the prophets, and especially in Christ, as in a temple.

R. L. Sample shows us how much Paul's Christology owed to Luke and the sermons in Acts. He indicates the way in which the Samosatene laid emphasis on the progress made by the Son until he finally became "Lord and Christ," and on his close relation to the prophets, also inspired by the divine Word and Wisdom. He even quotes Gregory of Nyssa (*Against Apollinaris* 9) for Paul's view that "out of heaven the Lord was made divine." All this, and much more, is close to what Theophilus had taught. The Lucan passages of Theophilus recur in Paul, as indeed do ideas about the name Christ and the "name above every name." And the divinization of the Lord is just what Theophilus maintained was a possibility for the First Adam as for the Second.

Further comparison between Theophilus and Paul will show that the later bishop was essentially maintaining what had been orthodox (because episcopal) at Antioch in the old days, not the ancient times of Ignatius but the middle ages of Serapion.

Marcellus of Ancyra

It is hard to see exactly how the position of Marcellus of Ancyra was linked to Antioch. It is clear, however, that he used some important terms related to this special Antiochene tradition. Klostermann's Fragment 60[38] proves our point.

> Before making the world the Logos was in the Father. When the omnipotent God proposed to make everything in the heavens and on earth, the genesis of the world required effective energy. Therefore, when there was no one else but God—for it is acknowledged that everything was made by him—then the Logos came forth and became maker of the world. Previously within God he mentally prepared it, as the prophet Solomon teaches us, saying, "When he prepared the heaven I was with him," and "As he laid secure the springs of what is under heaven, when he made strong the foundations of the earth, I was with him binding them fast. I was the one in whom he rejoiced" [Prov. 8:27–30]. For presumably the Father rejoiced with Sophia and Power [cf. 1 Cor. 1:24] when he made everything through the Logos.

This is essentially the doctrine of Theophilus.[39] Marcellus also calls Solomon a prophet and cites texts that Theophilus used for the same purpose. Daniélou noted his surprising backward look to a Jewish-Christian picture of Christ as "Day."[40] Eusebius criticized this Marcellan item too.[41]

The "Low" Christology and the Ebionites

In some respects this Antiochene Christology was close to the ideas of the Jewish-Christian Ebionites as discussed by Eusebius.[42]

> They regarded Christ as a simple, ordinary person, a man justified by progress in character and that alone. He was born of the intercourse of a man with Mary. Observance of the law was absolutely necessary, since merely faith in Christ and a corresponding way of life would not save them.

Relying on Origen,[43] Eusebius also mentioned Ebionites who regarded Mary as a virgin but did not recognize Christ as "God the Logos and Sophia." It looks as if Theophilus stood fairly close to these people as well as to Lucan strands in early Christian theology and to his successor Paul of Samosata. His theology apparently superseded that of Ignatius for a time but then was superseded itself. This is not to say it really was Ebionite. It expressed one of the many shades of doctrinal variety to be found within early catholic Christianity.

It seems undeniable that these views were understood and accepted as "orthodox" at Antioch at least from 180 to 260, though under pressure from Origenist bishops, synods finally condemned them. Our point is that in the early centuries the Christian doctrines about God—Father, Son, and Spirit—were remarkably flexible and that at least the emphases changed from one generation to another.

11

Also the Holy Spirit

The Spirit in the Bible

Biblical statements about spirit or the Spirit come from various ages and reflect divergent points of view and interests. At the beginning of Genesis the Spirit, or a spirit, or the breath of God is brooding over the chaotic waters. Something different, but called by a similar name, appears in the story of Samson, the divinely empowered fighter against the Philistines. We hear of this empowerment in the prophets both as present and as a future gift. Such diversity continued in Judaism and Christianity alike.

In his great study of Judaism, G. F. Moore clarified and contrasted the pictures of "spirit" in the Old Testament and later.

> In the Old Testament superhuman strength, courage, skill, judgment, wisdom, and the like, are attributed to "the spirit of God," or of "the Lord," which suddenly comes upon a man for the time being and possesses him, or more permanently rests upon him and endows him. In old narratives it is more common of physical power and prowess and the gift of leadership (not a personal agent); in the prophets it is occasionally used of prophetic inspiration. The equivalent phrase "the holy spirit" is very rare, and is never associated with prophecy.
>
> In Judaism, on the contrary, the holy spirit is specifically the spirit of prophecy. When the holy spirit was withdrawn from Israel, the age of revelation by prophetic agency was at an end. The scribes, interpreters of the word of God written and custodians of the unwritten law, succeed.[1]

First Maccabees (14:41) tells us that Simon Maccabeus was to be "leader and high priest for ever, until a trustworthy prophet should arise." In similar vein, Moore quotes *Tosefta Sotah* (13.2): "When the last prophets, Haggai, Zechariah, and Malachi, died, the holy spirit ceased out of Israel; nevertheless, it was granted them [their successors] to hear [communications from God] by means of a mysterious voice." The outpouring of the spirit would be a manifestation of God's presence in the last times (Joel 3:1), a prediction which in Acts 2:16 is treated as fulfilled at Pentecost.

The presence of the "spirit" obviously implied that God himself was present with his people, as in such passages as these from prophets and a psalm. "The spirit of the Lord is upon me" (Isa. 61:1, cited by Jesus in Luke 4:18f.). "I will put a new spirit within you; . . . they shall be my people, and I will be their God" (Ezek. 11:19f.; cf. Rev. 21:7). "I have poured out my spirit upon the house of Israel, says the Lord" (Ezek. 39:29). "Take not thy holy spirit from me" (Ps. 51:11).

Two comments in New Testament books make one wonder whether Christian ideas about the Spirit were entirely continuous with Jewish traditions. According to Acts 19:2, Paul asked some disciples of John the Baptist whether they had received the Holy Spirit when they believed. They told him they had never heard of the existence of the Holy Spirit. Again, John 7:39 states that Jesus spoke enigmatically about the future gift of the Spirit and comments that "there was as yet no Spirit, for Jesus had not yet been glorified." These statements do not seem to take the Old Testament into account.

In the Christian Gospels themselves we can trace some development in the teaching about the Spirit. The Spirit is prominent in the account of Jesus' baptism. According to all the evangelists, it descended upon him like a dove ("in bodily form," says Luke). John insists that it "remained" on him but does not explain what he means. The three earlier evangelists quote a "voice" which gives their primary interpretation of the event. The Father says of the Son, "You are ["this is," according to Matthew] my beloved Son" or even, according to early versions of Luke 3:22, "You are my Son; today I have begotten you"—a quotation from Psalm 2. Thereupon the Spirit drives Jesus out into the desert for his temptation by the devil.

The evangelist Luke lays strong emphasis on the presence and work of the Spirit. Holy Spirit was responsible for the conception of Jesus from the Virgin Mary (Luke 1:35).[2] It came upon him at his baptism and drove him into the desert (Luke 4:1); it inspired him to treat his life as the fulfillment of prophecy (Luke 4:18–21); he could "rejoice in the Holy Spirit" (Luke 10:21). He gave it back to the Father at his death (Luke 23:46). For Luke, Jesus was thus guided by the Spirit throughout his ministry, though Jesus is not the only person whom Luke calls "full of Holy Spirit" (Luke 4:1); there are also Elizabeth and Zacharias, the mother and father of John the Baptist (Luke 1:41, 67).

The Holy Spirit is also very prominent in Acts, filling such persons as the apostle Peter (Acts 4:8), the seven "deacons" (Acts 6:3) —among them the first martyr Stephen (Acts 6:5; 7:55)—and the Jerusalem Christian Barnabas (Acts 11:24). The Spirit was "poured forth" upon the apostles at Pentecost in a crucial experience described in Acts 2. To be sure, the story is told in terms somehow related to Philo's account of the giving of the law on Sinai.[3] But what counts in Acts is the gift of the Spirit.

The relationship of the Spirit to baptism was important for the apostolic church. Did baptism result in the gift of the Spirit, or come after it with the imposition of hands? Or did Spirit come first, baptism later? All three ideas are depicted in various parts of Acts, and we must conclude that the author was willing to accept any of them. The letters of Paul show that problems arose within the churches after baptism, especially when, as at Corinth, "spiritual" experience was highly valued. Paul had to devote a whole chapter of his first letter to the Corinthians to the question of spiritual gifts and to the excitement they produced at worship, as well as another chapter to the phenomenon of "glossolalia" or "uttering mysteries in the Spirit" (1 Cor. 12; 14). Obviously there were those who under the inspiration of a spirit, or the Spirit, would make pronouncements in God's name or identify themselves with him. It is hard to classify those who "spoke in tongues" at Corinth and presumably elsewhere in early churches. Paul insists that their utterances have to be explained by others and warns that a visitor would suppose the speakers were crazy. Ignatius sets forth God's will about church organization "in a loud voice, with God's own voice."[4] John the author of Revelation is "in the Spirit on the Lord's Day" when he hears voices and sees visions.

Perhaps the best-known text along these lines comes from Celsus, the pagan critic of second-century Christianity. He claimed to know people in Phoenicia and Palestine who often said

> I am God [or a son of God, or a divine Spirit]. And I have come. Already the world is being destroyed. And you, O men, are to perish because of your iniquities. But I wish to save you. And you shall see me returning again with heavenly power. Blessed is he who has worshipped me now! But I will cast everlasting fire upon all the rest, both on cities and on country places. And men who fail to realize the penalties in store for them will in vain repent and groan. But I will preserve for ever those who have been convinced by me.[5]

The passage seems to be partly modeled, or parodied, after some sayings of Jesus, but the self-proclamatory note at the start is found in pagan and Christian materials alike.[6] To D. E. Aune's examples we add a few oracles ascribed to the second-century prophet Montanus: "I am the Lord God omnipotent dwelling in man"; "I am neither an angel nor an envoy, but I the Lord God the Father have come"; and "I am the Father and the Son and the Paraclete." Similarly the prophetess Maximilla claimed to be "word, spirit, power." And Prisca described the Montanists' ecstatic technique. "Continence brings harmony, and they see visions; when they bow their heads, they also hear distinct voices, saving and mysterious." She was the prophetess to whom Christ appeared as a woman to inform her about the descent of the heavenly Jerusalem.[7]

A sectarian teacher could of course insist on his superiority without calling himself a prophet. The Gnostic Basilides apparently used exegesis for this purpose. "We are men, and the others are all swine and dogs. Therefore it says, 'Cast not pearls before swine nor give what is holy to the dogs.' "[8] It is remarkable, however, how many such teachers were influenced by "spiritual" ideas. Thus Valentinus was said to have seen a newborn child (in a dream) and asked who it was. The child identified itself as the Logos. Hence came the whole Gnostic system, says Hippolytus.[9] Valentinus' numerologist disciple Marcus also had a vision. The supreme Tetrad in female form (like the Christ of Prisca) came down to him and described the origin of the world, "which she had never revealed to any among men or gods."[10] In addition, Marcion's disciple Apelles was accompanied by a virgin named Philumene, whose ecstatic revelations Apelles recorded in a book called *Manifestations.* [11]

Paul himself, like Origen later, "would rather speak five words with his mind, in order to instruct others, than ten thousand words in a tongue" (1 Cor. 14:19). Prophecy is better than ecstasy. He does not deny that all Christians received the Spirit when they believed, but he insists that they must "walk" by the Spirit and its moral requirements (Gal. 3:2; 5:16). The Holy Spirit motivates them to say, "Jesus is Lord," not "Jesus be cursed!" (1 Cor. 12:3). At the same time Paul comes close to treating spiritual experience related to paganism as analogous to similar experience in the church. "You know that when you were heathen you were led astray to mute idols, however you may have been moved. *Therefore* I want you to know" about the utterances made under the inspiration of the Holy Spirit (1 Cor. 12:2–3).

The kind of "prophetic" or oracular ecstasy Paul was trying to avoid appears clearly in the case of the oracle of Apollo at Delphi.

In Greek views the spirit of inspiration was involved in the utterances of the priestess there. She sat on a tripod near a crevice in the earth from which vapor was said to come up.[12] Then, says the author of the first-century treatise *On the Sublime*, she "becomes pregnant from the divine power and is inspired to utter oracles" (13.2). Such pregnancy was obviously metaphorical, but in a malicious attack Origen took it literally, claiming that the spirit of Apollo entered her womb before she gave oracles.[13] Two centuries later John Chrysostom added the fantasy that on such occasions she would become drunk and crazy.[14] Presumably pagans neither provided nor accepted such explanations.[15]

In the Roman world her counterpart was the Sibyl of Cumae near Naples. Virgil gives the classic description of her inspiration. "She goes mad in the cavern so as to shake the god [Apollo] from her breast, and all the more he wearies her raving mouth, taming her wild heart, and moulds her by his control." When she speaks "she sings from the shrine her fearful enigmas, and echoes from the cavern, wrapping true predictions in obscure sayings."[16]

A famous collection of written oracles, used by the Roman state, was ascribed to the Sibyl, but there were so many oracles available that lists of Sibyls had to be compiled. There was the "official" Sibyl from Cumae near Naples, whose books, bought by King Tarquin, were consulted only by order of the senate. Destruction led to new compilations, as well as to official attempts to keep such oracles under control. Augustus had about two thousand of them burned in 13 B.C., while Tiberius made another investigation in A.D. 19 and later looked into the case of a supposedly official volume.[17] The Christian apologist Justin is the only author to claim that the death penalty has been imposed on readers of the books of Hystaspes (supposedly a Persian prophet) or the Sibyl or the prophets. No other testimony confirms this fantasy. Both Jews and Christians regularly read the prophets, not to mention the oracles forged by Jews and Christians in the Sibyl's name. Theophilus calls her "a prophetess for the Greeks and the other nations," while Clement says "the prophetic and poetic Sibyl" is "the prophetess of the Hebrews."[18] Origen had sense enough not to use them.

In this context Paul had to insist on correlation with the Christian gospel as well as rational guidelines. He accepted his converts' emphasis on freedom but insisted on theological content. He was quite willing to say that "the Lord is the Spirit, and where the Spirit of the Lord is, there is freedom" (2 Cor. 3:17). He thus spoke of "Spirit" in the context of "Lord," and indeed could define "Spirit" as "Spirit of the Lord" or even as "Lord." Another famous passage provides further interpretations of the work of the Spirit. "You are not in the flesh but in the Spirit, if the Spirit of God dwells in you. If anyone does not have the Spirit of Christ, he does not belong to him. If Christ is in you, the body is dead on account of sin but the Spirit is life because of righteousness. If the Spirit of him who raised Jesus from the dead dwells in you, he who raised Christ from the dead will also make your mortal bodies alive through his Spirit indwelling in you" (Rom. 8:9–11). Paul thus identifies the Spirit of God with the Spirit of Christ and, in turn, with the inward Christ. He is concerned with correlations, not distinctions, for he does not believe in a Spirit unrelated to Christ and the gospel.

The evangelist John tries to make a distinction between the ministry of Jesus, in which the Spirit was not active (in spite of its "remaining" on him after his baptism) and the time after his glorification (crucifixion) (John 7:39; cf. 12:23). Jesus predicts the coming of the Paraclete, the divine intercessor or helper identified with the Holy Spirit (John 14:26). The Spirit is once called "another Paraclete" (John 14:16) and is therefore not different in category from Jesus Christ himself, who is called the Paraclete in 1 John 2:1. After the resurrection, the Lord "breathes" Holy Spirit upon the disciples (John 20:22).

The Spirit and the Conception of Jesus

The account of the conception of Jesus by the Holy Spirit was not completely alien to Greek converts. The Gospels of Matthew and Luke, as well as Ignatius of Antioch, stated that Jesus Christ was begotten by the Spirit. How was this to be explained? The apologist Justin gave a rather inadequate explanation when he stated that the Logos became a man when, as "Spirit and power" (Luke 1:35), he himself came upon Mary from God.[19] Presumably he was fusing the account in Luke, to which he referred, with the "becoming flesh" of John 1:14. Justin's difficulty was due to two problems he had in view. On the one hand, he had to admit the parallel between the Gospel stories and the Greek tale of how Zeus begot Perseus from Danae.[20] On the other hand, he insisted that the Christian account had nothing in common with poets' stories of how Zeus came upon women for the sake of sexual pleasure.

Justin's older pagan contemporary Plutarch discussed similar cases but made points that Christians would not have accepted. In his *Table-talk* (8.1) he set forth his own view as well as that of "the Egyptians." Through a Platonist speaker he says, "I do not consider it strange if the god does not approach [a woman] like a man but alters mortal nature and by another kind of contact or touch, through other means, makes it pregnant with a more divine off-spring." He then refers to the Egyptians, who hold that a male god can have intercourse with a mortal woman, but a mortal man cannot "provide a female divinity with the principle of birth and preg-nancy." The substance of the gods consists of "air and breath (*pneumata*) and certain heats and moistures," evidently incapable of giving birth.

Plutarch, in his *Life of Numa* (4.4), apparently written later, says again that according to the Egyptians a male mortal could not have sexual intercourse with a goddess, but "a spirit of a god could approach a woman and insert in her certain principles of genera-tion." He personally rejects this distinction between god and god-dess, for sex involves participation and sharing by both parties.

There were also Christians whose ideas about the Spirit and the origin of Jesus did not win broad favor. These people, especially in Egypt, read the *Gospel of the Hebrews*, which expresses a singular doctrine of the work of the Spirit, notably in fragments that came down in Coptic or were cited by Jerome or Origen.[21] The Coptic fragment—not necessarily primitive—reads thus:

> When Christ wished to come upon the earth to men, the good Father summoned a mighty power in heaven, which was called Michael, and entrusted Christ to the care thereof. And the power came into the world and it was called Mary, and Christ was in her womb seven months.

This kind of story leaves no place for the work of the Holy Spirit. A more trustworthy fragment of *Hebrews* from Jerome reads thus:

> And it happened that when the Lord was come up out of the water the whole fount of the Holy Spirit descended upon him and rested on him and said to him, "My Son, in all the prophets I was waiting for you that you might come and I might rest in you. For you are my rest; you are my first-begotten Son who reigns forever."

This text makes it clear that Christ is the son of the Holy Spirit. Finally, both Origen and Jerome provide this fragment: "Even so did my mother, the Holy Spirit, take me by one of my hairs and carry me to the great mountain Tabor." Origen, in his *Commentary on the Gospel of John* (2.12), inquires how the Holy Spirit, owing its exis-tence to the Logos, can be called the mother of Christ. He suggests that since anyone who does Christ's will can be called his mother (Matt. 12:50), this could apply to the Holy Spirit. Here and in a homily on Jeremiah (15.4) he tends to accept the saying just because it cannot be taken literally. It should be added that in the Nag Hammadi *Apocryphon of James* the risen Lord says to the apostles, "Become better than I; make yourselves like the son of the Holy Spirit," probably like himself.[22]

Scholars have often suggested that the background of this saying lies in a Semitic language in which the word for "spirit" was *ruach*, a feminine noun. This would make the identification as "mother" easier. We may find this strange, but to call the Spirit "he" is no more satisfactory; the word *spiritus* is masculine in Latin, but its Greek original, *pneuma*, is neuter.

Spirit in the Apostolic Fathers and the Apologists

Christians only gradually worked out what the Holy Spirit meant. In the relatively popular religion of the *Shepherd* of Hermas, the Holy Spirit is identified with the Son of God or is called "the preexistent Holy Spirit which created the whole creation, which God made dwell in flesh."[23] Martin Dibelius said Hermas has no theology. Thus our text may mean no more than what we find in the contemporary sermon called 2 Clement (9.5): "If Christ, the Lord who saved us, was at first spirit and became flesh and thus called us, so also we shall receive our reward in this flesh."

Ignatius provides vivid pictures of the work of the Spirit. In his view the Old Testament prophets were Christ's "disciples in the Spirit," which must have inspired them as it did the bishop. In a vivid metaphor Ignatius refers to the Spirit as the "rope" that carries Christians to the heights of the temple of which they are stones.[24] Presumably he refers to the force and direction the Spirit gives. Justin too speaks of prophetic inspiration and the conception of Christ, as we have seen, and explicitly states that "we honor the prophetic Spirit in the third rank, with the Logos."[25]

The late second-century apologists Tatian and Theophilus try to work out a doctrine of the Spirit. Tatian emphatically rejects the Stoic view of God as spirit (he has to be emphatic in view of John 4:24, "God is Spirit") and says that while God is spirit, he does not pervade matter but is the "constructor of material spirits." If he pervaded matters he would "turn up in sewers and worms and doers of things unmentionable." Thus "the spirit that pervades matter is inferior to the more divine spirit." The lower one "is called soul" while the superior one "is the image and likeness of God." The latter was "originally the soul's companion, but gave it up when the soul was unwilling to follow it."[26] Evidently Tatian is using Genesis as a base for his speculations.

He goes farther with a doctrine much like that of the "world soul": "There exists spirit in luminaries, spirit in angels, spirit in plants and waters, spirit in men, and spirit in animals; though it is one and the same it possesses differences within itself."[27] He is trying to bring order out of the chaotic doctrine of the Spirit found in his predecessors—for example, in Hermas, but not only there.

Theophilus speaks of the Spirit as inspirer of prophets and evangelists as well as that which separated darkness from light at creation.[28] He also seems to equate Spirit with Logos and thus remains in some confusion. He clearly has Genesis in mind. "If I call God Spirit I speak of his breath" (*To Autolycus* 1.3)—the breath first breathed at creation (Gen. 1:3). God "gave a spirit to nourish the earth; his breath gives life to everything; if he held his breath everything would collapse" (alluding to Job 34:14f.), and humankind breathes God's breath (*To Autolycus* 1.7). More than that, "the whole creation is enclosed by the spirit of God, and the enclosing spirit together with the creation is enclosed by the hand of God" (*To Autolycus* 2.5). The picture—Theophilus adds a comparison with a pomegranate—seems to imply something rather definite and even material.

When we reach his exegesis of the creation story the point becomes clear. "The 'spirit borne over the water' was the one given by God to give life to the creation, like the soul in man, when he mixed subtle elements together (for spirit is subtle and water is subtle)[29] so that the spirit might nourish the water and the water with the spirit might nourish the creation, penetrating it from all sides." This spirit, he adds, "was situated between the water and the heaven." It was obviously material in essence. When Theophilus elsewhere notes the Stoic doctrine, "The spirit extended through everything is God," he does not deny its truth but simply points out that other philosophers disagree.[30] The philosopher Numenius took the text in Genesis as a reference to souls in generation settling upon water animated by the divine breath.[31] This is not exactly Theophilus' doctrine but the approach is similar. Clement of Alexandria, on the other hand, gives explicitly Christian exegesis of the verse. For him it proves that the Spirit participates in creation (*genesis* = birth) as in rebirth. Origen too refers the verse to the Holy Spirit.[32]

Irenaeus knew and used the work of Theophilus, but he tried to clear up the apologist's ambiguities by setting forth the more traditional Christian faith in Father, Son, and Holy Spirit. Though in his struggle against Gnosticism he usually spoke only of the Father and the Son, he clearly affirmed the faith of the church in the one omnipotent God, in the Son of God, Jesus Christ our Lord, and "in the Spirit of God, who gives knowledge of the truth [cf. John 16:13], who has explained the divine plans of the Father and the Son before men in every generation as the Father wills." All Christians, he says, recognize the same gift of the Spirit.[33]

The church's situation around 170 to 180 was one in which theological ideas about the Spirit had not been carefully worked out, and in facing the Gnostic danger leaders had neglected the problems of popular piety.

The Montanists and Ecstatic Prophecy

Just at this time, in the third quarter of the second century, new problems arose in regard to the inspiration of the prophets, both ancient and modern, and of church leaders. It may be significant that the eruption took place in the mountains of Phrygia. The second-century Roman historian Arrian says that the Phrygians "go mad for Rhea [the Great Mother] and are possessed by the Corybants [her demonic helpers]. When the deity possesses them they are driven and shout and dance as they predict the future, inspired and crazed."[34] It was a Christian in Phrygia named Montanus ("the mountain man")—a recent convert from paganism, said his critics —who believed in a fresh outpouring of the Spirit, beginning with himself. The gift did not, then, belong to the bishops as a gift passed down from one generation to the next, as Bishop Irenaeus said it was. Instead, Montanus believed that the Spirit produced prophetic ecstasy. He was able to persuade two married women (both, oddly, with Latin names like his) to leave home and become prophetesses; they then practiced exorcism and predicted the imminent end of the age.

Much excitement resulted in the province of Asia, especially in the area where their activities were centered. The conservative bishop of nearby Hierapolis convoked synods and produced literary works against them, but their final enemy was time, which took away much of the force of their predictions. Irenaeus, who did not like them, disliked their opponents more and referred back nostalgically to the great days when Paul was at Corinth and the Spirit was manifest in the church.

The idea that prophecy takes place in a trance was common not only among oriental prophets but also at Greek oracles and is expressed by many early Greek writers, notably Democritus and Plato.[35] Indeed, Origen describes as Greek the view that "the art of poetry cannot exist without madness."[36] The problem of ecstatic utterance and talking in tongues gives us some understanding of the controversy. Some of the most important Old Testament prophets did make pronouncements when in an ecstatic state.[37] The stories about Jesus suggest that his disciples regarded him as one who spoke thus, as some of them did. The accounts of the baptism, the temptation, the transfiguration, and the resurrection point toward ecstatic experience, as does the ascension, especially when compared with Paul's language about his own ascent to the third heaven or paradise.[38] In Acts we have the stories of Pentecost, the work of the Spirit with Philip, and the visions of Paul and Peter. As we saw, Paul was eager to keep this kind of experience from getting out of control. "I would rather say five words in church with my mind than ten thousand with a 'tongue.' " He was against abuses, however, not the phenomenon as such. The bishop Ignatius claimed that he could speak with "a loud voice, God's own voice" and could rely on special information given him by the Spirit.[39] Around 150, Justin did not hesitate to refer to the *ekstasis* of the Old Testament prophets.[40] Evidently he followed an authority like Philo of Alexandria, who similarly insisted on the irrationality of ecstasy[41] but viewed it as above reason, not below it.

Montanus' "new prophecy" was hard to handle in this environment. His opponents had to insist upon rather new distinctions as they tried to keep the movement within limits. They admitted that he was moved by some kind of spirit or other, but claimed that "he suddenly fell into a state of 'possession' and abnormal ecstasy, and became frenzied (*enthousian*) and began to babble and utter strange sounds." His prophesying was different from the traditional practice found in the church, says an anonymous opponent.[42] In addition, he filled the two women already mentioned with the same "spurious spirit" so that they "chattered in a frenzied, inopportune, and unnatural manner." Critics reported "the spirit that speaks through Maximilla" as saying, "I am driven away like a wolf from the sheep; I am not a wolf; I am word and spirit and power." Appropriate stories were circulated about the women's demise: "A maddening spirit drove both of them to hang themselves, though not at the same time."

As for another Montanist leader, rumor held that "on being lifted and raised heavenwards, he fell into abnormal ecstasy and, entrusting himself to the spirit of error, was whirled to the ground and so met a miserable end." The anonymous critic referred to his own ally Miltiades as having shown "that a prophet must not speak in ecstasy" and claimed, presumably following this source, that no prophet under either the Old Covenant or the New had ever spoken thus. These false prophets moved from voluntary ignorance to involuntary madness and abnormal ecstasy and ended in license and boldness. When the African church leader Tertullian became a Montanist he wrote seven books "on ecstasy" but none of them survive. It is fairly clear that the opponents of Montanism were developing Paul's attack on the tongue-talkers of Corinth. Paul had more tactfully suggested that outsiders coming upon Christians speaking in tongues would think they were crazy, whether they were or not.

Not all Christian leaders joined the attack, however. The apologist Athenagoras wrote shortly after the rise of Montanism and was willing to speak of the prophets as God's musical instruments, specifically flutes. W. R. Schoedel notes the same imagery in Philo and Plutarch.[43] Irenaeus severely criticized those who drove the gifts of prophecy out of the church (though he does not seem to have expressed a view on Montanus himself) and noted that Paul "knew men and women in the church who prophesied."[44]

Even churchmen could speak ecstatically at times. In his paschal sermon, Melito bishop of Sardis speaks in the name of the risen Lord, ascribing novel sayings to him. "I released the condemned; I brought the dead to life; I raise up the buried," he begins.[45] This is not the individualistic prophecy of the Montanists, however. Montanists could tell the difference. In Tertullian's Montanist treatise *On Ecstasy* "he criticized Melito's mind as elegant and rhetorical and said that he was considered a prophet by many Christians."[46] Obviously the Montanists did not so regard him.

We must be careful, however, not to draw dividing lines too sharply. Irenaeus denounced not the Montanists but those who rejected the Gospel of John (against the Montanists) and prophetic grace at the same time. He supposed that they would not accept Paul either, for in 1 Corinthians he spoke of prophetic gifts and knew men and women in the church who prophesied. People who thus drive out prophecy "sin against the Spirit of God and fall into unforgivable sin."[47] According to Tertullian, a bishop of Rome had already sent conciliatory letters to the churches on Montanism when a certain Praxeas persuaded him to recall them. If "Praxeas" is a pseudonym for Callistus,[48] the bishop may have been Zephyrinus, though he could have been as early as Victor, who we know dealt with the churches of Asia. Whoever he was, the Montanists were convinced that at one time he favored their view.

Alexandria and After

In scholastic Alexandria, on the other hand, Christian critics tended to denounce ecstasy and favor rationality. Clement claimed that only false prophets spoke "in ecstasy" and appealed to the eleventh *Mandate* of Hermas to prove that the divine Spirit works in the church while a false, earthly spirit works in self-willed "prophets."[49] Origen similarly differentiated spirits, finding the worse kind among the insane people cured by the Savior or in Judas Iscariot and the better one in the prophets and the apostles, who spoke "without a disturbance of the mind."[50] He did not share the view that poetry required ecstasy.

Interestingly enough, legend tells us that Origen's father recognized this kind of inspiration in his son. "Often he would stand over the sleeping boy and uncover his breast as if a divine spirit were enshrined in it, and kissing it with reverence would consider himself happy in his noble offspring."[51] Latin poets use similar language when they use expressions like *deus in pectore* of divine inspiration.[52] The divine spirit of the boy Origen was that of divination or poetic creation, well known among philosophers after Democritus.[53]

In Origen's treatise *On First Principles* (preface 4) he discusses some of the difficulties in regard to the Spirit.

> The apostles handed down the tradition that the Holy Spirit is associated with the Father and the Son in honor and rank. It is not so clear whether it was generated or not and whether it is to be considered Son of God or not. But we must inquire into all that as we are able, beginning with holy scripture and investigating wisely. This Spirit inspired all the holy prophets and apostles: the ancients did not possess another Spirit than did those who were inspired at Christ's coming; this is most clearly proclaimed in the Church.

Later Origen explains that the Holy Spirit works only in beings that are animate, capable of speech, rational, and good (*On First Principles* 1.3.5). It is the "principle of sanctity," delivered by the Savior to the apostles (John 20:22) and transmitted by their hands to believers "after the grace and renewal brought by baptism" (*On First Principles* 1.3.7). Still later, a very brief section in his work discusses the one Holy Spirit as the Paraclete in the Gospel of John, as the inspirer of the allegorical method of exegesis, and as the donor of various spiritual gifts—though not among the Montanists, who are unintelligent and quarrelsome (*On First Principles* 2.7). The Spirit thus works in the church but not among outsiders or heretics.

The doctrine of the Spirit was fairly important to Origen, but we are not surprised to find that his *Dialogue with Heraclides* was subtitled

On the Father, the Son, and the Soul—without mention of the "third person." The passage in 1 Corinthians which we earlier called creedal or at least semicreedal shows Paul trying to bring order out of chaos in regard to the one God the Father and the one Lord Jesus Christ (1 Cor. 8:6), but not the Holy Spirit. As late as 325 the Nicene Creed ended abruptly with the words, "Also the Holy Spirit,"[54] but by the end of the fourth century the subjects of theological debate included the Spirit as well as the Son, and in 381 the creed of Constantinople contained a fairly elaborate statement of belief on the subject. "And in the Holy Spirit, the Lord and the Lifegiver, proceeding from the Father, worshipped and glorified together with the Father and the Son, who spoke through the prophets." Shortly before that date, there were those who emended the text of 1 Corinthians in order to provide a more definite notice about the Spirit. Some manuscripts refer to the Father and the Son and then add mention of "one Holy Spirit, in whom are all things and we in him."

One might regard the theological development as based on attempts to rationalize spiritual phenomena. Some of the biblical texts treat "spirit" not as personal but as a force, or even an experience, not clearly definable. Such difficulties do not mean that the doctrinal goal was wrong. The category of personal divine being shared by the Father and the Son is not quite the same as that shared with the Spirit, and this is one reason why Eastern theology speaks of the Spirit as "proceeding from the Father" and in the West we hear of "proceeding from the Father and the Son." We may not share the speculations of some of the fathers about triads or be able to understand exactly what they meant by coequality.

On the other hand, we should not try to reduce doctrines to their presumed origins and assume that the nature of the Spirit must be limited to force or experience. We do not suppose that the *Gospel of the Hebrews* was right when it spoke of the Holy Spirit as Christ's mother. Like the Father and the Son, the Spirit transcends our limited powers of description and analysis as well as our experience.

12

Three Gods in One

As Jews, the earliest Christians believed there is one God. Jesus himself asserted that there were two commandments, requiring first of all love of the one God, then love of one's neighbor (Mark 12:29–31 and parallels). In the early second century the Jewish-Christian *Shepherd* of Hermas, later often regarded as scripture, insists on the primacy of monotheistic belief. "First of all, believe that there is one God who founded and created all things and made everything exist from the non-existent, and contains everything, alone being not contained." Hermas is on the direct line of belief that goes from Hellenistic Judaism to many of the Fathers.[1] It should also be noted that Hermas never mentions Jesus or Christ.

The Three

The New Testament

In the early church we do not hear of baptism "in" or "into" the name of this one God. If the rite of John the Baptist was in the name of anyone, it would have been in this name (cf. Acts 18:25). But Christian baptism, as we meet it in Paul and the book of Acts, is in the name of Jesus.[2] There was obviously a close relation between the God worshiped by Christians and the Jesus in or into whose name they were baptized. The various Christological titles we discussed earlier attempt to explain this relation. Indeed, the "creedal formula" of 1 Corinthians 8:6 looks like such an explanation. For us—that is, for baptized Christians—there is one God, and there is one Lord. This looks like an interpretation of the Shema of Deuteronomy 6:4: "Hear, O Israel, the Lord our God, the Lord, is one." Christians could find both the one God and the one Lord in this crucial verse.

Such musings may have been satisfactory as long as most converts came from Judaism and already believed in the one God. Christians simply explained that there was also one Lord, who (as, for example, in 1 Corinthians and the Gospel of John) was God's agent in creation. In a Jewish environment they could also speak of the Holy Spirit in the rather unspecific manner to which we have referred.

The movement toward triadic formulas in Pauline rhetoric does not explain the nascent doctrine of the Trinity, but we note that. Paul likes threes, such as "apostles, prophets, teachers" (1 Cor. 12:28) or "faith, hope, love" (1 Cor. 13:13); or "the grace of the Lord Jesus Christ and the love of God and the fellowship of the Holy Spirit" (2 Cor. 13:14). Only at the end of Matthew (28:19), however, is the risen Lord depicted as saying, "Go . . . and make disciples of all nations, baptizing them in the name of the Father and of the Son and of the Holy Spirit." The passage is important because the three names are given equal status. Now for the Gentiles three names are needed. They must be baptized in the name of the Father as well as in the name of the Lord Jesus and of the Spirit. The passage is also important for what it does not say. Three names are provided, but no explanation of the plurality is supplied. This is not a trinity (though trinity is not excluded) but a triad.

A somewhat later passage in 1 John (5:6–8) also reflects a liking for threes. The author begins with Christology and passes on to a doctrine of the Spirit, essentially relying on themes found in the Fourth Gospel.

> This is he who came by water and blood, Jesus Christ, not with the water [of his baptism] only but with the water and the blood [of his crucifixion]. And the Spirit is witness, because the Spirit is the truth. There are three witnesses, the Spirit, the water, and the blood; and these three agree.

To this mysterious but not theologically useful passage a Spanish Priscillianist in the late fourth century added explicitly trinitarian language so that it would mention three witnesses "on earth" and end thus: "And there are three witnesses in heaven, the Father, the Word, and the Spirit, and these three are one." The addition is suitable in a Johannine context, for it refers to Logos as John does and is ultimately based on "I and the Father are one" (John 10:30). Unfortunately it is not genuine, since it appears in no old manuscripts or versions or in any early fathers.

After the New Testament

Justin Martyr

We must be content with listings of the three persons as long as we are in the New Testament or early patristic period, and even with a certain incoherence of order. Thus the apologist Justin claims that Christians are not godless and states that "we confess the most true God, the Father of righteousness and chastity and the other virtues, untouched by wickedness [as contrasted with the pagan gods]; we honor and worship him and the Son who came from him and taught us these things, and the army of good angels who follow and resemble him, and the prophetic Spirit" (*Apology* 1.6.2). What is the army of good angels doing here?[3] Apparently the Spirit is less significant than this army.

In another passage about the God whom Christians worship, however, Justin explicitly states that worship is due to Jesus Christ the Son of God in the second place and to the prophetic Spirit in the third place (*Apology* 13.3). When he describes Christian baptism and eucharist he says that in both rites the names of Father, Jesus Christ, and Holy Spirit are invoked, though in different ways. Baptism is "in the name" of all three (*Apology* 61.3), whereas at the eucharist praise and glory are offered to the Father of all "through the name of the Son and of the Holy Spirit" (*Apology* 65.3). The irregularity over the army of angels, while surprising, is therefore not as important as the movement toward uniformity.

Justin and Numenius

In the second century the most prominent advocates of triadic doctrine were the Neopythagoreans and the Middle Platonists. Justin already recognized the possibility of an alliance when he could claim that Plato was relying on Moses (!) in order to assign second and third places to the Son and the Spirit. Plato found the soul of the universe like a *chi* (the cross) in the universe (*Tim.* 36BC). This world soul was the Logos, said Justin, and Plato ascribed the place after the first God to it, as well as the third place to the Spirit, which in Genesis was said to be borne above the waters. All this was supposedly indicated in a bit of mystification in the so-called *Second Epistle* of Plato (312E) which was much admired by Platonists and early Christians.[4] The text is this: "All things are related to the King of all, and they exist for him and he is the cause of all good things.[5]

And the second are related to the Second, and the third to the Third." Later the apologist Athenagoras provided exegesis of the passage (*Leg.* 23.7) and insisted that Plato "came to understand the eternal God apprehended by mind and reason." The parallel does not really prove anything.

There is an important alternative set of categories in an allegorical exercise by Philo. The Jewish exegete is discussing the names "father" and "mother," and he finds that "the Demiurge who made this universe was also the Father of what came into existence, while its Mother was the knowledge which the Maker possessed. God had intercourse with her (in no human fashion) and sowed coming-to-be. After Knowledge received the seeds of God and completed her birth-pangs she bore the only and beloved Son, this world." Philo finds the scriptural source of his notion in the book of Proverbs: "God obtained me [wisdom] first of all his works and founded me before the age." He continues by interpreting it Platonically: "Everything that came into existence had to be younger than the Mother and Nurse of the All." It is hard to tell what Philo thought was literal, what figurative, in this picture of creation, but in it there is obviously a triad of Father, Mother, and Son. The Mother is the divine Wisdom and also the "nurse of becoming" as in the *Timaeus.* [6] None of the early Christian apologists paid any attention to a doctrine like this.

A Platonic anticipation or parallel of Christian belief can be found in the influential theology of Numenius, the most prominent Platonist and Pythagorean of the second century. His date is often set in the late second century, but if he taught around 150—as is quite possible—he could have influenced Justin, especially since he probably taught at Rome.[7] Numenius was the source for much of Plotinus' thought, according to ancient critics,[8] but the Christian authors Clement and Origen knew him as well. He evidently influenced both Neoplatonism and Christianity.[9]

In his thought, there is a combination of monotheism and polytheism, of the one and the many, which is quite similar to what we find among Christians. Numenius reserved the term "good in himself (*autoagathos*)" for the supreme First God, who does not create but is the Father of the Second God, the Demiurge or creator. The First is Father, the Second Creator (*poiētēs*), and the Third what is created (*poiēma*). "The First God is at rest, while the Second, on the contrary, is in motion; the First is concerned with the intelligible realm, the Second with both the intelligible and sensible. . . . In place of the motion inherent in the Second, I declare that the stability (*stasis*) inherent in the First is an innate motion, from which derives the order of the cosmos and its eternal permanence, and preservation is poured forth upon all things."[10]

When Numenius relates the First to intelligibles and the Second to both intelligibles and sensibles, we are reminded of Origen's speculations about the Father as source of being, the Son as source of rationality, and the Spirit as source of sanctity.[11] In Origen's view, Greek philosophers could and did acknowledge "one unbegotten God who created and governs the universe and is 'the Father of the universe,' . . . and that everything was created by the Logos of God."[12] H. Crouzel notes that "Origen evidently refers to the second God of the Platonic triad," and refers to *Epistle* 2.312E and to Numenius. But he also points out that the Holy Spirit is not really comparable to the *anima mundi* of Platonic thought.[13] In this regard, Origen's scheme is virtually the reverse of Numenius'.

The Christian authors insist that the Father is the Creator, but since they treat the Son or Logos as the mediator of creation, the consequence is that for them the Creator, as far as human knowledge goes, even if given by revelation, is really the Son. The role of the Holy Spirit in creation is limited to the giving of breath and life. But Numenius cannot have criticized the Christian triadic scheme too harshly. John Dillon notes that his own scheme is "rather forced" and suggests that "those who adopted it were following some model," imperfectly adapted.[14] Is it possible that philosophers followed Christians?

Numenius went farther into speculation than did the earlier Christians. "If the Demiurge of Generation is good, then in truth the Demiurge of Being will be the Good Itself, this being inherent in his essence. For the Second, being double, creates his own Ideal Form and the universe, being a demiurge. But the first is wholly contemplative."[15] The quotation shows the difficulty of locating the functions of the Third.

We should add that two more passages in Justin's *Apology* may be related to Numenius' thought. Plato spoke of the "Third," says Justin, because he had read that "the spirit of God was borne over the waters" (Gen. 1:2), and he assigned the second place to the Logos, in the whole in the shape of the letter *chi* (*Apology* 60.5–7). Numenius himself interpreted "the prophet" (i.e., Moses) as referring to souls settling upon the water which is god-infused. His exegesis, at least as Porphyry described it, had to do with the nymphs or Naiads, powers presiding over waters.[16] The exegesis was obviously not Christian, but it showed a concern for the sacred text.

One may compare this with the discussion of the verse in Clement's *Excerpts from Theodotus* 47, where archangels and angels of archangels come forth from the "psychic and luminous substance," a mixture of the "pure" substance "borne above" the waters and the heavy and material substance ("earth") borne below. Numenius is not responsible for the Gnostic details, but he may have pointed toward this kind of allegorization.

Perhaps in relation to such a view, Justin complains about those who erect statues of Kore (Athena), the daughter of Zeus, at springs. "They said that Athena was the daughter of Zeus not from intercourse, but when the god had in mind the making of the world through a word (*logos*) his first thought was Athena" (*Apology* 64.5). The underlying exegesis is clearly related to what Plato wrote in the *Cratylus* (407B), that Athena is mind and intellect or even "mind of God." But it is also related to something Jewish or Christian with the idea of creation by a word. It is Porphyry, not provably Numenius, who similarly identifies Athena with "forethought."[17] But Numenius could have spoken thus; compare his reference to "more noble souls who are nourished by Athena" (frag. 37).

One more passage may help us to assess the place of Numenius in relation to the Christians.[18]

> Since Plato knew that among men the Demiurge is the only divinity known, whereas the Primal Intellect, which is called Being-in-Itself, is completely unknown to them, for this reason he spoke to them, as it were, as follows: "O men, that Intellect which you imagine to be supreme is not so, but there is another Intellect prior to this one which is older and more divine."

This passage expresses an attitude toward Platonic theology much like that found in Athenagoras. Plato anticipated the Christian doctrine of God.[19]

Numenius was no Jew or Christian, even though he admired Moses and Jesus and took the Bible allegorically. As a good Pythagorean or Platonist, he remained a polytheist. Johannes Lydus, a sixth-century pagan, preserves a fragment on the gods which was neglected by Christian writers. "Numenius says that the god at Jerusalem is without communion with others but is father of all the gods and is unwilling that anyone should share in his honor" (frag. 56). Three more fragments from Lydus and one from Macrobius show Numenius using the usual allegorical explanations of the gods, though another from Macrobius tells how the Eleusinian goddesses (Demeter, Persephone, Kore) reproached him for giving publicity to the rites (frags. 55, 57–59).

Finally, a statement in Lucian's *Icaromenippus* (ch. 9) shows how the satirist may have viewed Numenius' speculations. "Some lavishly declared the gods to be many and differentiated them. They called one a first god and assigned to others the second and third ranks of deity." We dimly discern the text which Middle Platonists took from the *Second Epistle* of Plato.

What we see in all these passages is the attempt to systematize the earlier triadic doctrine, on the part of pagans and Christians alike. These first steps cannot be viewed as successful, but at least they were being taken.

A passage in Theophilus of Antioch is sometimes invoked for the doctrine of the Trinity, but it proves nothing. He is offering symbolical exegesis of the "days" of creation in Genesis and suggests that as the sun is a figure of God and the moon of humanity, "similarly the three days prior to the luminaries are figures of the triad of God and his Logos and his Sophia. In the fourth place is man, who is in need of light—so that there might be God, Logos, Sophia, Man. For this reason, the luminaries came into existence on the fourth day" (*To Autolycus* 2.15). The passage is an exercise in numerology and 4 is just as important as 3.

What we find in these early authors, then, is not a doctrine of the Trinity—a term we reserve for a doctrine that tries to explain the relation of the three Persons to the one God—but a depiction of the three Persons. In other words, we find the materials for such a doctrine but not a doctrine as such.

Indeed, it might not be completely wrong to suggest that the Christian triad developed out of three different categories of being: the Father who creates, preserves, redeems, judges; the Son, the historical and human revealer and redeemer who somehow transcends humanity; and the Holy Spirit, essentially a spiritual experience that came to be personified. Even if this could be viewed as a correct picture of the earliest stages of doctrinal development, the meaning of the doctrine was not necessarily—or one might say "necessarily not"—expressed in its initial stages. We cannot apply some sort of cultural primitivism to the history of Christian doctrine. To be sure, trinitarian doctrine has continued to provide difficulties, but again, simplicity is not the criterion we should wish to apply in dealing with them.[20]

The Three in One

The doctrine of the trinity in unity is not a product of the earliest Christian period, and we do not find it carefully expressed before the end of the second century. When the Gnostic author of the

Apocryphon of John reports a revelation of one who said, "I am the Father, I am the Mother, I am the Son," the relationships of the three to the one are left in paradox.[21]

The Trinitarianism of Athenagoras

The first Christian author to deal with the specific problems of trinitarian doctrine was Athenagoras, an apologist from either Athens or Alexandria, whose work was later known only to Methodius and therefore was not very influential. Athenagoras knew Justin's *Apology* and apparently tried to make some of its arguments more convincing. His thought is notable for its philosophical concerns.

Athenagoras uses rational arguments in support of his various claims and begins with a proof of the unity of God. Two or more gods, he says, would be either in the same category or in different categories. They would not be in the same category, for gods, being uncreated, would be dissimilar. And they would not be in different categories (or places), for there is no place in or over which two gods could rule. After proving this point to his own satisfaction, he adds proof texts from scripture (*Embassy for the Christians* 8–9) and concludes that "we have brought before you a God who is uncreated, eternal, invisible, impassible, incomprehensible, and infinite, who can be apprehended by mind and reason alone, who is encompassed by light, beauty, spirit, and indescribable power, and who created and now rules the world through the Logos who issues from him" (10.1). In *Embassy* 16.1 he adds that "God is himself all things to himself: inaccessible light, a complete world, spirit, power, reason." These Platonic statements call to mind Aelius Aristides' description of Zeus.

Next Athenagoras explains what Christians mean by "Son of God." He is "the Logos of the Father in ideal form (*idea*) and energizing power (*energeia*); for like him (*pros autou*) and through him (*di autou*) all things came into existence [John 1:3], since the Father and the Son are one [John 10:30]. Now since the Son is in the Father and the Father in the Son [John 10:38] by a powerful unity of spirit, the Son of God is the mind (*nous*) and reason (*logos*) of the Father" (*Embassy* 10.2).

As the "first offspring" of the Father, the Son came into existence thus (*Embassy* 10.3–4):

"God, who is eternal mind, had in himself his Logos from the beginning, since he was eternally logical." The Son "came forth to serve as ideal form and energizing power for everything material which as an entity without qualities and[22] underlies things in a state characterized by the mixture of heavier and lighter elements.[23] The prophetic Spirit also agrees with this account. 'For the Lord,' it says, 'made me the beginning of his ways for all his works" [Prov. 8:22].

Finally, "this same Holy Spirit, which is active in those who speak prophetically, we regard as an effluence of God (Wisd. 7:25) which flows forth from him and returns like a ray of the sun." Christians "bring forward God the Father and God the Son and the Holy Spirit and proclaim both their power in the unity and their diversity in rank." In addition, God through the Logos set "a host of angels and ministers in their places." These are "concerned with the elements (or, planets), the heavens, and the world with all that is in it and the good order of all that is in it" (*Embassy* 10.4–5; cf. 24.2).

What is especially noticeable here is the use of the terms "ideal form" and "energizing power" to explain the functions of the Son. The former clearly relates to Platonic philosophy, while the latter is the kind of Aristotelian term that turns up in Middle Platonism after the late second century B.C. After that time, the Platonic ideas often turn out to be the thoughts of God. Thus Athenagoras views the "thoughts" as the one thought, or the sum total of the ideas, "identified . . . with the Stoic Pneuma-Logos."[24] Athenagoras bypasses the doctrine of the incarnation as he argues that Christian theology sets forth "a plural conception of deity."[25]

This is to say that in beginning to develop the doctrine of the Trinity Christians made use of the methods already worked out among Platonists and Pythagoreans for explaining their own philosophical theology, in harmonious accord with pagan polytheism.

Theologians less intelligent than Athenagoras sometimes used more anthropomorphic models. Theophilus refers to the "two hands" of God. His doctrine, as we have seen, provides a strange mixture of literal interpretation and symbolism.

The First Book on the Trinity: Novatian

From Theophilus we move to one of the first writers to use his work: Novatian of Rome, author of the earliest treatise explicitly concerned with the Trinity.[26] Perhaps Novatian employed Theophilus' work because he had heard he used the word *trias.* A sixteenth-century copyist of Theophilus seems to have reproduced all of Book III under the mistaken impression that it dealt with the three Persons.[27]

Novatian's work was preserved only because it was handed down among the writings of Tertullian. It relies on the church's "rule of truth" for its outline, beginning with God the Father and laying emphasis on his transcendence with language taken from Theophilus. The same rule teaches us about the Son, who in the incarnation became both God and man. For these chapters Tertullian seems to be a primary source, even for the rather unusual discussion of Philippians 2:5–11, a passage taken to involve the assumption of limits by the divine Son.[28] The discussion of the Holy Spirit, as always before the fourth century, is very brief and, oddly enough, says that the work of the Spirit in the prophets consisted of making accusations against the Jewish people.

In the last two chapters of the book, Novatian finally justifies the title *On the Trinity* by discussing the unity of God and the three Persons.[29]

> The belief that Christ is God does not contradict the belief that there is one God, even though heretics have wrongly used logical arguments to prove him either God the Father or mere man. [Thus the true Christ is once more crucified between two thieves!] They are blind to the plain statements of scripture. We hold that there is one God, maker of heaven and earth, but since we may not neglect any portion of scripture, we rely on plain scriptural proofs of Christ's deity. A mixture of reverence and logic will reconcile apparent contradictions. There is only one God; yet Christ was addressed as "My Lord and my God" [John 20:28]. Think of analogous situations. Scripture states that there is one Lord [Deut. 6:4], yet Christ is Lord; one Master [Matt. 23:8], and yet the apostle Paul is called Master [2 Tim. 1:11]; one God alone is good [Matt. 19:17], yet Christ is good ["in the scriptures"]. If apparent contradiction is reconciled in those cases, why not also in the question of deity?

Novatian now passes beyond argument to affirmation.

> God the Father is the creator of all, without origin, invisible, immeasurable, immortal, eternal, one God. When he willed it he generated the Logos. The secret of generation is known to none but Father and Son. He is always in the Father. The Son is before all time; the Father is always Father, without origin and therefore prior to the Son, who is generated by him and therefore less than him.
>
> Through that divine being, the Logos, all things were made. The Son is therefore before all things but after the Father. He is God proceeding from God, the Second Person as being the Son. His deity does not deprive the Father of the glory of being the one God. Christ is God, not as a being unborn, unbegotten, without origin. He is not the Father, invisible and incomprehensible. To give him these attri-

butes would be to affirm the existence of two gods. The Son is what he is not of himself but from the Father. He is the Only-begotten (John 1:14) and First-begotten (Col. 1:15), the Beginning of everything, who attests the one God as First Origin of being. He does nothing of his own counsel but serves the will of the Father, by obedience proving the truth of the one God.

Christ, then, is God begotten to be God and Lord and Angel. There is no discordance of attributes that would imply the existence of two gods. The divine virtue of the one God bestowed on the Son returns upon himself in the community of the divine substance (*substantiae per communionem*). The Son is Lord and God of all else, by his authority received from the Father. Thus the Father is rightly proved to be the one and only and true God (cf. John 17:3).

Novatian finally ends his treatise with allusions to the passage in 1 Corinthians (15:24–28) that speaks of the final subjection of the Son to the Father, "that God may be all in all." His own stance is thus subordinationist and can be explained in reference to his reliance on biblical passages. Apparently the work is difficult to interpret toward the end because a later orthodox reviser has tinkered with the text.

Arianism

Before Nicaea, Christian theology was almost universally subordinationist. Theology almost universally taught that the Son was subordinate to the Father (see, for example, chapter 8), but Arius expressed this kind of Christology in a provocative way. It was especially offensive at Alexandria, where Origen had tried to overcome subordinationism even though he shared many aspects of it. Presumably Arius' true views can be seen in his letter to his ally Eusebius of Nicomedia.[30] He objected to the slogans of his own bishop, Alexander of Alexandria, such as

> Ever God ever Son, together Father with Son, the Son exists unbegottenly with God, ever begotten, unbegotten in kind, not by a thought or a moment does God precede the Son, ever God ever Son, from God himself the Son.

Arius vigorously criticized contemporaries who called the Son a "belch" (presumably in reference to Ps. 45:2; see chapter 10) or an "emanation"[31] or "alike [to the Father] ungenerated."

More soberly, Arius claimed to "say and think and have taught and teach that the Son is not ungenerated nor a portion of anything ungenerated in any way or out of any substratum. Instead, by choice and will he originated before times and before ages, fully God, only begotten, immutable. And before he was begotten [Ps. 2:7] or created [Prov. 8:22] or defined [Rom. 1:4] or founded [Prov. 8:23], he was not. He was not ungenerated. We are persecuted because we say, The Son has a beginning but God is without beginning." The bishop of Nicomedia agreed with him. "It is obvious to anyone that what has been made was not before coming into existence. What comes into existence has a beginning of being." The slogan of Arius and his allies soon came to be this: "There was when he was not."

Whether or not the theology of Origen was still Alexandrian orthodoxy (Peter of Alexandria seems to have criticized it, but he was martyred in 311), the great theologian had expressed his diametrically opposite opinion in his treatise *On First Principles* (1.2.9), in reference to the Son as Wisdom. *"Non est quando non fuerit."* Later in the treatise he had insisted that even the words "when" and "never" had a temporal meaning that could not be used in regard to the Trinity (*On First Principles* 4.4.1). Here, as H. Crouzel notes, he follows Plato (*Tim.* 37E). In any event, Arius' ideas were not acceptable to the bishop of Alexandria.

The Council of Nicaea in 325 saw the Alexandrian bishop and his allies decisively win a battle (though not a war) over the theology of Arius, heir and more than heir of the traditional doctrine that the Son was subordinate to the Father. We need not enter into all the theological details or even the political ones. It is important, however, to note that the bishops who met at Antioch in the winter of 324–325 issued a creed in which they already rejected Arius' Christology. Both Antioch and Nicaea used creeds for the first time as doctrinal tests. Kelly quotes C. H. Turner: "The old creeds were creeds for catechumens, the new creed was a creed for bishops."[32]

At Antioch the majority insisted (several times) that the Son was begotten from the Father and that the mode of the generation was incomprehensible. "We anathematize those who say or think or preach that the Son of God is a creature or has come into being or has been made and is not truly begotten, or that there was when he was not."[33] Similar but more fully worked out statements occur in the creed of Nicaea itself. The section concerning the Lord Jesus Christ runs as follows:

> And in one Lord Jesus Christ, the Son of God, begotten from the Father, God from God, light from light, true God from true God, begotten not made, *homoousios* with the Father, through whom all things came into being, things in heaven and on earth, who because of us men and because of our salvation came down and became incar-

nate, becoming man, suffered and rose again on the third day, ascended to the heavens, and will come to judge the living and the dead.

Almost every word of this formulation needs exegesis, though the
anti-Arian thrust is obvious. "Begotten from the Father" speaks of
the Son's origin in generation (presumably eternal, as in Origen's
working out of the doctrine), and "begotten not made" makes the
point fully clear. This is to say that for the creation language about
Sophia in Proverbs 8:22 we now firmly substitute the generation
language required by the metaphor "Son." In the first chapter of
Hebrews, God addresses the preexistent Son with the text, "Thou
art my son, this day have I begotten thee" (Ps. 2:7; Heb. 1:5). In
consequence, it could be said that the Son as Son "sprang from the
Father's substance *(ousia),*" as Theognostus of Alexandria had put
it.[34]

"True God from true God" involves rejection of the old philosophical distinction between the perfect God (a term shared by
Tatian, Clement, and the Valentinian Ptolemaeus and implied by
Numenius), and the subordinate Demiurge. The phrase also rejects
distinctions between "God" and "the God" and between "God"
and "the only true God" of John 17:3.

The term *homoousios* was of course not scriptural,[35] though Origen
had long ago shown that nonscriptural terms could represent scriptural ideas, as when he discussed the word "incorporeal."[36] He
himself had used the word in reference to the Father and the Son,
explaining that an "emanation or vapor" (terms from Wisdom of
Solomon 7:25–26) was "of one substance with that body from which
it is an emanation or vapor." Dionysius of Alexandria had used
similar language for the same purpose. According to Athanasius,
the bishops who condemned Paul of Samosata also condemned the
use of the term because of the way Paul used it. H. C. Brennecke
has argued, however, that this was an error based on the confusion
of the views of Paul with those of Marcellus of Ancyra, a confusion
fostered by Eusebius of Caesarea, hostile toward both.[37] Athanasius
himself militantly defended the term and, as G. W. H. Lampe notes,
regarded it as defining the "full and absolute deity of the Son" and
also implying the "substantial identity of Father and Son as the
solution of the problem of the divine unity."

According to Eusebius of Caesarea, whose orthodoxy had been
approved by the emperor Constantine, the emperor himself proposed the term *homoousios* to the Nicene synod. He explained that
it did not refer to corporeal passions and did not mean that the Son
originated from the Father by any division or abscission. "The im-

material and intelligible and incorporeal nature could not undergo any corporeal passion, and such matters must be understood as bearing divine and ineffable meanings." Eusebius concludes his description thus: "So our most wise and pious king philosophized."[38] It is unlikely that Constantine himself discovered the term, and ancient authors preferred to blame or praise others for it. The Arians generally blamed Ossius of Cordoba; Philostorgius apparently named both Ossius and Alexander; Hilary mentioned Athanasius. All agree that though Constantine was a Christian, he was not a theologian.

What the Nicene Creed did was maintain the picture of trinitarian theology as nonrational, not irrational but beyond reason, and based firmly on selected complexities of scripture and tradition. It rejected the position of Arius with its evident use of logic, in favor of a more traditional or flexible logic that had been employed since the time of the apostle Paul onward through Ignatius, Tertullian, and the later Origen.

What the classical and patristic scholar Benedict Einarson said is generally true: "An early Christian was not often considered unorthodox if he maximized claims made for Christ." References to Christ's human life occur in very few early creeds. At Caesarea, Eusebius included the note that the Son "lived among men," while half a century later the *Apostolic Constitutions* (7.41) state creedally that he "lived in holy fashion according to the laws of God his Father."[39] In the Nicene Creed nothing specific is said of the humanity of Christ.

In chapters 8 and 10 we traced aspects of the Logos Christology which was highly regarded in the second and third centuries. In the creed of Nicaea, however, there was no use of the term "Logos," presumably because it did not really explain what it purported to explain. It raised more problems than it solved. The council preferred the metaphors of personal relation (Son-Father) to those of linguistic analysis (Word-Thought). In a way, it recapitulated the work of the evangelist John, who began his Gospel with Logos but then turned to Father and Son and ended (as he had begun) with God.

In our final chapter we shall be concerned with the creeds in their broader outlines and with the question why early Christians, unlike adherents of other religions in their time, made use of creeds at all. Answering this question will bring us back to the conflicts with non-Christian religions with which our study began.

13

Creeds and Cult

Our consideration of the gods and God cannot end with the complexities of trinitarian philosophical theology. Paganism and Christianity alike were based on foundations of religious faith and experience as well as on the logical or illogical speculations of the learned minority. The philosophical theologies acquired strength from their rootage in the faith and worship shared with priests and peoples alike. In Christianity itself speculation could be checked in relation to basic affirmations of faith that gradually developed into creeds.

Affirmations of Faith

The earliest affirmations of faith imply the future existence of creeds. To say with Peter "You are the Christ" (Mark 8:29) means that Jesus is *the* Christ and that other possible Christs are being rejected. Similarly, to be baptized in or into the name of Jesus means turning away from other names. The explicit purpose of John is the implicit purpose of all the Gospels. "This is written so that you may believe that Jesus is the Christ, the Son of God, and by believing may have life in his name" (John 20:31).

We have repeatedly referred to 1 Corinthians 8:6, with its affirmations about the one Father and the one Lord, the former as ultimate ground of creation, the latter as mediating Demiurge. From the Pauline epistles we can reconstruct something like the statements of the future creeds concerning the nature and mission of Christ. The hymn in Philippians 2:5–11 tells us that he was "in the form of God [and] emptied himself, assuming the form of a slave, coming to be in the likeness of men and found in fashion as a man; he humbled himself and became obedient unto death." Another way of describing his incarnation occurs in Galatians 4:4: "When the fulness of time came, God sent his Son, born of a woman, born under the law, to redeem those under the law so that we might receive adoption." Or this: "Though he was rich he impoverished himself for you, that you might become rich by his poverty" (2 Cor. 8:9). These statements use different metaphors to convey a basic notion of the divine condescension.

Paul says little about Jesus' ministry or teaching, chiefly because he was concerned with problems within the churches with which much of the teaching was not concerned. He does cite sayings about marriage (1 Cor. 7:10, 12, 25) and sets forth "from the Lord" the tradition about the Last Supper as the model for the Lord's Supper (1 Cor. 11:23–25). He describes another such tradition, or cluster of traditions, as "the gospel" which is necessary for salvation. It consists of a summary of the purpose of Christ's death "in accordance with the [Old Testament] scriptures" and accounts of the burial and the resurrection appearances, ending with one to Paul himself (1 Cor. 15:1–8). Beyond this lies a "word of the Lord" in 1 Thessalonians 4:16–17: "The Lord will come down from heaven with a cry of command, with the archangel's call, and with the sound of the trumpet of God. And the dead in Christ will rise first; then we who are left alive shall be caught up together with them in the clouds to meet the Lord in the air; and so we shall always be with the Lord." Similarly, in 1 Corinthians 15:51–52, Paul tells his converts a "mystery," a secret of revelation: "We shall not all sleep, but we shall all be changed, in a moment, in the twinkling of an eye, at the last trumpet. For the trumpet will sound, and the dead will be raised imperishable, and we shall be changed." Scholars often note that the musical accompaniment is typical of Jewish apocalyptic. Paul and his converts accepted it as part of the picture whatever its source may have been.

In these materials we find an outline of the saving mission and ultimate return of Christ which anticipates much of the language of the Apostles' Creed. Some of it is explicitly treated as "gospel" or "tradition," but Paul must have considered all of it as authoritative Christian doctrine. He was not accustomed to idle speculation. This must have been *the* gospel for him. "If we, or an angel from heaven, should preach to you a gospel contrary to that which we preached to you, let him be accursed. As we have said before, so now I say again, If any one is preaching to you a gospel contrary to that which you received, let him be accursed" (Gal. 1:8–9; cf. 1 Cor. 15:1–2).

There is thus a standard of "orthodoxy" in Paul's thought. It is his gospel, for which indeed he claims a divine origin. "I would have you know, brethren, that the gospel which was preached by me is not man's gospel. For I did not receive it from man, nor was I taught it, but it came through a revelation of Jesus Christ" (Gal. 1:11–12). This is to say that all must accept it without raising questions.

In the later pastoral epistles we find a modification of the first Pauline formula. "There is one God, and there is one mediator between God and men, the man Christ Jesus, who gave himself as a ransom for all." This is the message for which Paul was "appointed a preacher and apostle" (1 Tim. 2:5–7) and therefore it is a basic expression of "the knowledge of the truth" (1 Tim. 2:4).

Around the same time, or perhaps a little later, the author of Jude urges his readers to "contend for the faith which was once for all delivered to the saints" (Jude 3). This is hardly a novelty in view of the firmness and intensity of the Pauline message. The author of 2 Peter goes a little farther when he predicts the rise of "destructive heresies" (2 Peter 2:1), criticizes those who "scoff" at the promise of the second coming and the last judgment (2 Peter 3:3–4) and "twist" passages in the letters of Paul and "the other scriptures" (2 Peter 3:15–16). The reference to the Pauline epistles as in a collection and as scripture shows that 2 Peter is rather late. It does not show that its doctrine on orthodoxy is markedly different from what came earlier.

Finally, at the end of the Revelation to John (Rev. 22:18–19) we find the book itself being maintained in its pure and original state. A curse is provided for anyone who either adds to the words of the prophecy or subtracts from them. Precedent for such a curse could be found in the book of Deuteronomy (Deut. 4:2; 13:1). It reinforces the authority of the Revelation, though quite a few Christians later rejected the whole book.

What we have said about these New Testament authors is hardly surprising. If we say that they defended "orthodoxy," we say no more than that they meant what they said and were sure they were right. We may add that they had no idea that Christian doctrine would have a history or that their thought would be part of it.

The Trinity and the Creeds

According to the evangelist Matthew, the risen Lord Jesus commanded baptism in the threefold name: "All authority has been given me in heaven and on earth. Therefore go forth and make disciples of all nations, baptizing them in the name of the Father and of the Son and of the Holy Spirit, and teaching them to keep all the commandments I gave you. And behold, I am with you always, until the end of the age" (Matt. 28:18–20).

Within a few centuries the formulas used in baptism were expanded and developed into what was called the Apostles' Creed. According to a picturesque legend relayed by Rufinus, each apostle "contributed the clause he judged fitting."[1] In fact, the creed is closely related to the baptismal promises made in the church at Rome. There is another creed, commonly called Nicene but really promulgated by the Council of Constantinople in 381 in order to set forth the Nicene faith.[2] We have already discussed significant points in it.

These creeds and their antecedents in "rules of truth" or "rules of faith" were highly important from the time when churches began testing the beliefs of their members. We see the process in effect at Rome at least by the year 140, when Marcion's predecessor Cerdo got into difficulties. Irenaeus tells us that under Hyginus (A.D. 138–141) Cerdo "often came into the church and made a confession but ended up thus: sometimes he taught in secret, sometimes he made a renewed confession, but sometimes he was convicted of false teaching and removed from the assembly of the brethren."[3] Apparently what Cerdo "confessed" was the common faith of the Roman church. Elsewhere Irenaeus explains the deviation. Cerdo, like Marcion, taught that the known and just God of the Old Testament was not the good but unknown Father of Christ.[4] (For this kind of doctrine, see chapter 7.) In this instance the baptismal formula seems to have served as a doctrinal test.

No doubt among the Marcosian Gnostics the baptismal formula served a similar function, for it is similar to those in use among more orthodox Christians. "Into the name of the unknown Father of everything, into Truth the mother of all, into the one who descended to Jesus; for unity and redemption and communion with the powers." A Syriac formula which Irenaeus calls "Hebrew" (and misunderstands completely) might mean, "In the name of Wisdom, Father and Light, called Spirit of Holiness, for the redemption of the angelic nature,"[5] and thus stands farther away from Christianity.

Do the baptismal formulas and creeds set forth a doctrine of the Trinity? Those we have thus far described do not. A literal translation of the Apostles' Creed reads thus:

> I believe in (1) God, the Father Almighty, creator of heaven and earth; and in (2) Jesus Christ, his only Son, our Lord, who was conceived by the Holy Spirit, born from the Virgin Mary, suffered under Pontius Pilate, was crucified, dead, and buried. He descended into hell. On the third day he rose again from the dead, ascended to heaven, sits at the right hand of God the Father Almighty, thence he will come to judge the living and the dead. I believe in (3) the Holy Spirit . . .

In spite of Rufinus' claim,[6] the creed contains no explicit reference to trinitarian belief and in fact does not support it.[7]

The Apostles' Creed is a simple proclamation of a triad, as is the formula at the end of Matthew and in the *Didache,* not an interpretation of the relationships of the persons, much less a philosophical or theological analysis. The Father is God, and the risen Lord sits at his right hand. The section about Jesus Christ confirms this point. It is a reflection of the apostolic preaching about the life of Christ, with a few additions. These additions do not bear upon the purpose of the mission of Jesus, whether the proclamation of the kingdom of God or the redemptive sacrifice of the cross. Earlier scholars sometimes supposed that this section was especially antiheretical and that the conception and birth were mentioned in opposition to Marcion. He held that Christ came down from heaven as a saving spirit. More probably, however, the miraculous events were mentioned because they seemed striking and important.

It should be noted that the first section of the creed serves a secondary apologetic purpose. Many pagans interested in theology shared the belief in a god who could be called Father and Maker of heaven and earth.

Eastern creeds, on the other hand, emerged out of theological and Christological conflict. "We believe in (1) one God the Father almighty, maker of heaven and earth, and of all things visible and invisible; and in (2) one Lord Jesus Christ, the only-begotten Son of God, begotten from the Father before all ages, light from light, true God from true God, begotten not made, of one substance with (*homoousios*) the Father; through whom all things came into existence, who because of us men and because of our salvation came down from the heavens, and was made flesh from the Holy Spirit and the Virgin Mary and was made man, and was crucified for us under Pontius Pilate and suffered and was buried, and rose again on the third day according to the scriptures and ascended to the heavens and sits at the right hand of the Father and is coming again with glory to judge living and dead; of whose kingdom there will be no end; and in (3) one Holy Spirit, the Lord and life-giver, who proceeds from the Father, who together with Father and Son is worshiped and glorified, who spoke through the prophets . . ."[8]

The Apostles' Creed had spoken of God the Father and of his Son Jesus Christ. The Nicene Creed, on the other hand, lays emphasis on the *one* God and the *one* Lord as in 1 Corinthians 8:6, but now not so much against polytheism as against various heresies.[9] In Greek there are 44 words about Father and Spirit, 110 about the Son. Emphasis is laid on the origins and interrelationships of all three Persons. The Father is the source of absolutely everything that is, including both Son and Spirit. The Son as Son, however, is eternal ("before all ages") and *homoousios* with the Father—they have the same "substance" or "essence"—as "light from light" (an analogy favored by the apologists from Justin onward) and "true God from true God" (language intended to exclude Eusebius' exegesis of John 17:3). The Son was also the instrument of creation, as Paul indicated in 1 Corinthians 8:6. The statement that his kingdom will have no end comes from Luke 1:33 and is directed against the exegesis of 1 Corinthians 15:23–28 maintained by Marcellus of Ancyra. The language about the Holy Spirit also deals with origins: the Spirit proceeds from the Father, as in John 15:26 (cf. 1 Cor. 2:12), and is worshiped and glorified with Father and Son, as both Athanasius and Basil of Caesarea had stated.[10]

If we compare the two creeds a little more generally, we find Constantinople more philosophical and more theological, farther away from the more primitive Christian doctrines, frequently echoing biblical language but doing so in order to promote fourth-century emphases. Nearly half the article about the Son is concerned with his preexistence, a topic not mentioned in the Apostles' Creed.

The creed of Constantinople, like the Nicene before it, was trinitarian not only in intent but in actuality. J. N. D. Kelly has defined the difference between West and East, between Constantinople (and others) and Apostles' (and others) thus: "In Western creeds the centre of interest is the primitive kerygma about the Saviour, whereas in Eastern creeds the cosmic setting of the drama obtrudes itself more obviously."[11] In addition, cosmological concern almost inevitably leads to trinitarian doctrine.

The Nicene Creed and its tributaries, as C. H. Turner said, were intended to test the orthodoxy of bishops, not the simpler faith of persons being baptized. From the fourth century onward, creeds like it were used for just this purpose, and in some places they were introduced to the eucharist a century later.

The Idea of Unity Against Diversity

We have now traced the passage from religion to theology in the Greco-Roman pagan world and in early Christianity and have seen the similar use of cosmic terms in the interpretations of the divine. Philosophical theology was no Christian invention but was commonplace, along with rhetoric, in Greco-Roman religious thought. Even the doctrine of the Trinity was to some extent anticipated in

Platonic circles. Does this mean that early Christian theology was "nothing but" paganism with a biblical accent? Or, to paraphrase Numenius, was Christianity no more than Plato with a faint Palestinian accent? Here we must differentiate our historical analysis of origins from the more durable images of the transcendent, not fully dependent on circumstances of time and place. The rise of Christian theology took place under strong pressures from the leading philosophies of the time. We should not say that it was "no more than" the sum of its parts, but the reality of the pagan environment cannot be neglected.

As Christians dealt with this environment they tried to achieve a certain fixity in their intellectual position. This was made necessary by two factors. First, and most important, Christians were trying to present a relatively unified front to the outside world, especially the world of the state and its sporadic persecutions. Second, for the sake of church discipline and harmony it was necessary to limit the range of opinions. The more peculiar aberrations had to be disavowed. During the second century, emphasis was laid on the history of the church as a "pure virgin" later led astray by heretics. The search for the original dream was conducted by all sides. My one true faith or orthodoxy was prior to heterodoxy, your diverse and inconsistent developments.

Such a picture was soon associated with similar treatments of the history of philosophy, if it did not develop out of them. The first Christian to sketch the history of philosophy was the sometime Platonist Justin, who in his *Dialogue with Trypho* found original unity followed by complexity. According to him,

> originally there were no Platonists or Stoics or Peripatetics or Theoretics or Pythagoreans, since this knowledge was one. I wish to state why it became manifold. It happened that those who first touched on philosophy and therefore became famous had successors who did not investigate the truth but, merely impressed by the constancy and self-control and novel terminology of their teachers, regarded their teaching as true and handed down to their own successors such doctrines and others like them. Therefore they were called by the name of the father of the doctrine.[12]

Justin's account resembles Numenius' description of post-Platonic Platonism. In his view, later Platonists departed from the pure doctrine of Plato himself. Naturally Numenius supposed that he was restoring the pure doctrine.[13] School succession lists like those provided by Clement of Alexandria[14] and Diogenes Laërtius served to show who were the "orthodox" members. The Christian episcopal lists make the same point. Gnostics too went back through correct successions to the beginning. The Valentinian Ptolemaeus speaks of his school's "apostolic tradition, received by succession," while Valentinus himself traced his spiritual genealogy back through a certain Theodas to Paul, and Basilides went through Glaukias to Peter.[15] As for the "unity" of true philosophy, the Middle Platonist Atticus argues that Plato was the great teacher of a philosophy combining all the virtues of the pre-Socratics.[16] Disunity came later.

A different and highly critical picture is given by Diodorus Siculus. "The Greeks, aiming at the profit to be made out of the business, keep founding new schools and, wrangling with one another over the most important matters of speculation, bring it about that their pupils hold conflicting views, and that their minds, vacillating throughout their lives and unable to believe anything at all with firm conviction, simply wander in confusion." This is the line that Irenaeus takes against the Gnostics. He says they claim to have found something new every day.[17]

Another way of dealing with heresies was to explain that whereas "the tradition of all the apostles has been one and the same, the heresies derived their names sometimes from a founder, or a place of origin, or a nationality, or a practise, or peculiar opinions, or from admired personages, or immoralities." Clement of Alexandria gives this analysis. It is almost exactly the same as the classification used for philosophical schools by Diogenes Laërtius.[18]

Diversity to a philosopher or a Christian is wrong in itself, while unity is right. Given this basic axiom, it was simple enough to attack heretics who followed various teachers. Justin explains that all heresies arose after the ascension of Christ, when Simon, Menander, and Marcion came to the fore.[19] Hegesippus goes farther by explaining that one heterodoxy led to another. There were no heresies in Christianity before a certain Thebuthis, around the year 62, introduced one or more out of the seven sects in Judaism.[20] Irenaeus too believes that the way to attack complex heresies like Valentinianism is to start with the simpler errors of Simon, Menander, Saturninus, and their immediate successors.[21]

All these discussions are based on the axiom that there was an original unified Christianity, later spoiled when diversity came in. At Alexandria, only Origen seems to have opposed this view. He conceded that the apostles delivered a uniform message, but he held that they left the philosophical analysis of its content to later exegetes, of whom he was the chief.[22]

Later theologians were quite sure there were clear and sharp lines between orthodoxy and heresy, and they insisted on their own orthodoxy. An unusual exception occurs in the case of the unbaptized emperor Constantine, who severely criticized both Arius and his bishop Alexander, not only for raising in public the theological questions that divided them but for raising them at all.[23] The subsequent Council of Nicaea did not take up this problem.

At the beginning of his reign, Julian was eager to restore pagan religion and he therefore recalled from exile the bishops and other Christian leaders who had been exiled by Constantine's son Constantius, a loyal Arian. He restored churches to Novatianists and rights to the Donatist clerics. He urged heretics to express their beliefs freely, so that as Christians fought among themselves they could not unite against him. He "knew from experience that no wild animals are so hostile to mankind as most Christians are in their deadly hatred of one another."[24]

By the year 374, Epiphanius, the bishop of Salamis on Cyprus, was composing an enormous treatise against the eighty heresies he believed he could find. His virulent work provides extensive quotations and paraphrases based on much older sources, but his own judgments are usually mistaken. A principal value of his work is for studying lore about snakes, since he lists and describes eighty species of them.[25]

Church battles continued with outsiders as well as insiders. The church was on the verge of a complete victory over the forces of paganism. In 384, when Christians were removing treasure and ornaments from the temples, the pagan orator Symmachus, prefect of the city of Rome, defended toleration without convincing the emperors or other Christians.[26] He first asked the emperors to restore Roman religious institutions, venerated by earlier rulers and not abolished by the later (Christian) ones. Indeed, though the emperor Constantius "followed other rites, he preserved established rites for the empire." "*Suus cuique mos, suus ritus est,*" says Symmachus, echoing the words of Cicero more than four centuries earlier (see chapter 2). "Everyone has his own customs, his own religious practises." This is the foundation of Symmachus' argument. "Man's reason moves entirely in the dark," he continues. "His knowledge of divine influences can be drawn from no better source than from the recollection and the evidences of good fortune received from them." This is the traditional popular and Stoic argument based on the use of historical examples to prove the case for the gods as well as on the avoidance of rigorous logical proofs.

Symmachus also adheres to tradition when he suggests that "whatever each of us worships is really to be considered one and the same." And he asks, "What does it matter what practical system we adopt in our search for the truth?" This is so because "not by one avenue only can we arrive at so tremendous a secret" *(uno itinere non potest perveniri ad tam grande secretum)*. Some have claimed that Symmachus suffers from mixed motives and that he is trying to persuade the emperors to pay for pagan worship. Such a charge neglects the extent to which human motives are always mixed, even among the Christians of the fourth century.[27]

The return to Ciceronian sentiment is interesting because among educated Christians a similar return was under way. We find it in both Ambrose and Augustine, but for our purposes most notably in the early fifth century, in the *Commonitorium* of Vincent of Lérins. Vincent was trying, at long last, to set forth a theoretical basis for orthodoxy that might go beyond personal prejudices and whims. He found it in the idea of *consensus* as developed in Cicero's *Tusculan Disputations*. The ultimate authority was "the divine law," interpreted by "the tradition of the Catholic church." Opposing Augustine's doctrine of predestination, Vincent naturally rejected diversity in favor of "the norm of the ecclesiastical and Catholic understanding," and he quoted Stephen of third-century Rome as having said, "No innovation except what is handed down." There may have to be development *(profectus)*, but not alteration *(permutatio)*.

What of Cicero? Vincent clearly relies on the *Tusculan Disputations* when he writes provocatively that he would rather be wrong with Origen than right with others. Cicero had said this about Plato, and in the section of the disputations where he was discussing antiquity and consensus.[28] Again, Vincent clearly had in mind the *consensus* not of a majority of Christians but of "the holy fathers." He thus followed Cicero's idea of appealing to the agreement of philosophers, not people in general.[29]

Whether or not *consensus* as promoted by either Cicero or Vincent is workable, we see from this important example that in order to escape from the morass of accusations and slanders provided by men like Epiphanius the church had to try to recover the higher ground of classical moderation. By the fifth century it could often afford to do so.

The pagan appeal for diversity and toleration was opposed, at least superficially (for the moment we neglect the grand continuities in Mediterranean religious history), by Christian insistence on the unity of God, of faith, of cult, and of the church itself. The emphasis on the one God had been made in opposition to the many gods of paganism, whether in remote Old Testament times or in the Greco-

Roman world itself. The Second Isaiah makes the point vigorously: "I am Yahweh [the Lord], and there is no other, besides me there is no God. . . . I form light and create darkness, I make weal and create woe, I am the Lord, who do all these things" (Isa. 45:5–7). Or again, in the Decalogue: "You shall have no other gods but me" (Ex. 20:3). And in Deuteronomy 6:4 once more: "The Lord our God, the Lord, is one; and you shall love the Lord your God with all your heart, and with all your soul, and with all your might." There is an exclusiveness about Old Testament religion. The Gnostics imagined that statements about Yahweh and his jealousy proved that he was ignorant of the real plethora of gods. Both Jews and Christians strongly disagreed. As an obvious example we cite 1 Timothy 2:5: "There is one God, and there is one mediator between God and men, the man Christ Jesus." Or again, in Ephesians 4:4–6: "There is one body and one Spirit, just as you were called to the one hope that belongs to your call, one Lord, one faith, one baptism, one God and Father of us all, who is above all and through all and in all." The unity of God found its earthly counterpart in the unity of believers, bound together against a hostile world. John puts the motif of exclusiveness as strongly as anyone. "No one has ever seen God; the only Son, who is in the bosom of the Father, has made him known" (John 1:18). He insisted that no one comes to the Father but through Jesus (John 14:6). And Christians had to be right, because the Johannine Christ had promised that the Holy Spirit would lead them into the whole truth (John 16:13).

The Latin author Tertullian understands this kind of leading not as a continuing search (typical, he thought, of Gnostics) but as an appropriation of truth already obtained. He expresses the view of most patristic theologians, and points the way to Cyprian's statement that outside the church there is no salvation.

Other religions had no creeds. As far as we can tell, they had no councils with debates over philosophical theology. Oddly enough, the Christian debates were deeply influenced by the training of the debaters in rhetoric and philosophy—as we have tried to show throughout this book—but the influence was usually denied or neglected. As we saw, even Origen refrains from quoting the philosophers who influenced his thought so much.[30]

Christianity took the faith traditional in the second century—largely derived from the Old Testament but reinterpreted in the light of the experience of Jesus and the Spirit—and insisted that persons seeking baptism had to express it, especially in opposition to their native "idolatry." As time went by, the logical implications of the faith were worked out on the basis of the leading philosophies of the time, often in ways remarkably similar to such workings out in other religions. The religious impulses and their expressions turned out to be much the same. The various Christian syntheses as they emerged were different because of the unique synthesis of revelation by God the Father and the Son and the Holy Spirit.

We began with militant opposition to idolatry and then moved through the thicket of religious and philosophical analysis and interpretation of various pagan gods. The upshot was that the development of the Christian doctrine of the Trinity was, to say the least, not alien to philosophical or even rhetorical statements made by pagans about the pagan gods. We have no intention of equating Christian theology with pagan analysis of the various pagan deities. Nevertheless, it is clear that there were resemblances. If we move into the sphere of temples and churches, what we have observed in the intellectual realm corresponds remarkably well with the almost universal Mediterranean urge to preserve the temples of the old gods and with a few modifications use them as churches of the new religion. The result was eminently satisfactory both for the grandparents who had preserved the temples and for the new generation which regarded the gods as outmoded or, for that matter, false. In most cases, the marvelous religious buildings of the Greco-Roman world could be preserved and redirected for the new worship.

Notes

Chapter 1: Gods in the Book of Acts

1. Cf. P. J. Koets, *Deisidaimonia* (Purmerend, 1929).

2. Cf. E. Derenne, *Les procès d'impiété intentes aux philosophes à Athènes au Ve et au IVe siècles avant J.-C.* (Liège and Paris, 1930).

3. *SVF* II 1019; Plutarch, *On Superstition* 167D; Bodo von Borries, *Quid veteres philosophi de idololatria senserint* (Göttingen, 1918), 90.

4. This is strikingly similar in outline to 1 Thess. 1:9–10; see chapter 3.

5. Strabo 14.683; Herodotus 1.199; Plutarch, *Theseus* 20.

6. Cf. M. P. Nilsson, *Griechische Feste von religiöser Bedeutung* (repr. Darmstadt, 1957), 364–74.

7. Cf. Diogenes Laërtius 6.46.

8. Strabo 8.378–79.

9. Pausanias 2.5.1.

10. In Dio Chrysostom, *Orations* 37.34.

11. Aelius Aristides, *Orations* 46.25, p. 370, 11–12 Keil.

12. C. W. Blegen et al., *Corinth*, III.i (Cambridge, Mass., 1930), 20–21; cf. G. Roux, *Pausanias en Corinthie* (Paris, 1958), 129.

13. Athenaeus 13.574BC (see the whole passage beginning 573C); cf. E. Will, *Korinthiaka* (Paris, 1955), 232.

14. On festivals of Aphrodite, see Nilsson, *Griechische Feste von religiöser Bedentung*, 362–82, and also note the experiences of Lucius at Corinth in Apuleius, *Golden Ass* 10.19ff.

15. Lenschau, "Korinthos," *RE* Suppl. IV (1924), 1034.

16. B. Keil, "Ein LOGOS SYSTATIKOS," Nachrichten . . . Göttingen, Philol.-hist. Kl. (1913), 1–41.

17. Apuleius, *Golden Ass* 10.18; Lucian, *Demonax.*

18. Ovid, *Metamorphoses* 8.620–724.

19. W. M. Calder, "A Cult of the Homonades," *Classical Review* 24 (1910), 76–81; "Zeus and Hermes at Lystra," *Expositor* VII, 10 (1910), 1–6.

20. F. Knoll, *Denkmäler aus Lykaonien, Pamphylien und Isaurien,* Deutsche Gesellschaft der Wissenschaften und Künste für die Tschechoslowakische Republik in Prag (Brünn, 1935), 72–73, no. 146.

21. *CIG* 2462, 2796, 2963c, 3194, 3211 (= *IGR* IV 1415), 3493; *BCH* 1 (1877), 136; 11 (1887), 464, no. 29; T. Wiegand, *SAB* 1906, 259; Calder as above; *IGR* IV 1406.

22. *SVF* II 1024, 1079; III 90; Cornutus 16, p. 20, 18 Lang; Justin, *Apology* 1.21.2; 22.2; Clement, *Stromata* 6.132.1.

23. S. Loesch, *Deitas Jesu und antike Apotheose* (Rottenburg, 1933), 30–34, 42–46.

24. H. J. Cadbury, *The Book of Acts in History* (New York, 1955), 5f.; examples in *OGI* 9, 5; 10, 15; cf. H. Bellen in *KP* IV 56f.

25. Pliny, *Epistles* 10.96.10.

26. H. Wankel, ed., *Die Inschriften von Ephesos,* 1a (Bonn, 1979), nos. 17–19 (p. 115, tr. p. 120).

27. A. Wardman, *Religions and Statecraft Among the Romans* (Baltimore, 1982), 128.

28. *SIG* 867.

29. F. J. Foakes Jackson and Kirsopp Lake, eds., *The Beginnings of Christianity,* V (London, 1933), 255.

30. Strabo 3.4.8, 160; 4.1.4–5, 179.

31. On a relief, cf. E. Akurgal, *Ancient Civilizations and Ruins of Turkey* (Istanbul, 1973), 165.

32. Minucius Felix, *Octavius* 22.5; Jerome, *Commentary on Ephesians, Prologue* (*PG* 26.270BC); cf. R. Fleischer, *Artemis von Ephesos and verwandte Kultstatuen aus Anatolien und Syrien* (Leiden, 1973), 74–88.

Chapter 2: Mediterranean Religions Westward

1. *CIL* X 1552.

2. *ILS* 5317, 6.

3. Josephus, *Antiquities* 17.328.

4. *IGR* I 422; A. Audollent, *Defixionum tabellae* (Paris, 1904), 278–80.

5. For the translation, see C. C. Torrey, "The Exiled God of Sarepta," *Berytus* 9 (1949), 45–49.

6. *OGI* 594.

7. *CIL* X 1601, 1553, 1563–64.

8. *OGI* 595.

9. Pliny, *Epistles* 10.96.6.

10. Dionysius of Corinth in Eusebius, *Ecclesiastical History* 4.23.10.

11. Livy 10.47.6f.

12. Livy, Book XI, summary; for later accounts, cf. Emma and Ludwig Edelstein, *Asclepius*, I, 431–50 (Test. 845–54). For Delphic participation, H. W. Parke and D. E. W. Wormell, *The Delphic Oracle*, II (Oxford, 1956), 142f. (no. 355).

13. Ibid., 250f. (Test. 43B = *SIG* 1173 = *IGR* I 41).

14. Livy 29.11.7; cf. 38.18.9.

15. Augustus, *Monumentum Ancyranum* 4, 19.

16. Lydus, *On the Months* 4.59; cf. K. Latte, *Römische Religionsgeschichte* (Munich, 1960), 261; M. J. Vermaseren, *The Legend of Attis in Greek and Roman Art* (Leiden, 1966).

17. *SIG* 280, 32–45.

18. Greeks generally called the god Sarapis; Romans, Serapis. We follow Greek usage.

19. Tertullian, *Apology* 6.8.10.

20. G. Wissowa, *Religion und Kultus der Römer*, 2d ed. (Munich, 1912), 351–53.

21. Dio Cassius, 47.15.4.

22. Josephus, *Antiquities* 18.65–80.

23. Tacitus, *Annals* 2.85; so also Suetonius, *Tiberius* 36.

24. Juvenal 6.489, 526–41. Like other Roman authors, Juvenal goes on to speak of Jewish superstition: 6.542–47.

25. *ILS* 6419f, 6420b.

26. Apuleius, *Golden Ass* 11.17.

27. Eusebius-Jerome, *Chronicle*, p. 129 Helm.

28. Cf. Parke and Wormell, *The Delphic Oracle*, II, 117, no. 286.

29. Tacitus, *Histories* 4.83f.

30. Plutarch, *On Isis and Osiris* 361E.

31. Ibid., 361F–362A.

32. Ibid., 29, 362c.

33. Clement, *Exhortation to the Greeks* 48.

34. Origen, *Against Celsus* 5.38; Numenius, frag. 53 Des Places.

35. Aelius Aristides, *Orations* 45.29–30.

36. Text and translation in A. Deissmann, *Light from the Ancient East*, rev. ed. (New York, 1927), 152–57; A. D. Nock, *Conversion*, 49f.

37. O. Weinreich, *Neue Urkunden zur Sarapis-Religion* (Tübingen, 1919), 19f., 31–33; *IG* XI 4 1299 = *SIG* 663 (without the hymn); Nock, *Conversion*, 51f.; H. Engelmann, *Die delische Sarapisaretalogie* (Meisenheim am Glan, 1964).

38. Athenaeus v.196A; *OGI* 54, 5–6; Clement, *Exhortation to the Greeks* 54.2.

39. The fragment is preserved by Theophilus, *To Autolycus* 2.8, and in an Oxyrhynchus papyrus (XXVII 2465). Cf. P. Perdrizet in *REA* 12 (1910), 217–47.

40. *BGU* 1211; A. S. Hunt and C. C. Edgar, *Select Papyri*, II (Cambridge, Mass., 1934), no. 208.

41. Plutarch, *Antony* 24.3–4; 54.6; 60.3.

42. Dio Cassius 48.39.2; cf. 50.5.3, 25.3–4.

43. F. Cumont, *Les religions orientales dans le paganisme romain*, 4th ed. (Paris, 1929), 197.

44. A. Vogliano and F. Cumont, "La grande iscrizione bacchica del Metropolitan Museum," *AJA* 37 (1933), 215–31, 232–63.

45. Tertullian, *Apology* 6.7, 10.

46. Plutarch, *Pompey* 24.5.

47. Dio Cassius 63.5.2.

48. Justin, *Apology* 1.66.4; *Dialogue with Trypho* 70.1; 78.6.

49. *ILS* 659, of the year 308.

50. I read thus: (au)GGGG / (deo soli i)NVICTO / (mithrae — ab oriente) AD / (occide)NTEM.

51. Perhaps the last inscription was *ILS* 4197, the restoration of a Mithraeum at Noricum (Klagenfurt) in 361.

52. Strabo 16.2.34–36.

53. Cicero, *On Behalf of Flaccus* 69.

54. Augustine, *City of God* 6.11.

55. Tacitus, *Histories* 5.3–5.

56. Diodorus Siculus, *Historical Library*, Books 34/35.1.3.

57. Josephus, *Against Apion* 2.80.

58. Ibid., 92–96.

Chapter 3: Christian Missionaries Against Idolatry

1. Eusebius, *Preparation for the Gospel* 5.36.2; cf. Ramsay MacMullen, *Paganism in the Roman Empire*, 31.

2. Hesiod, *Works and Days* 252.

3. *Codex Theodosianus* 16.10.21.

4. Bodo von Borries, *Quid veteres philosophi de idololatria senserint*, 88–106.

5. Aelius Aristides, *Apology* 13.3 as against Celsus in Origen, *Against Celsus* 7.62.

6. *Didache* 6.3; 2 Clement 3.1; cf. 1 Cor. 8:4; 10:19.

7. Maximus of Tyre, *Orations* 11.5a.

8. L. Spengel, *Rhetores Graeci*, II (Leipzig, 1854), 126,2–128.1.

9. Plato, *Apology* 24B; Xenophon, *Memorabilia* 1.1.2; Favorinus in Diogenes Laërtius 2.40.

10. Frag. 4 in Eusebius, *Preparation for the Gospel* 13.12.6–7.

11. Clement, *Stromata* 6.39.2–3.

12. Ibid., 6.40–41.

13. C. Schmidt, *PRAXEIS PAULOU* (Hamburg, 1936), 24, Seite 1, 17–22; cf. p. 30, Seite 2, 32–34.

Chapter 4: Functions of Gods and Goddesses

1. The expression comes from W. W. Tarn, *Hellenistic Civilisation*, 3d ed. (London, 1952), 351; he used it of Gnosis.

2. M. Rostowzew, "Epiphaneiai," *Klio* 16 (1920), 203.

3. C. Blinkenberg, *Die lindische Tempelchronik* (Bonn, 1915), 34–40; F. C. Grant, *Hellenistic Religions*, 9–13; compare the epiphanies of Vesta in Dionysius of Halicarnassus 2.68–69.

4. P. Oxy. XI 1381, 219; E. and L. Edelstein, I, 172, no. 331.

5. Origen, *Against Celsus* 7.35.

6. Ibid., 8.45.

7. See chapter 13, section "The Idea of Unity Against Diversity."

8. Cicero, *On the Nature of the Gods* 2.162–67; cf. *On Divination* 1.84.

9. Cicero, *On Divination* 1.37f., 79.

10. L. Spengel, *Rhetores Graeci*, III (Leipzig, 1856), 4–6; F. C. Grant, *Hellenistic Religions*, 166–67.

11. Pausanias 2.26.7.

12. Dio Chrysostom, *Orations* 33.47.

13. A. S. Hunt and C. C. Edgar, *Select Papyri*, I (London, 1932), nos. 111–12, 120–21, 133–34, 136–37; 125.

14. *SIG* 1160–66; F. C. Grant, *Hellenistic Religions*, 34–35.

15. Albinus, *Introduction to Plato* 15, p. 171, 18 Hermann.

16. Plutarch, *On Isis and Osiris* 361D.

17. Artemidorus, *Dream Book* 2.34, p. 157, 4 Pack.

18. Ibid., p. 158, 14.

19. Ibid., 2.39, p. 175, 8.

20. Whether or not Galen wrote the *Physician* (XIV 674, 676 Kühn), the sentiment is like what he expresses elsewhere.

21. Galen, *Whether the Embryo Is Animate* 5, XIX 179.

22. Galen, *Commentary on the Prognostic of Hippocrates*, I. 4, XVIII B 17.

23. Galen, *On the Doctrines of Hippocrates and Plato* 3.8, V 348.

24. Galen, *On the Composition of Drugs According to Place* 9.4, XIII 271.

25. Galen, *On Sperm* 1.5, IV 531.

26. *OGI* 458, 31–45.

27. J. P. V. D. Balsdon, *Roman Women* (London, 1962, 1974), 301, n. 112.

28. Suetonius, *Augustus* 98.2.

29. For later stories about it, see Suetonius, *Augustus* 94.3–6.

30. Cf. S. Loesch, *Deitas Jesu und antike Apotheose* (Rottenburg, 1933); L. Bieler, *THEIOS ANER* (Vienna, 1935).

31. Suetonius, *Vespasian* 23.4.

32. Cf. Justin, *Apology* 1.29.4; J. Beaujeu, "Les apologètes et le culte du souverain," *Entretiens*, Fondation Hardt, 19 (Geneva, 1972), 101–42.

33. Cf. Melito of Sardis in Eusebius, *Ecclesiastical History* 4.26.9.

Chapter 5: The Deeds of Individual Gods and Heroes

1. P. Roussel in *BCH* 55 (1931), 70–116.

2. M. P. Nilsson, *Geschichte der griechischen Religion*, II, 2d ed. (Munich, 1961), 227.

3. Dio Cassius 71.8.4; Eusebius, *Ecclesiastical History* 5.5.1–4.

4. See the learned discussion in Macrobius, *Saturnalia* 1.17.

5. Cf. 1 Cor. 7:23–24 and W. L. Westermann, "The Freedmen and the Slaves of God," Proceedings of the American Philosophical Society, 92 (1948), 55–64.

6. See F. Bömer, *Untersuchungen zur Religion der Sklaven*, Abhandlungen der Akademie der Wissenschaften, Mainz, Geistes- und Socialwiss. Kl. (1960), 133–41.

7. Cicero, *On Divination* 1.38; Strabo 9.420.

8. H. W. Parke and D. E. W. Wormell, *The Delphic Oracle*, I (Oxford, 1956), 274–82.

9. Dio Cassius 63.14.2; Suetonius, *Nero* 40.3.

10. Eusebius, *Preparation for the Gospel* 5.18–36; 6.7.

11. Julian, *Orations* 6.199A; 7.209B.

12. L. Robert, "Trois oracles de la Theosophie," Comptes-rendus de l'Académie des Inscriptions 1968, 568–99.

13. Lactantius, *De mortibus persecutorum* 11.7; Eusebius, *Preparation for the Gospel* 4.2.11.

14. Origen, *Against Celsus* 1.37; 6.8; cf. H. Chadwick, *Origen Contra Celsum* (Cambridge, 1953), 321.

15. Jerome, *Against Jovinian* 1.42, *PL* 23, 285.

16. Plutarch, *Table-talk* 8.2–3, 717D; Apuleius, *On Plato* 1.1; Olympiodorus, *Life of Plato* 1, p. 191 Hermann.

17. Cf. H. J. Rose, *A Handbook of Greek Mythology* (New York, 1929), 50.

18. J. H. Oliver, *The Civilising Power*, Trans. Amer. Philos. Soc. 58. 1 (Philadelphia, 1968), 50 (sec. 39).

19. Ibid., 194 (sec. 276).

20. C. Blinkenberg, *Die lindische Tempelchronik* (Bonn, 1915), 4 (A 3), 34–40; *SIG* 725.

21. *OGI* 331, IV 52.

22. Diodorus Siculus 3.66.2; Pliny, *Natural History* 2.231; Pausanias 6.26.2.

23. *SVF* II 1024, 1079, III (Diogenes) 90; Cornutus 16, p. 20, 19 Lang.

24. Justin, *Apology* 1.21.2; cf. 22.2; cf. Clement, *Stromata* 6.132.1; Hippolytus, *Refutation of All Heresies* 4.48.2; 5.7.20.

25. Sextus Empiricus, *Against the Schoolmasters* 1.260–62.

26. Strabo 8.374; Pausanias 2.27.3.

27. R. Herzog, *Die Wunderheilungen von Epidauros* (Leipzig, 1931), 2.

28. Eusebius, *Life of Constantine* 3.56; cf. Sozomen, *Ecclesiastical History* 2.5; E. and L. Edelstein, I, 419–20.

29. *IG* 4th ed. 2, 1, 438.

30. Zonaras 13.12C–D; E. and L. Edelstein, I, 420–21.

31. For the latter, cf. P. MacKendrick, *Roman France* (London, 1971), 178–80.

32. A.-J. Festugière, *Personal Religion Among the Greeks*, 85–104; C. A. Behr, *Aelius Aristides and the Sacred Tales.*

33. G. Michenaud and J. Dierkens, *Les rêves dans les "Discours sacrés" d'Aelius Aristide* (Brussels, 1972).

34. For all this, cf. Apollodorus, *Library* 2.4.8—7.8.

35. Justin, *Dialogue with Trypho* 69.3; cf. *Apology* 1.54.9.

36. Justin, *Apology* 1.21.2.

37. Dio Chrysostom, *Orations* 8.28–35; 31.16; 2.78.

38. Epictetus, *Discourses* 1.6.32–36; 2.16.44. On his complete obedience, 3.22.57.

39. Ibid., 3.26.32.

40. Ibid., 3.24.13, 16 for the moral meaning; in between, the problem of Heracles' offspring.

41. Diodorus Siculus, *Historical Library* 1.27.2–4; cf. 22.2–6.

42. Cf. F. C. Grant, *Hellenistic Religions*, 130–31.

43. Ibid., 131–33.

44. C. H. Oldfather on Diodorus notes that according to Pseudo-Eratosthenes, *Catasterismi* 33 (p. 40 Olivieri), Isis is a bright star in the head of the Dog constellation.

45. O. Weinreich, *Neue Urkunden zur Sarapis-Religion* (Tübingen, 1919), 10f.; cf. M. Dibelius, *Die Formgeschichte des Evangeliums*, 2d ed. (Tübingen, 1933), 93; J. Amann, *Die Zeusrede des Ailios Aristeides* (Stuttgart, 1931), 19.

46. Aelius Aristides, *Orations* 42.4–5 Keil; 45.29–30.

47. T. A. Brady and P. M. Fraser, "Sarapis," OCD (2d ed.) 951; cf. F.

Cumont, *Les religions orientales dans le paganisme romain,* 4th ed. (Paris, 1929), 260f., n. 68.

48. E.g., Wilcken, *Chrestomathie* 97, a letter to a man *en katochei* in the Sarapieion at Memphis.

49. For the last meaning, cf. Vettius Valens, *Anthology,* p. 73, 24 Kroll.

50. *OGI* 262, 25.

Chapter 6: The Philosophical Doctrine of God

1. Wilcken, *Chrestomathie* 116.

2. Cf. A. S. Pease, *M. Tulli Ciceronis De Natura Deorum,* II (Cambridge, Mass., 1958), 1092–94.

3. For example, Theophilus, *To Autolycus* 1.3–4; *Corpus Hermeticum* 2.14.

4. Plutarch, *On Isis and Osiris* 372E; *ILS* 1859, 4361, 4376a.

5. Apuleius, *Golden Ass* 11.5; cf. P. Oxy. XI 1380.

6. For the background, cf. W. Jaeger, *The Theology of the Early Greek Philosophers.*

7. Diels-Kranz 21 B (fragments) 10, 23, 26, 25.

8. Aeschylus, *Suppliant Women* 100–3.

9. Xenophanes, B 12, 14, 15, 16.

10. Clement, *Stromata* 5.109.1; 7.22.1.

11. A. B. Cook, *Zeus: A Study in Ancient Religion,* I-III (Cambridge, 1914–1940).

12. H. J. Rose, *A Handbook of Greek Mythology* (New York, 1929), 47.

13. K. Ziegler, "Zeus," in W. H. Roscher, ed., *Ausführliches Lexikon der griechischen und römischen Mythologie,* VI (Leipzig and Berlin, 1937), 685–702.

14. Homer, *Iliad* 1.544.

15. Clement, *Stromata* 5.114.4.

16. Frag. 480 Nauck; cf. N. Zeegers-Vander Vorst, *Les citations des poètes grecs chez les apologistes chrétiens du IIe siècle* (Louvain, 1972), 90–91, 98, 166.

17. Pseudo-Justin, *On the Unity of God* 5.

18. Lucian, *Zeus the Tragic Poet* 41; Athenagoras, *Embassy for the Christians* 5.2.

19. Plutarch, *The Amorous Man* 13, 756B–C.

20. *SVF* I 527, 537.

21. Cornutus 9, p. 9, 1 Lang.

22. Plutarch, *Table-talk* 8.3, 718A.

23. Aelius Aristides, *Orations* 43; cf. J. Amann, *Die Zeusrede des Ailios Aristeides* (Stuttgart, 1931).

24. Pseudo-Aristotle, *On the Universe* 397B–401A.

25. Ibid., 7, 401AB.

26. O. Kern, *Orphicorum fragmenta* (Berlin, 1922), F 21a.

27. Plato, *Laws* 4.715E–716A.

28. Plutarch, *On the E at Delphi*, ch. 20, 393Bff.

29. Ibid., ch. 10, p. 164, 27 Hermann.

30. Frag. xvi = Stob. 1.41.4.

31. Albinus, *Introduction to Plato* p. 171, 18.

32. Ibid., ch. 16, p. 172, 2.

33. Apuleius, *On the Teaching of Plato* 1.5.

34. Eusebius, *Preparation for the Gospel* 15.5.3.

35. Albinus, *Introduction to Plato* 28, p. 181, 36 Hermann.

36. Numenius, Frag. 17 Des Places; of. J. Dillon, *The Middle Platonists*, 366–67f.

37. Numenius, Frag. 12; cf. E. des Places, *Numenius: Fragments* (Paris, 1973), 10–14. See Chapter 12 on the Trinity.

38. Text in L. Spengel, *Rhetores Graeci*, III (Leipzig, 1856), 331–67, 368–446; rev. by C. Bursian, *Der Rhetor Menandros und seine Schriften*, Abhandlungen der königlichen bayerischen Akademie der Wissenschaften, Philosophisch-philologische Kl., 16, 3 (1882), 30–151.

39. Cf. G. Soury, *Aperçus de philosophie religieuse chez Maxime de Tyr* (Paris, 1942).

Chapter 7: Christian Doctrines of God

1. Josephus, *Against Apion* 2.192.

2. J. Dillon, *The Middle Platonists*, 128.

3. Plutarch, *Platonic Questions* 2, 1000E; Cherniss, note ad loc.

4. Plutarch, *On the Procreation of the Soul in Timaeus* 4, 1013E–14B.

5. E.g., Philoponus, *On the Eternity of the World*, 211, 11 Rabe (Plutarch and Atticus); 529, 22ff.

6. On this, cf. G. Stroumsa, "The Incorporeality of God," *Religion* 13 (1983), 345–58.

7. Hippolytus, *Refutation of All Heresies* 7.20.

8. Nag Hammadi Codex II 1, 25–3, 35.

9. Tertullian, *Prescription of Heretics* 7.3.

10. E.g., Philo, *On the Special Laws* 1.307; cf. N. Dahl and A. F. Segal, "Philo and the Rabbis on the Names of God," *JJS* 9 (1978), 1–28.

11. Epiphanius, *Against Eighty Heresies* 33 in G. Quispel, *Ptolémée: Lettre à Flora* (Paris, 1949), ch. 7.

12. L. W. Barnard, *Justin Martyr: His Life and Thought* (Cambridge, 1967), 79–84.

13. Justin, *Apology* 2.6.1–2.

14. Irenaeus, *Against Heresies* 1.3.1, 3, 4.

15. Athenagoras, *Embassy for the Christians* 10.1, tr. W. R. Schoedel.

16. The Marcionite Marcus taught that "the Good does not condemn those who have disobeyed him" (A. von Harnack, *Marcion. Das Evangelium vom fremden Gott,* 2d ed. [Leipzig, 1924], 265*).

17. Cf. Ex. 20:5–6; Deut. 5:10; 7:9.

18. Plutarch, *Conspectus of the Essay on "The Stoics"* 35, 1050E = *SVF* II 1176.

19. Compare Pseudo-Aristotle and Dio Chrysostom as cited in chapter 6.

20. Irenaeus, *Against Heresies* 1.12.2.

21. Ibid., 2.13.3, partly repeated in 8.

22. Ibid., 3.25.5, because of what Plato said in the *Laws,* 715E, and the *Timaeus,* 29E.

23. Ibid., 2.28.4.

24. Cf. *Sources chrétiennes* 293, 240–44.

25. Irenaeus, *Against Heresies* 4.11.2.

26. Cf. S. R. C. Lilla, *Clement of Alexandria: A Study in Christian Platonism and Gnosticism* (Oxford, 1971), 212–26.

27. Clement, *Stromata* 4.155.2.

28. Lilla, *Clement of Alexandria,* 221–22.

29. Origen, *Commentary on the Gospel of Matthew* 10.23, p. 33 Klostermann.

30. Origen, *Homilies on the Gospel of Luke* 6; *Exposition of the Song of Solomon, Prologue.*

31. Philo, *On the Sacrifices of Abel and Cain* 101.

32. Compare the analogies in Matt. 7:9–11; Luke 11:11–13.

33. The expression "for us" recalls Ignatius, *Epistle to Polycarp* 3.2.

34. Cf. H. Crouzel, *Origène: Traité des principes*, II (Paris, 1978), 165–66.

Chapter 8: Christ: Deeds and Names

1. Cf. W. Bauer, *Das Leben Jesu im Zeitalter der neutestamentlichen Apokryphen* (Tübingen, 1909), 360–68.

2. On miracle stories, cf. the "classical' analyses by R. Bultmann, *Die Geschichte der synoptischen Tradition*, 2d ed. (Göttingen, 1931), 223–60; M. Dibelius, *Die Formgeschichte des Evangeliums*, 2d ed. (Tübingen, 1933), 49–53, 66–100.

3. Bultmann, *Die Geschichte der synoptischen Tradition*, 253.

4. Compare the discussion of Dionysus in chapter 4.

5. Except for the folk tale of the coin in the fish's mouth, Matt. 17:27.

6. F. Braudel, *The Mediterranean and the Mediterranean World in the Age of Philip II* (New York, 1976), I, 241, 255–67.

7. Dibelius, *Die Formgeschichte des Evangeliums*, 232.

8. Justin, *Apology* 1.22.

9. Tertullian, *Apology* 21.17.

10. Origen, *Against Celsus* 2.48.

11. F. J. Foakes Jackson and H. J. Cadbury, *The Beginnings of Christianity*, I.i (London, 1922), 362.

12. Compare the book of Ezekiel, where the prophet is addressed as "son of man."

13. Even if the sequence is wrong, there was a development of some sort.

14. Codex Bezae; Old Latin; Justin, *Dialogue with Trypho* 103.6; Clement, *Tutor* 1.25.2.

15. It recalls similar expressions in Isa. 49:1 and Jer. 1:5.

16. On what follows, see "The Book of Wisdom at Alexandria," in R. M. Grant, *After the New Testament* (Philadelphia, 1967), 70–82; "Les êtres intermédiaires dans le judaïsme tardif," *Le Origini dello gnosticismo*, Supplements to *Numen*), XII, ed. U. Bianchi (Leiden, 1967), 141–57.

17. Sirach 24:3–4, 6–7, 9; cf. 1 Enoch 42.

18. Wisd. of Sol. 7:22–23; *SVF* I 557, cited by Clement of Alexandria; Wisd. of Sol. 7:25–26, 8:3.

19. Wisd. of Sol. 9:1–2. Are the events depicted as consecutive or parallel?

20. H. A. Wolfson, *Philo*, I, 256, citing Philo, *On Flight and Finding*, 50–52.

21. Philo, *Questions and Answers on Genesis* 4.97; *Quod deterius potiori insidiari solet* 115–16; *On Flight and Finding* 109; *On Drunkenness* 30–31; Plato, *Timaeus* 49A, 51A.

22. Philo, *Questions and Answers on Genesis* 4.145; *Questions and Answers on Exodus* 2.3.

23. J. Dillon, *The Middle Platonists*, 164.

24. W. L. Knox, "The Divine Wisdom," *JTS* 38 (1937), 230–37; cf. also H. Conzelmann, "Die Mutter der Weisheit," *Zeit und Geschichte*, ed. E. Dinkler (Tübingen, 1964), 225–34.

25. W. Peek, *Der Isishymnos von Andros und verwandte Texte* (Berlin, 1930).

26. J. Bergman, *Ich bin Isis, Studien zum memphitischen Hintergrund der griechischen Isis-Aretalogien*, Acta Universitatis Upsaliensis, Historia religionum, 3 (1968).

27. D. Müller, "Ägypten und die griechischen Isis-Aretalogien," Abhandlungen der sächsischen Akademie der Wissenschaften zu Leipzig, Phil.-hist. KI., 53, 1 (1961); review of Bergman in *Orientalische Literaturzeitung* 67 (1972), 117–30.

28. The editors of P. Oxy. XI note Diodorus Siculus 1.27 on Isis and the power of Egyptian women.

29. Y. Grandjean, *Une nouvelle arétalogie d'Isis a Maronée* (Leiden, 1975), 120f.

30. Plutarch, *On Isis and Osiris* 373B, 372E.

31. Bergman, *Ich bin Isis*, 169f.

32. Ibid., 289–92.

33. Only in Rom. 9:3, if there.

34. Ignatius, *Epistle to the Magnesians* 6.1; 7.2.

35. Ibid., 8.2; *Epistle to the Smyrneans* 1.2; *Epistle to Polycarp* 3.2; *Epistle to the Ephesians* 7.2 as cited by Athanasius, *On the Synods of Arminium and Seleucia* 47.1.

36. Ignatius, *Epistle to the Trallians* 5.

37. Irenaeus, *Against Heresies* 1.24.1–2.

38. Tertullian, *Against Valentinians* 4.3.

39. Irenaeus, *Against Heresies* 1.6.1.

40. Hippolytus, *C. Noet.* 1; for a sermon, cf. E. Schwartz, *Zwei Predigten Hippolyts* (*SBAW*, Philol.-hist. K1. 1936, 5), 5–18.

41. Epiphanius, *Against Eighty Heresies* 57.1.8.

42. Hippolytus, *Refutation of All Heresies* 10.17.1–2.

43. Cf. E. Kroymann, *Tertullian Adversus Praxean* (Tübingen, 1907), ix–xiii.

44. Irenaeus, *Against Heresies* 5.28.4.

45. Eusebius, *Ecclesiastical History* 5.28.3.

46. Hippolytus, *Refutation of All Heresies* 9.7.1–2; 11.3.

47. Tertullian, *Against Praxeas* 1.5; 29.3, 5.

48. Eusebius, *Ecclesiastical History* 5.28.4–5, 11–12.

49. Justin, *Apology* 1.63.15; Tatian, *Oration to the Greeks* 13, p. 15, 5 Schwartz; Clement, *Exhortation to the Greeks* 110.1.

50. See also A. Houssiau, *La christologie de saint Irénée* (Louvain, 1955), 230–32.

51. Clement, *Stromata* 3.59.3.

52. Frag. 24, *Clemens Alexandrinus*, III, p. 210 Stählin.

53. Frag. 23, Vol. III, p. 202 Stählin.

54. J. N. D. Kelly, *Early Christian Doctrines*, 153–54.

55. J. Scherer, *Entretien d'Origène avec Héraclide* (Paris, 1960), 54–62.

56. Origen, *Commentary on the Gospel of John* 2.1–2; Philo, *On Dreams* 1.229; Clement, *Stromata* 3.81.6.

57. Numenius, frags. 16, 20 Des Places

Chapter 9: The Cosmic Christ

1. *Apostolic Constitutions* 8.12.6ff.; F. E. Brightman, *Liturgies Eastern and Western*, I (Oxford, 1896), 14ff.; my note in *ATR* 30 (1948), 91–94 = *Christian Beginnings* (London, 1983), art. 19.

2. Justin, *Apology* 1.26.3; Irenaeus, *Against Heresies* 1.23.4; Epiphanius, *Against Eighty Heresies* 33.7.3–4.

3. Plutarch, *On Isis and Osiris* 352C; A. D. Nock, *Essays on Religion and the Ancient World*, ed. Z. Stewart (Oxford, 1972), 460.

4. Plutarch, *On the E at Delphi* 391F, 393C, 394A, C.

5. L. Spengel, *Rhetores Graeci*, III 446, 2.

6. Ibid., 43B, 11; 441, 1; 442, 30.

7. Julian, *Orations* 4, 136A; cf. Macrobius, *Saturnalia* 1.18.18.

8. R. MacMullen, *Paganism in the Roman Empire*, 12–13 (from Oenoanda).

9. *SVF* II 908–9; Cicero, *On the Nature of the Gods* 1.41; Minucius Felix, *Octavius* 19.12.

10. Justin, *Apology* 1.64.5; Athenagoras, *Embassy for the Christians* 22.8.

11. Aelius Aristides, *Orations* 43.7–9, p. 340, 14–30 Keil.

12. Ibid., 37.2–4, pp. 304–5.

13. Cf. R. M. Grant, *After the New Testament* (Philadelphia, 1967), 66f.; for further speculations, 70–82.

14. F. W. Lenz, "Der Athenahymnos des Aristides," *Rivista di Cultura Classica e Mediaevale* 5 (1963), 329–47, esp. 339–40.

15. Plutarch, *On the E at Delphi* 388E, 389A.

16. Aelius Aristides, *Orations* 41.4, p. 13 Keil.

17. H. Brandenburg, "Meerwesensarkophage und Clipeusmotiv," *JDAI* 82 (1967), 195–245.

18. A. Geyer, *Das Problem des Realitätsbezuges in der dionysischen Bildkunst der Kaiserzeit* (Würzburg, 1977).

19. A. D. Nock, "Sarcophagi and Symbolism," *AJA* 50 (1946), 140–70.

20. Julian, *To the Cynic Heraclides* 220D, 221C.

21. *Kore Kosmou* 23, 29–30 Nock-Festugière.

22. D. L. Page, *Greek Literary Papyri*, I (London, 1942), no. 136.

23. Cf. E. and L. Edelstein, *Asclepius: A Collection and Interpretation of the Testimonies*, I, 169–75 (no. 331).

24. Aelius Aristides, *Orations* 42.4 Keil; E. and L. Edelstein, *Asclepius*, 156, 159–60 (no. 317); cf. no. 303 and II, 106–7.

25. Aelius Aristides, *Orations* 50.56; E. and L. Edelstein, *Asclepius* 150 (no. 302).

26. See also C. Bonner, "Some Phases of Religious Feeling in Later Paganism," *HTR* 30 (1937), 119–40, and C. A. Behr, *Aelius Aristides and the Sacred Tales*.

27. Cornutus 31, p. 62, 23; p. 64, 15 Lang; *SVF* I 514, emending "logos" to "tonos"; cf. P. Decharme, *La critique des traditions religieuses chez les grecs* (Paris, 1904), 33–34.

28. Porphyry, *On the Worship of Images*, in Eusebius, *Preparation for the Gospel* 3.11.25.

29. Julian, *To the Cynic Heraclides* 219D–220A.

30. Athenagoras, *Embassy for the Christians* 18.4–5; O. Kern, *Orphicorum fragmenta* (Berlin, 1922), F 57 (Athenagoras), F 54 (Damascius).

31. *Orphic Hymns* 12, pp. 13–14 Quandt.

32. Apuleius, *Golden Ass* 11.25. Such "mouths and tongues," ultimately derived from Homer, are often mentioned by rhetoricians, e.g. Aelius Aristides (*Orations* 45.16; 47.1) praising Sarapis or Asclepius, or the Christian Theophilus praising the creation in Genesis (*To Autolycus* 2.12).

33. Athenagoras, *Embassy for the Christians* 22.8.

34. Plutarch, *On Isis and Osiris* 358EF.

35. As at Philae, *OGI* 695.

36. Plutarch, *On Isis and Osiris* 372EF.

37. G. Showerman, *The Great Mother of the Gods* (Madison, 1902), 234.

38. Ibid., 289–92.

39. Plutarch, *On Isis and Osiris* 369E.

40. Porphyry, *On the Cave of the Nymphs* 6, p. 60, 7 Nauck 2; J. Bidez and F. Cumont, *Les mages hellénisés* (Paris, 1938), II 29.

41. Frag. dub. 60 Des Places.

42. Porphyry, *On the Cave of the Nymphs* 24, p. 73, 4.

43. M. Simon, "Mithra, rival du Christ?" *Études mithraïques* (Teheran and Liège, 1978), 457–78.

44. Aelius Aristides, *Orations* 45.16f., 24.

Chapter 10: Divergent Christologies at Antioch

1. Cf. W. A. Meeks and R. L. Wilken, *Jews and Christians in Antioch;* D. S. Wallace-Hadrill, *Christian Antioch: A Study of Early Christian Thought in the East* (Cambridge, 1982).

2. The only possible exception is the ambiguous Acts 20:28; cf. H. Conzelmann, *Die Apostelgeschichte* (Tübingen, 1963), 119.

3. Cf. P. Nautin, "Les citations de la 'Predication de Pierre' dans Clément d'Alexandrie," *JTS* 25 (1974), 98–105, with a reference to C. Andresen, *Logos und Nomos* (Berlin, 1955), 189, n. 1.

4. Clement, *Stromata* 6.39.2–3.

5. Ignatius, *Epistle to the Magnesians* 6.1; 7.2.

6. Tatian, *Oration to the Greeks* 42; notably by Lucian, *On the Syrian Goddess* 1, etc.; cf. C. Clemen, *Lukians Schrift über die syrische Göttin* (Leipzig, 1938), 7.

7. Herodotus 7.63.

8. Tatian, *Oration to the Greeks* 29, tr. Whittaker.

9. Clement, *Excerpts from Theodotus* 16; *Stromata* 2.36.1.

10. Both Marcion and *P46* read the text as "the likeness of a man."

11. 1 Clem. 61.2 also took the psalm in reference to humanity; cf. R. M. Grant and H. H. Graham, *First and Second Clement* (New York, 1965), 95.

12. Philo, *On the Creation of the World* 170–72; E. Goodenough, *Introduction to Philo Judaeus*, 2d ed. (Oxford, 1962), 37f.

13. Justin, *Apology* 2.6.1; Theophilus, *To Autolycus* 1.3; cf. *Corpus Hermeticum* 2.14.

14. Theophilus, *To Autolycus* 1.7; 2.22.

15. Ibid., 1.4–5, 7; 2.10, 16, 18, 22.

16. Valentinians in Irenaeus, *Against Heresies* 1.8.5; Clement, *Excerpts from Theodotus* 6.3; Tatian, *Oration to the Greeks* 5, p. 5, 21; Irenaeus, *Against Heresies* 3.8.3; Clement, *Exhortation to the Greeks* 7.3; 110.1; *Tutor* 1.62.4; Tertullian, *Against Praxeas* 5.2; Origen, *Commentary on the Gospel of John* 1.17, p. 22, 9 Preuschen.

17. Tertullian, *Against Praxeas* 21.2; Paulinists in Epiphanius, *Against Eighty Heresies* 65.1.5; Marcellus, frag. 60 Klostermann.

18. Note the timeless present participle in John 1:18: "being in *(eis)* the bosom of the Father."

19. Theophilus, *To Autolycus* 2.10, 22.

20. Irenaeus, *Against Heresies* 2.28.6; Origen, *Commentary on the Gospel of John* 1.24, p. 29, 23; cf. R. Cadiou, *Commentaires inédits des Psaumes* (Paris, 1936), 77.

21. Tertullian, *Against Hermogenes* 18.6; *Against Praxeas* 7.1; *Against Marcion* 2.4.1.

22. Cf. M. Mühl, "Der Logos endiathetos und prophorikos in der älteren Stoa bis zur Synode von Sirmium," *Archiv für Begriffsgeschichte* 7 (1962), 7–56; for rhetoric, Hermogenes, 2.7, pp. 352–62 Rabe.

23. Irenaeus, *Against Heresies* 2.12.5; 13.8; Origen, *Against Celsus* 6.65.

24. Justin, *Apology* 1.36.

25. Cf. G. Quispel and R. M. Grant, "Note on the Petrine Apocrypha," *VC* 6 (1952), 31f.

26. Frag. 4 von Dobschütz; cf. Matt. 12:1–15.

27. Justin, *Apology* 1.33.6.

28. Cf. Acts 1:9; Luke 24:51.

29. Theophilus, *To Autolycus* 2.25, with allusions to Luke 1:80; 2:40, 52.

30. Contrast Irenaeus *Against Heresies* 3.21.10.

31. Theophilus, *To Autolycus* 2.10, 28, 30, 35, 38; 3.13.

32. Eusebius, *Against Marcellus* 1.2.25ff.

33. Irenaeus, *Against Heresies* 5.28.4 (from Ignatius, *Epistle to the Romans* 4.1).

34. Serapion in Eusebius, *Ecclesiastical History* 6.12.

35. G. Bardy, *Paul de Samosate*, 2d ed. (Louvain, 1929); F. Loofs, *Paulus von Samosata* (Leipzig, 1924); H. de Riedmatten, *Les Actes du procès de Paul de Samosate* (Fribourg, 1952); and T. E. Pollard, *Johannine Christology and the Early Church* (Oxford, 1970).

36. R. L. Sample, *The Messiah as Prophet: The Christology of Paul of Samosata*, diss. Northwestern, 1977; directed by D. Groh. See also F. W. Norris, "Paul of Samosata: *Procurator Ducenarius*," *JTS* 35 (1984), 50–70.

37. From *Doctrina Patrum* 41, VI.

38. Eusebius, *Ecclesiastical Theology* 3.3.43–44.

39. Theophilus, *To Autolycus* 2.10, 22.

40. J. Daniélou, *Théologie du Judéo-Christianisme* (Tournai, 1958), 222f.

41. Eusebius, *Against Marcellus* 1.2.23f.

42. Eusebius, *Ecclesiastical History* 3.27.

43. Origen, *Commentary on the Gospel of Matthew* 16.12.

Chapter 11: Also the Holy Spirit

1. G. F. Moore, *Judaism*, I (Cambridge, Mass., 1927), 421f.

2. Luke's narrative owes something to the story of the birth and spirit empowerment of Samson (Judg. 13ff.); compare the summaries (Luke 2:40, 52) with Judg. 13:24 and 1 Sam. 2:26. Matthew also mentions the Holy Spirit (Matt. 1:18, 21) in this regard.

3. Cf. H. Conzelmann, *Die Apostelgeschichte* (Tübingen, 1963), 27, citing Philo, *On the Decalogue* 33.46.

4. Ignatius, *Epistle to the Philadelphians* 7.1.

5. Origen, *Against Celsus* 7.9, tr. Chadwick.

6. Cf. D. E. Aune, *Prophecy in Early Christianity and the Ancient Mediterranean World*, 70–72.

7. Cf. R. M. Grant, *Second-Century Christianity* (London, 1946), 95–96.

8. Ibid., 21.

9. Ibid., 27.

10. Irenaeus, *Against Heresies* 1.14.1.

11. A. von Harnack, *Marcion. Das Evangelium vom fremden Gott*, 2d ed. (Leipzig, 1924), 177, 405*.

12. Cf. Plato, *Laws* 4.719C: "When a poet is seated on the Muses tripoa he is not in his senses but resembles a fountain."

13. Origen, *Against Celsus* 3.25; 7.3.

14. Chrysostom, in *Homily on I Corinthians* 29.1, *PG* 61, 242.

15. For the vapor, cf. L. B. Holland, "The Mantic Mechanism at Delphi," *AJA* 37 (1933), 201–14. There is no trace of it today.

16. Virgil, *Aeneid*, 6.77–80, 98–100.

17. Suetonius, *Augustus* 31.1; Dio Cassius 57.18.4; Tacitus, *Annals* 6.12.

18. Justin, *Apology* 1.44.12; Theophilus, *To Autolycus* 2.36; Clement, *Exhortation to the Greeks* 27.5; 71.4.

19. Ignatius, *Epistle to the Ephesians* 18.2; Justin, *Apology* 1.32.10; 33.6.

20. Justin, *Apology* 1.22.5.

21. E. Hennecke, W. Schneemelcher, and R. McL. Wilson, *New Testament Apocrypha*, I (Philadelphia, 1963), 158–65.

22. J. M. Robinson, ed., *The Nag Hammadi Library* (San Francisco, 1977), 32.

23. *Similitudes* 9.1.1; 5.6.5.

24. Ignatius, *Epistle to the Magnesians* 9.2; *Epistle to the Philadelphians* 7; *Epistle to the Ephesians* 9.1.

25. Justin, *Apology* 1.13.

26. Tatian, *Oration to the Greeks*, pp. 5, 2; 4, 3; 5, 10; 12, 18; 14, 26 Schwartz.

27. Ibid., p. 13, 28.

28. Theophilus, *To Autolycus* 2.9, 13.

29. Theophilus has in mind air and water among the four elements.

30. Theophilus, *To Autolycus* 2.4; *SVF* II 1033.

31. Numenius, Frag. 30 Des Places.

32. Clement, *Selections from the Prophets* 7.1; Origen, *On First Principles* 1.3.3.

33. Irenaeus, *Against Heresies* 4.33.7; 5.20.1.

34. Arrian, *Bithyn.* frag. 9, p. 199 Roos.

35. Cf. R. M. Grant, *The Letter and the Spirit*, 2–6.

36. Origen, *On First Principles* 3.3.3.

37. E.g., Isa. 6:1ff.; Ezek. 1:4ff.; Dan. 7:1; cf. Rev. 1:10.

38. 2 Cor. 12:14; cf. 1 Cor. 14:13–14; Gal. 1:15–16; 2:20.

39. Ignatius, *Epistle to the Philadelphians* 7.1–2.

40. Justin, *Dialogue with Trypho* 115.3.

41. Philo, *The Heir of Divine Things* 249–65.

42. Eusebius, *Ecclesiastical History* 5.16.3–17.4

43. Athenagoras, *Embassy for the Christians* 7.3; 9.1; W. R. Schoedel, *Athenagoras* (Oxford, 1972), 21.

44. Irenaeus, *Against Heresies* 3.11.9.

45. Melito, *Homily* 101(–3), tr. Hall.

46. Jerome, *On Illustrious Men* 24.

47. Irenaeus, *Against Heresies* 3.11.9.

48. Cf. T. D. Barnes, *Tertullian* (Oxford, 1971), 278–79.

49. Clement, *Stromata* 1.85.3.

50. Origen, *On First Principles* 3.3.4.

51. Eusebius, *Ecclesiastical History* 6.2.11.

52. Cf. Ovid, *Metamorphoses* 2.641; Virgil, *Aeneid* 6.46–48; Statius, *Thebais* 4. 542.

53. *FVS* 68 B 18 = Clement, *Stromata* 6.168.2; G. Verbeke, *L'évolution de la doctrine du pneuma,* 271.

54. A. and L. Hahn, *Bibliothek der Symbole und Glaubensregeln der alten Kirche,* 3d ed. (Breslau, 1897), 161.

Chapter 12: Three Gods in One

1. R. Joly, *Hermas: Le Pasteur* (Paris, 1958), 144.

2. 1 Cor. 1:12–14; 6:11; Rom. 6:3; Gal. 3:27; Acts 2:38; 8:16; 19:5.

3. Cf. F. Andres, *Die Engellehre der griechischen Apologeten des zweiten Jahrhunderts* (Paderborn, 1914), 13–16; W. Michaelis, *Zur Engelchristologie im Urchristentum* (Basel, 1942), 146f.

4. Cf. Numenius in Eusebius, *Preparation for the Gospel* 11.18.3; 14.5.6; Clement, *Stromata* 5.103.1; Origen, *Against Celsus* 6.18; see Lucian as cited below.

5. This may be the source of the Platonizing addition to Xenophanes to be found in Irenaeus; see chapter 6.

6. Philo, *On Drunkenness* 30; Plato, *Timaeus* 49a, 52d, 88d.

7. J. Dillon, *The Middle Platonists*, 361–62

8. Porphyry, *Life of Plotinus* 17.

9. For Numenius' influence on Clement and perhaps Tatian, cf. J. H. Waszink, "Some Observations on the Appreciation of 'The Philosophy of the Barbarians' in Early Christian Literature," *Mélanges offerts à Mlle C. Mohrmann* (Utrecht, 1963), 41–56, esp. 53–56.

10. Numenius, frag. 15 Des Places; tr. Dillon, 368.

11. Origen, *On First Principles* 1.3.5–8.

12. Ibid., 1.3.1.

13. H. Crouzel, *Origène: Traité des principes*, II (Paris, 1978), 57–58.

14. Dillon, *The Middle Platonists*, 367.

15. Numenius, frag. 16; tr. Dillon, revised, 369.

16. Porphyry, *On the Cave of the Nymphs* 10, p. 63, 7 Nauck 2d ed.; Numenius, frag. 30.

17. Porphyry, *On the Cave of the Nymphs* 32, p. 78, 14.

18. Numenius, frag. 17; tr. Dillon, 363; possibly a paraphrase of Plato, *Timaeus* 28C.

19. Cf. A. D. Nock, "The Exegesis of *Timaeus* 28C," *VC* 16 (1962), 79–86.

20. See C. C. Richardson, *The Doctrine of the Trinity* (New York and Nashville, 1958); see Chapter 10 above.

21. W. C. Till, *Die gnostischen Schriften des koptischen Papyrus Berolinensis 8502*, TU 60 (Berlin, 1955), 82; M. Krause and P. Labib, *Die drei Versionen des Apokryphon des Johannes* (Wiesbaden, 1962), 112, 201.

22. Here there is a gap in the manuscript tradition.

23. Heavier: water, earth; lighter: air, fire.

24. Cf. Dillon, *The Middle Platonists*, 95.

25. W. R. Schoedel, *Athenagoras* (Oxford, 1972), xviii; cf. *JTS* 31 (1980), 356–67.

26. Irenaeus and Tertullian also used Theophilus.

27. See R. M. Grant in *VC* 6 (1952), 152, reprinted in *Christian Beginnings: Apocalypse to History* (London, 1983).

28. Cf. J. Gewiess, "Zum altkirchliche Verständnis der Kenosisstelle," *Theologische Quartalschrift* 128 (1948), 463–87.

29. I follow and modify the summaries of W. Y. Fausset, *Novatiani Romanae vrbis presbyteri De trinitate liber* (Cambridge, 1909), 111, 115f.

30. Epiphanius, *Against Eighty Heresies* 69.6; H. G. Opitz, *Urkunden zur Geschichte des arianischen Streites* (Berlin, 1935), no. 1.

31. Tertullian defended the term, *Against Praxeas* 8, but Origen rejected it, *On First Principles* 4.4.1.

32. J. N. D. Kelly, *Early Christian Creeds* (London, 1950), 205, 209f.

33. Ibid., 210.

34. Athanasius, *On the Decrees of the Synod of Nicaea* 25.2, p. 21, 2 Opitz; Theognostus used the old analogies of light and water and spoke of "emanation of the *ousia* of the Father."

35. What follows is based largely on the article in G. W. H. Lampe, *A Patristic Greek Lexicon*, 959; on Gnostic usage, Kelly, *Early Christian Creeds*, 245.

36. Origen, *On First Principles*, preface 8–9.

37. "Zum Prozess gegen Paul von Samosata," *ZNW* 75 (1984), 270–90.

38. *Urkunden* 22 Opitz.

39. Kelly, *Early Christian Creeds*, 182, 186.

Chapter 13: Creeds and Cult

1. Cf. J. N. D. Kelly, *Rufinus: A Commentary on the Apostles' Creed*, 100f.

2. Cf. J. N. D. Kelly, *Early Christian Creeds*, 296–331; see also A. and L. Hahn, *Bibliothek der Symbole und Glaubensregeln der alten Kirche*, 3d ed. (Breslau, 1897).

3. Irenaeus, *Against Heresies* 3.4.2.

4. Ibid., 1.27.1.

5. Ibid., 1.21.3; F. Graffin in A. Rousseau and L. Doutreleau, *Irenée de Lyon Contre les Hérésies Livre I*, I (Paris, 1979), 270.

6. Kelly, *Rufinus*, 71, 134.

7. Kelly, *Early Christian Creeds*, 372.

8. Ibid., 297–98.

9. Cf. Irenaeus, *Against Heresies* 1.3.6.

10. Kelly, *Early Christian Creeds*, 341–42.

11. Ibid., 194.

12. Justin, *Dialogue with Trypho* 2.1–2.

13. Eusebius, *Preparation for the Gospel* 14.5; on "restoration," see R. M. Grant, *The Letter and the Spirit*, 15–30.

14. Clement, *Stromata* 1.63.2–64.4; 6.57.3.

15. Epiphanius, *Against Eighty Heresies* 33.7.9; Clement, *Stromata* 7.106.4.

16. Eusebius, *Preparation for the Gospel* 11.2.2.

17. Diodorus Siculus 2.29.6; Irenaeus, *Against Heresies* 1.21.5.

18. Clement, *Stromata* 7.108; Diogenes Laërtius 1.17.

19. Justin, *Apology* 1.26.

20. Eusebius, *Ecclesiastical History* 4.22.5, 7.

21. Irenaeus, *Against Heresies* 1.22–23.

22. Origen, *On First Principles*, 1, preface.

23. Eusebius, *Life of Constantine* 2.64.

24. Ammianus Marcellinus, 22.5.3f.; cf. J. Bidez and F. Cumont, *Ivliani imperatoris epistvlae et leges* (Paris, 1922), 50–52.

25. Cf. J. Dummer, "Ein naturwissenschaftliches Handbuch als Quelle für Epiphanius von Constantia," *Klio* 55 (1973), 289–99.

26. Symmachus, *Relation* 3; R. H. Barrow, *Prefect and Emperor* (Oxford, 1973), 32–47; for the context, cf. A. H. Armstrong, "The Way and the Ways: Religious Tolerance and Intolerance in the Fourth Century A.D.," *VC* 38 (1984), 1–17.

27. Cf. Grazia Lo Menzo Rapisarda, *La personalitá di Simmaco e la III relatio* (Catania, 1967).

28. Vincent of Lérins, *Commonitory* XVII (23); Cicero, *Tusculan Disputations* 1.39.

29. Cf. A. S. Pease, *M. Tulli Ciceronis De Natura Deorum*, I (Cambridge, Mass., 1955), 294f.

30. Cf. also E. Ivanka, *Hellenisches und christliches im frühbyzantinischen Geistesleben* (Vienna, 1948).

Reading List

Students and others may wish to look up some of the ancient authors cited, since I have generally tried to base my statements on such primary evidence. The easiest way for most will be to rely on the volumes of the Loeb Classical Library for non-Christian authors, and some Christians as well, such as the apostolic fathers and some works by Clement, Tertullian, Minucius Felix, Eusebius, and Augustine. It is customary to criticize the texts printed in Loeb as somewhat outmoded, but advances in either classical or patristic philology are less common than one might suppose.

Thus readers are not led far astray when using the Ante-Nicene Christian Library of 1867–1897 or the Nicene and Post-Nicene Fathers of 1886–1900 (both reprinted since), though the translations in the Library of Christian Classics, edited by John Baillie, John T. McNeill, and Henry P. van Dusen, are generally better. One should also mention the series Ancient Christian Writers and its rival Fathers of the Church, both usually of high quality. In addition, there are texts and translations of some important authors in the series edited by Henry Chadwick, *Oxford Early Christian Texts: Acts of the Christian Martyrs, Athanasius, Athenagoras, Cyprian, Melito, Tatian, Theophilus*. One cannot do without Chadwick's annotated translation, *Origen Contra Celsum* (Cambridge, 1953), or G. W. Butterworth, *Origen on First Principles* (London, 1936). The "apocryphal New Testament" is translated by R. McL. Wilson after W. Schneemelcher and E. Hennecke, 2 vols. (Philadelphia, 1963, 1965), while James M. Robinson edited translations of *The Nag Hammadi Library* (San Francisco, 1977). Other Gnostic documents are translated by me in *Gnosticism: An Anthology* (New York, 1961) or by R. McL. Wilson after W. Foerster, *Gnosis*, 2 vols. (Oxford, 1972, 1974). For a good survey, see K. Rudolph, *Gnosis* (Edinburgh, 1983).

The reading list that follows is no more than that. It is limited to works in English and does not correspond to the works used in preparing this volume. More work is published on the church fathers, for example, in French and German, not to mention Italian, than in English. The list is arranged by chapters, though obviously there is some overlapping. Much gratitude goes to my colleague Dr. Arthur Droge for his help in preparing the list.

I should add that F. C. Grant, *Roman Hellenism and the New Testament* (Edinburgh, 1962), not only gives an admirable introduction to the subject but also provides a chronological table and a more complete bibliography up to that time, while there is an inclusive bibliography on Greco-Roman religion in Ramsay MacMullen, *Paganism in the Roman Empire* (New Haven, 1981).

Chapter 1: Gods in the Book of Acts

F. J. Foakes Jackson and Kirsopp Lake, eds., *The Beginnings of Christianity*, I (London, 1920–1933) (there never was a II), remains the largest and best commentary in English. The most useful volumes are the fourth (commentary on Acts) and the fifth (short essays on various topics). Also recommended is E. Haenchen, *The Acts of the Apostles: A Commentary* (Philadelphia, 1971). A few studies of special subjects include C. F. Edson, "The Cults of Thessalonica," *Harvard Theological Review* 41 (1948), 153ff.; B. Gaertner, *The Areopagus Speech and Natural Revelation* (Uppsala, 1955); D. E. Aune, "Magic in Early Christianity," *Aufstieg und Niedergang der römischen Welt*, II.23.2, edited by H. Temporini and W. Haase (ongoing).

Chapter 2: Mediterranean Religions Westward

The studies of Franz Cumont remain basic for introductory purposes and stimulus, even though they are out of date and wrong in several regards (as Ramsay MacMullen has pointed out in his equally basic *Paganism in the Roman Empire*). Cumont's *Oriental Religions in Roman Paganism* is translated from the second edition of 1911, not the fourth of 1929 (where the notes are what matter), while *The Mysteries of Mithra* is well out of date. A. D. Nock, *Conversion* (Oxford, 1933), is not out of date; for detailed discussion of many points, see Nock's *Essays on Religion and the Ancient World*, 2 vols. (Oxford, 1972), edited by Zeph Stewart. In general, J. Ferguson, *The Religions of the Roman Empire* (Cornell, 1970); also J. Teixidor, *The Pagan God: Popular Religion in the Graeco-Roman Near East* (Princeton, 1977). On westward routes, compare P. Beskow, "The Routes of Early Mithraism" in *Études mithraïques* (Leiden, 1978), 7ff.

Two collections of translated texts are especially useful. These are F. C. Grant, *Hellenistic Religions: The Age of Syncretism* (New York, 1953), and *Ancient Roman Religion* (New York, 1957).

For particular cults, see above all B. F. Meyer and E. P. Sanders, eds., *Self-Definition in the Graeco-Roman World*, Vol. 3 of Jewish and Christian Self-Definition (Philadelphia, 1983), an admirable collection of essays. Here is an alphabetized list for various gods: Emma and Ludwig Edelstein, *Asclepius: A Collection and Interpretation of the Testimonies*, 2 vols. (Baltimore, 1945); A. Vogliano and F. Cumont, "The Bacchic Inscription in the Metropolitan Museum," *American Journal of Archaeology* 37 (1933), 215ff.; M. P. Nilsson, "The Bacchic Mysteries of the Roman Age," *Harvard Theological Review* 46

(1953), 175ff.; M. J. Vermaseren, *Cybele and Attis: The Myth and the Cult* (London, 1977); R. E. Witt, *Isis in the Graeco-Roman World* (Cornell, 1971); S. K. Heyob, *The Cult of Isis Among Women of the Hellenistic-Roman World* (Leiden, 1975); Michael Grant, *The Jews in the Roman World* (London, 1973); M. J. Vermaseren, *Mithras, the Secret God* (London, 1963); R. L. Gordon, "Mithraism and Roman Society: Social Factors in the Explanation of Religious Change in the Roman Empire," *Religion* 2 (1972), 92ff.; J. E. Stambaugh, *Sarapis Under the Early Ptolemies* (Leiden, 1972).

Chapter 3: Christian Missionaries Against Idolatry

On some of the problems, see Edwyn Bevan, *Holy Images: An Inquiry Into Idolatry and Image Worship in Ancient Paganism and in Christianity* (London, 1940), and N. H. Baynes, "Idolatry and the Early Church," in *Byzantine Studies and Other Essays* (London, 1955), 116–43. See also Martin Dibelius, *Studies in the Acts of the Apostles* (London, 1956); P. E. Corbett, "Greek Temples and Greek Worshippers: The Literary and Archaeological Evidence," *Bulletin of the Institute for Classical Studies* 17 (1970), 149ff.; and J. E. Stambaugh, "The Functions of Roman Temples," *Aufstieg und Niedergang der römischen Welt*, II.16.2, 554ff.

Chapter 4: Functions of Gods and Goddesses

On relations to the gods, see Martin P. Nilsson, *Greek Popular Religion* (New York, 1940), and *Greek Piety* (Oxford, 1948); A.-J. Festugière, *Personal Religion Among the Greeks* (Berkeley, 1954); H. J. Rose, *Religion in Greece and Rome* (New York, 1959); F. Brenk, *In Mist Apparelled: Religious Themes in Plutarch's Moralia and Lives* (Leiden, 1977); J. G. Griffiths, ed., *Plutarch's De Iside et Osiride* (University of Wales, 1970). For a contrast with Christians, R. Walzer, *Galen on Jews and Christians* (Oxford, 1949). On miracles, there is my *Miracle and Natural Law in Graeco-Roman and Early Christian Thought* (Amsterdam, 1952), as well as the more sociological study by H. C. Kee, *Miracle in the Early Christian World* (New Haven, 1983). See also much of the literature noted for Chapter 2, above.

There are helpful articles on deification in English by E. Bickerman, F. Millar, and G. W. Bowersock in the symposium of the Fondation Hardt (*Entretiens*, Vol. 19 [Geneva, 1972]) on *Le culte des souverains dans l'empire romain*. For more extensive studies, see Lily Ross Taylor, *The Divinity of the Roman Emperor* (Middletown, Conn., 1931), and J. R. Fears, *Princeps a diis electus: The Divine Election of the Emperor as a Political Concept at Rome* (Rome, 1977).

Chapter 5: The Deeds of Individual Gods and Heroes

Here Zeus is the most important. On Zeus, see A. B. Cook, *Zeus: A Study in Ancient Religion*, 3 vols. in 5 (Cambridge, 1914–1940), to be supplemented by L. R. Farnell, *Cults of the Greek States*, 5 vols. (Oxford, 1896–1909). On other figures, see H. Engelmann, *The Delian Aretalogy of Sarapis* (Leiden, 1975), and J. G. Griffiths, ed., *Apuleius of Madauros: The Isis-Book* (Leiden, 1975). Especially significant is C. A. Behr, *Aelius Aristides and the Sacred Tales* (Amsterdam, 1968).

Chapter 6: The Philosophical Doctrine of God

On the pre-Socratics see Werner Jaeger, *The Theology of the Early Greek Philosophers* (Oxford, 1947). He viewed them as beginning a process ultimately continued in Christianity. For a different view see F. M. Cornford, *Principium Sapientiae: The Origins of Greek Philosophical Thought* (Cambridge, 1952). Perhaps I should mention my own essay, "Early Christianity and Pre-Socratic Philosophy," in the *Wolfson Jubilee Volumes* (Jerusalem, 1965), 357ff. On critics of religion see H. W. Attridge, "The Philosophical Critique of Religion Under the Early Empire," *Aufstieg und Niedergang der römischen Welt*, II.16.1, 45ff. For the treatise *On the Universe* (*De mundo*), see J. P. Maguire, "The Sources of Pseudo-Aristotle De Mundo," Yale Classical Studies 6 (1939), 111ff. For the immediate philosophical background of Christian thought in Middle Platonism, R. E. Witt, *Albinus and the History of Middle Platonism* (Cambridge, 1937), is not as helpful as John Dillon, *The Middle Platonists* (Cornell, 1977); see also H. A. Wolfson, *Philo*, 2 vols. (Cambridge, Mass., 1947), and H. D. Betz, ed., *Plutarch's Theological Writings and Early Christian Literature* (Leiden, 1975). Highly important for the background is G. W. Bowersock, *Greek Sophists in the Roman Empire* (Oxford, 1969).

Chapter 7: Christian Doctrines of God

The best and most thorough treatment remains that of G. L. Prestige, *God in Patristic Thought* (London, 1936); see also my James W. Richard lectures on *The Early Christian Doctrine of God* (Charlottesville, 1966).

Chapter 8: Christ: Deeds and Names

The questions raised here are not new, and A. E. J. Rawlinson, *The New Testament Doctrine of the Christ* (London, 1926), is still valuable. One should also use Oscar Cullmann, *The Christology of the New Testament* (Philadelphia, 1959), and the New Testament Theology books by more recent authors such as Hans Conzelmann.

Chapter 9: The Cosmic Christ

For this kind of analysis not much is written in English. See Martin P. Nilsson, "The High God and the Mediator," *Harvard Theological Review* 56 (1963), 101–20. For this and succeeding chapters see J. N. D. Kelly, *Early*

Christian Doctrines (New York, 1958); R. P. C. Hanson, *Tradition in the Early Church* (London, 1962); and Henry Chadwick, *Early Christian Thought and the Classical Tradition* (Oxford, 1966).

Chapter 10: Divergent Christologies at Antioch

The student should look at W. Bauer, *Orthodoxy and Heresy in Earliest Christianity* (Philadelphia, 1971), since this chapter is partly directed against his basic theory. See also R. V. Sellers, *Two Ancient Christologies* (London, 1940). On Antioch, see Wayne A. Meeks and Robert L. Wilken, *Jews and Christians in Antioch*, SBL Sources for Biblical Study, 13 (Missoula, Mont., 1978). The principal problem is raised by the doctrinal move from Ignatius (W. R. Schoedel, *Ignatius of Antioch*, Philadelphia, 1985) to Theophilus (my text and translation, Oxford, 1970); see also "Scripture, Rhetoric and Theology in Theophilus," *Vigiliae Christianae* 13 (1959), 33ff.

Chapter 11: Also the Holy Spirit

Edwyn Bevan, *Sibyls and Seers* (Cambridge, Mass., 1929), gives a good introduction to the practice and theory of revelation and inspiration; more philosophically, G. Verbeke (in French), *L'évolution de la doctrine du pneuma* (Paris and Louvain, 1945); see also my study of allegorical interpretation, *The Letter and the Spirit* (London, 1957). Specifically on the Holy Spirit see G. W. H. Lampe, *The Seal of the Spirit* (London, 1951). On activities of the Spirit in the church and outside it see D. E. Aune, *Prophecy in Early Christianity and the Ancient Mediterranean World* (Grand Rapids, 1983).

Chapter 12: Three Gods in One

Again we turn back to A. E. J. Rawlinson, who edited *Essays on the Trinity and the Incarnation* (London, 1928); see also J. N. D. Kelly, *Early Christian Doctrines* (New York, 1958), and W. R. Schoedel, "A Neglected Motive for Second-Century Trinitarianism," *Journal of Theological Studies* 31 (1980), 356ff. Readers of German should consult G. Kretschmar, *Studien zur frühchristlichen Trinitätstheologie* (Tübingen, 1956).

Chapter 13: Creeds and Cult

Here we recommend J. N. D. Kelly, *Early Christian Creeds* (London, 1950), and *Rufinus: A Commentary on the Apostles' Creed* (Westminster, Md., 1955). The whole subject really demands going into early Christian history, for which the best study is W. H. C. Frend, *The Rise of Christianity* (Philadelphia, 1984)

Index